Commendations for *The Splash of Words*

This beautiful and wise meditation centred around Mark Oakley's anthology of the 'soul language' of poetry opens new windows in the shared house of both poetry and belief.
Dame Carol Ann Duffy, Poet Laureate

Some writers have the gift of simply letting you know you can trust them. Mark Oakley has this gift in abundance: in this book we read in his company a succession of very diverse poems; we listen to his honest, careful, demanding reflections on them; and we recognize that this is a deeply authentic voice that can be relied on not to give us either clichés or indulgent ramblings. A very moving book, opening all kinds of doors into a more compassionate, more truthful understanding.
The Rt Hon Dr Rowan Williams, Lord Williams of Oystermouth, Master of Magdalene College, Cambridge

Mark Oakley has a strong sense of language as sacrament, a sharp eye for telling phrases, and a warm heart with which to return echoes. *The Splash of Words* proves all these things on every page; it is a tribute to the persuasive power of enthusiasm.
Sir Andrew Motion, Homewood Professor of the Arts, Johns Hopkins University, Baltimore, and former Poet Laureate

The Splash of Words is a unique and inspirational book by a great man of faith, hope and humanity. Mark Oakley reminds us of the power of poetry as both metaphor and instrument for our best selves.
Shami Chakrabarti, barrister, former Director of Liberty

With a choice of poems that draws on many streams, from the well loved to the unfamiliar, from Gerard Manley Hopkins to Liz Berry to landays recited by Afghan women, Mark Oakley makes unexpected and electrifying connections. Navigating poem after poem, he gives us the chance 'to eavesdrop on the great/ Presences'.

Even believing in poetry, he still leaves space for unease and uncertainties, because he of all people recognizes that 'there is no/ Road that is right entirely'. In doing so he illuminates the way for those who think they know the territory as well as for those who may be wary of it. Dipping in to this book, the spirit is cleansed in the sparkle of language.

Imtiaz Dharker, poet, awarded the Queen's Gold Medal for Poetry

If poems were pictures, then Mark Oakley would be a top curator. He has gathered here a group of poetic masterpieces, and arranged them before us with rare discernment. And, as great exhibitions deserve brilliant catalogues, so this book offers an invaluable complement to the works themselves. In his opening essay as well as in his reflections on the individual poems, Oakley offers context, commentary and insight into his choices. It's a book that 'interrupts our snoring', challenging us to countenance life's vividness and complexity through art – and not just any art, for (of course) poems *aren't* pictures; they're poems. Oakley's exceptional feel for the distinctiveness of the poetic medium – and his ability to articulate it – is another of the special gifts of this book.

Professor Ben Quash, Professor of Christianity and the Arts, King's College London

THE SPLASH OF WORDS

Believing in poetry

MARK OAKLEY

CANTERBURY
PRESS
Norwich

First published in 2016 by the Canterbury Press Norwich
Editorial office
3rd Floor, Invicta House
108–114 Golden Lane
London EC1Y 0TG, UK

Third impression 2017

Hymns Ancient & Modern® is a registered trademark
of Hymns Ancient and Modern Ltd

Canterbury Press is an imprint of Hymns Ancient & Modern Ltd
(a registered charity)
13A Hellesdon Park Road, Norwich
Norfolk NR6 5DR, UK

www.canterburypress.co.uk

British Library Cataloguing in Publication data

A catalogue record for this book is available
from the British Library

978 1 84825 468 8

Typeset by Regent Typesetting
Printed and bound in Great Britain by CPI Group (UK) Ltd

If we could get the hang of it entirely
    It would take too long;
All we know is the splash of words in passing
    And falling twigs of song,
And when we try to eavesdrop on the great
    Presences it is rarely
That by a stroke of luck we can appropriate
    Even a phrase entirely.

Louis MacNeice
from *Entirely*

There is much more to be said on this subject of which this
Is a mere fragment: *I count myself not to have apprehended.*

John Ash
from *Finding Prostanna (2)*

If prose is a river, poetry is a fountain.

Michael Longley

Tom Miller

whose faith, generosity and laughter always inspire

Contents

Believing in Poetry

If I knew where poems came from, I'd go there.
Michael Longley

'Poetry' is a divisive word. You can feel either excited by it or negative about it. The second response often has its roots in school memories of being made to plough through boring texts or recite poems to the rest of the class. Or it can be a consequence of having tried to read poetry later in life but finding it incomprehensible, all the hard work put into reading it seemingly not matched by what you get out. For many people poetry is a scary or a frustrating concept. There is even a word for it: 'metrophobia' – the fear of poetry.

I remember the day I realized I needed to start reading poetry again. I went to a poetry event with Wendy Cope and heard her read a poem about her grandmother. The poem is called 'Names'.[1]

She was Eliza for a few weeks
When she was a baby –
Eliza Lily. Soon it changed to Lil.

Later she was Miss Steward in the baker's shop
And then 'my love', 'my darling', Mother.

Widowed at thirty, she went back to work
As Mrs Hand. Her daughter grew up,
Married and gave birth.

Now she was Nanna. 'Everybody
Calls me Nanna,' she would say to visitors.
And so they did – friends, tradesmen, the doctor.

In the geriatric ward
They used the patients' Christian names.
'Lil,' we said, 'or Nanna,'
But it wasn't in her file
And for those last bewildered weeks
She was Eliza once again.

I listened to those few simple lines that capture the fragile life
cycle of a woman and that make you feel tender towards her after
just 107 words – and I found I was crying. I'm not alone in this
experience. An anthology has been published called *Poems that
Make Grown Men Cry* in which 100 famous men have named
the poem that first made them tearful (a companion volume of
poems that made 100 women cry has now followed).[2] Not all
poems make you start weeping, of course – far from it. There is,
though, a sense that when we start talking about poems we are
talking about a soul-language, a way of crafting words that distils
our experience into what feels like a purer truth. This sense of dis-
tillation, even cleansing, that poems have about them also pushes
on our contours. They bring epiphany or surprise moments of
recognition which then ask us to re-imagine the world in some
fresh way, our comprehension deepened. Creativity is contagious.

The title of this book comes from a poem by Louis MacNeice
called 'Entirely'. MacNeice was always something of a detached
bystander and unable to sign up to any neat and finalized sys-
tem of thought. In 'Entirely' he reveals this inability to summarize
anything or anyone. It begins:

If we could get the hang of it entirely
    It would take too long;
All we know is the splash of words in passing
    And falling twigs of song,

And when we try to eavesdrop on the great
    Presences it is rarely
That by a stroke of luck we can appropriate
    Even a phrase entirely.[3]

The phrase 'splash of words' is a good description of poetry. When you read a poem there is an initial splash like a pebble thrown into a lake. The words disturb your surface and have their impact. Then, as the poem begins to do its work, the ripples of meaning head out towards your shore, often slowly but relentlessly, and you realize that these words are shifting your perceptions and consequently even transforming who you are and how you understand. 'When I let go of what I am, I become what I might be', noted the Chinese poet Lao Tze. A poem's ultimate meaning is found not in the words but in us, in our response to the words. When you encounter this splash of words you understand that ultimately poetry is not about factual information but human formation. Like water, language goes stagnant if it doesn't move. The poet's task is to wage a war against cliché so that words take their rightful place in the development and growth of human lives and the world itself.

But what of those people mentioned at the start – and you might be one of them – for whom this splash of words is nothing but a meaningless verbal chaos? How can the ripples start out in them? What can be said to encourage them to give poetry another chance?

It might help to think about Belgium.[4] Consider the way you'd be thinking if you were planning a trip there. You might try to learn a few useful phrases, or read a bit of Belgian history, or thumb through a guidebook in search of museums, restaurants, flea markets. The important thing is that no matter how well you had prepared, you'd know that when you get to Belgium you are going to be a bit confused and occasionally at a loss. The important thing is that you'd accept the confusion as part of the whole experience. You would just accept that feeling a bit unsure about things is part of the fun of being away from home. What you wouldn't do is become paralysed with anxiety because you don't speak fluent Flemish. Nor would you decide in advance that you'd never understand Belgians because you can't immediately determine why their most famous public statue is that of a naked child peeing in a fountain. You'd probably say, 'That's what they like here and if I stay around long enough maybe it'll begin to make sense'. For those for whom poetry is as baffling as Antwerp on a Sunday night, you just need to stay with the confusion for a while and accept that the difficulty might be part of its importance. Of course, like learning Flemish, the more you use the language, the more it begins to make sense.

I must be clear from the start. This is not a scholarly book but it is an enthusiastic one and I just hope that some of its enthusiasm will catch. Its subtitle is 'Believing in poetry' and this has two possible meanings, of course. It can mean that we trust poetry, as you might believe in your doctor, and are sure that it is a worthwhile art form and one we should take seriously as well as enjoy. Or it might mean that we believe something through poetry, that things we believe and hold true are conceived, articulated and celebrated poetically. It probably won't surprise you to learn that it is both meanings that I want to celebrate here. This book has two very ambitious aims very modestly pursued.

First, I hope it will remind us that, in the words of the Irish poet Michael Longley, 'if prose is a river, poetry is a fountain'. Poetry is not always an easy read. We can't place it with all the consumerist reading that many of us do today. Poetry puts language in a state of emergency. What we are more used to is prose. Prose fills endless pages of lines in a continuous language that stops with a small dot, takes a breath and starts again. It travels with you, demanding little more than the occasional pause to have another quick thought. Prose begins with a capital letter, chugs along nicely and ends with a full stop. It communicated its meaning well or it didn't.

Poetry does not chug along. Words have been placed into relationships we are not used to them being in. They are surrounded by spaces, gaps appear, dashes pop up and sometimes punctuation has completely disappeared. It doesn't have a single view in mind but has multiple meanings in its sight, having discerned that truth is much richer in connectivity and conjunctions, more riotously vivid, than the 'prosaic' world of prose would have you believe. Language needs to stretch and exercise itself to do some justice to reality.

Each word of the poem, for example, has been listened to for its sounds and what they contain. Reading poetry aloud helps us hear these properly. The sounds of words are caught up in their communication. Meaning and melody are inseparable. You only need to say 'Hurry up!' or 'Slow down!' to hear how the sound of the words reflects what's being asked of you. Sometimes the echoing words are placed into a formal rhythm. Human beings are rhythmic by nature because as long as we are alive there is a beat playing itself out right in the centre of our bodies. It is what poets call an 'iamb' (the 'te-tum' sound of a light stress followed by a heavy one), a heartbeat rhythm. Place five iambs together in a line – which is about the length of a natural human breath – and you get the basic rhythmic line structure of so much English poetry. For example: 'Shall I compare thee to a summer's day?', 'Of Man's first disobedience, and the fruit', 'Batter my heart three-person'd God, for you'.

Poetry is not an easy running river. It is not a quick read. It is a fountain, a source from which meaning can be slowly, patiently drawn. We have all heard of 'creative writing' but poetry demands of us a creative reading. Poetry is a language that listens. There is no quick clarity. No seductive easy answers. There is no one meaning to be had either, no conclusive evidence to give to the court. Get a group of people together talking about a poem and you'll discover this very quickly. As you read a poem you have to persevere for the meanings that begin to work their way out, resonating and demanding in equal measure.

So, when you buy a poetry book you aren't getting many words for your money but you are getting more meaning for your money. You can't paraphrase poetry, though you can try to out-line its themes and effects. You could never easily paraphrase the poem by Wendy Cope I started with. Poems communicate some-where deep within us before they are intellectually or emotionally understood by us. That is why they are potentially transformative and are used in such a variety of places and times: from work to help rehabilitate young offenders to giving voice to unspoken grief at a funeral; from helping children see their world better to, similarly, stirring up adults to protest for change. Poetry is the more human voice. The meanings of a poem are always ahead of us naughtily calling back 'catch us if you can' – and we follow because it feels we are being taken somewhere new and important. The nineteenth-century American poet Emily Dickinson wrote:

A word is dead
When it is said,
Some say.

I say it just
Begins to live
That day.[5]

Second, I am writing this book for those who are committed to a religious faith, or who are intrigued by the possibility of such a commitment, in the hope it will remind us of our poetic home-land. Poetry is the person of faith's native language. We live in a Google world of facts on tap, quick information at the click of a mouse. There are some who argue that religious faith should equally give immediate and ready answers to every possible question and that religions have scriptures to be used as text-books to find out what those answers are. This approach fails to recognize, of course, that every text is filtered through the eyes of the reader. Also, as the novelist Marilynne Robinson has written in her novel *Gilead*, 'nothing true can be said about God from a posture of defence',[6] and we all know how biblical bullets can be fired in debates to score against the enemy. Such weaponized reading will never nurture souls. This 'simple answer' approach to faith fails to recognize something else – that from its very beginnings the human intuition that the world is a gift, that it has a divine origin, and that life and love come from this same source, was explored and shared poetically. No other language could possibly begin to do justice to these inspiring, daunting mysteries of reality itself.

Ever since priests and people of the world's religions have been aware of the numinous they have opened their arms to invoke the divine name and have done so with poetry pouring from their lips and dramatized into movement. It is also striking that the holy texts of the world's religions, believed by many to be revealed by God as holy wisdom from beyond the human mind, are often found in poetic form. It is acknowledged by the world's religions that God is very obviously a poet.

... God is the poetry caught in any religion,
caught, not imprisoned.
Les Murray

Hinduism's earliest sacred texts, known collectively as the Vedas and written in India between 1500 and 600 BCE, are in effect thousands of poems. Some are hymns addressed to the gods, some chants used by priests for rituals and some reflections on the nature of the Divine. Hindu scripture then incorporated the Upanishads, dating from around 700–500 BCE, composed in verse, as is that pinnacle of Indian poetry, the Bhagavad Gita, or Song of God, with its author and date unknown. In China, the classic Tao Te Ching was also composed in poetic form, probably by Lao Tsu in the sixth century BCE. The opening verse ends by calling the Tao 'the gate to all mystery'. It is a text that unapologetically celebrates the potency of poetic paradox.

Then the collection of writings known as the Hebrew Bible, what Christians often refer to as the Old Testament, composed over the centuries of the first millennium BCE, contain a huge variety of poetic discourses. The most obvious poetry is found in the 150 Psalms, in the noble language of the book of Job, the imagery, often sexual, of the Song of Songs and in the Wisdom literature of the Proverbs and their riddling insights into the good life. But poetry is found elsewhere, not least in the books of the Prophets who warn human beings of what they have turned into and what they are consequently doing to the world. This is done in gradual intensification of an image or in metaphor, so vital to

poetry and in all talk of God. The messengers of any needed trans-
formation in society require a language that offers poetic hope,
not prosaic plans, and this has continued right up into the poetic
speeches of more recent prophets such as Martin Luther King Jr.
He never said, 'I have a nightmare'. His dream was always voiced
in dignified and deeply lyrical imagery and cadence. Poetry helped
share his dream and began making it a reality.

The Christian Gospels (first to second century CE) are not so
obviously poetic until you study them closely. You then see the
artistry of each of the four writers, or evangelists, as well as the
persistently figurative preaching of Jesus himself.[7] Jesus, as it were,
often took people on that trip to Belgium, leaving them wonder-
ing, according to the Gospels, what on earth he meant and yet
being intrigued and drawn by his parabolic language that hovered
rather than came in to land. Storytelling reveals meaning without
committing the final error of defining it. Jesus was poetic. Here
is something a bit shocking – the Good Samaritan never existed.
Nor did the Prodigal Son. Jesus made them up. He was a verbal
artist. He used similes, metaphors and parabolic riddles all the
time. Maybe for this reason the Christian creeds found it difficult
to make succinct reference to them, no paraphrase possible again,
and so if you hear the Apostles' Creed or Nicene Creed recited in
a church service you will find that it doesn't mention Jesus' teach-
ings at all, simply that he was born, suffered, died and rose again.
His poetry defied succinct dogma. One scholar, Joachim Jeremias,
has argued that the original Aramaic of Jesus' sayings would have
been full of poetic alliteration and assonance, conveyed through a
four-beat rhythm. Likewise, the persistent and inventive imagery
of Paul and the baffling, evocative vision of John continued the
push beyond the literal into the heart of spiritual realities.

As regards the Qu'ran (610–632 CE) God is the poet and
speaker of the entire text. God alone is seen as the author of a text
so beautiful that Muslims have developed particular chant styles
for reciting it. Perhaps its most poetic verse is its much repeated
line that has become the key statement of Islam's *shahadah* or
confession of faith: 'There is no god but God'. In the Arabic,
transliterated as *la ilaha illa Allah*, the repetition of the double

consonant 'il' between the open 'a' vowels gives the verse a power-ful flowing rhythm and emphasis. This is poetry in motion as God is praised.[8]

With all these scriptures, truth is expressed through poetry for the faithful. It is not just a better way of saying truth but rather truth is found in this form. Truth for the person of faith is inseparable from the way it is spoken. In the poem 'Religion and Poetry' by the Australian poet Les Murray, who dedicates each of his collections to the glory of God, it notes:

> Religions are poems. They concert
> our daylight and dreaming mind, our
> emotions, instinct, breath and native gesture
>
> into the only whole thinking: poetry.[9]

You might say that truth is far too important to be literalistic with. We know this when we fall in love and try to express how we feel. Literalism won't do. We turn to every poetic device we can muster to try to ensure that our love is communicated and received. If poetry is the language of love, it must also be the language of faith, the language of the Church and the language of God. The curse of literalism is that it often misses meaning and turns reson-ant truth to stone. It stops the flight of the moth of sacred poetry and pins it down so that it no longer dances near the divine flame but becomes just another bit of controlled and routine argument like so much else. Speaking of his own Christian faith, the poet Padraig O'Tuama makes the point: 'Whatever Jesus of Nazareth's death means, it doesn't mean something that can be written on a fridge magnet'.[10]

. . . He is such a fast
God, always before us and
leaving as we arrive.
R. S. Thomas

I write as a Christian, and no matter how appealing all I have said might sound to some, it is no secret that much of my religion over the centuries – and today – has been anything but poetic. Christianity has a reputation in some parts for being very literalistic in its reading of that library of extraordinary texts known as the Bible and its historic creeds. It is when religion becomes literalistic that the troubles usually begin, including the physical or spiritual violence that it is frighteningly able to self-justify. To take the Bible seriously does not mean shrinking it into your own particular system of thinking about God, others and yourself. To take the Bible really seriously means engaging with the variety of its texts, its history, the cultural, interpretative and ethical questions that need addressing, as well as the similar questions they ask of us. It is to invite the comforts and unease of their inspiration, artistry, open-endedness and teasing of human pride. We mustn't close down the conversation with the texts. We spend a lot of time asking whether the Bible is 'true' and miss the fact that the biblical texts are often asking us, 'Are you true?' This is the real question that readers of the Bible should face – others are a distraction – and it is posed time and time again through the various literary and historically shaped genres of the biblical library.

Talk of the Bible being 'inspired' as if that means it has no human error or internal contradictions is as limiting as thinking that a love poem inspired by the existence and influence of a lover must be perfect in every way to be authentic and true. God's reality, love and being is the inspiration of the biblical writers, but God is not the 'author' of this library, dictating words on paper outside of human fallibility. The Bible is an often beautiful, often frustrating, sometimes alarming, endlessly nurturing and scrutinizing communication inspired by the truth of God's creative loving. It is authentic in its voice but it is inevitably coloured by human limitations too – as our language and thoughts always will be. At the end of the day, the Bible is a collage of writings that remind us that God is not to be the easy object of our knowledge but the deepest cause of our wonder.

I have come to understand language as sacramental. This means that for people of Christian faith the placing of our spaces, the metaphors, rhythms, cadences and chosen vocabulary is as vital to the transforming of the flat world of first impressions into the rich interconnectivity of the kingdom of God as the placing of bread and wine on the table and the pouring of water into the font. We may be working very hard to ensure that our Christian communication explains and clarifies biblical and religious metaphors, giving one meaning to a biblical text, and in doing so maybe depriving them of their sacramental effect. Identify the point, it is assumed, and no more need be said. But part of the point may well be that there is no single point but a range of possibilities to be brought into play as free and flowing as the font waters and as extravagant in meaning as the wedding vows, being allowed to filter into all the levels and invisible histories of those who listen. The Eucharist is the sacrament that feeds us by making us more hungry. It deepens our desire for God. Faith intensifies rather than satisfies our longing for God. Are our words to do the same, feeding by their refusal to be captured? In poetry, the poem never has the last word. To use an image of D. H. Lawrence, if you try to nail down the meaning of a poem, it either kills the poem or the poem gets up and walks away with the nail.[11]

Poetry reminds us that words are not just a medium for conveying something else but are themselves an essential constituent in the experience. Thomas Howard describes this well:

> A poem is a thing. It is not a set of fancy trimmings to an otherwise obvious truth. Many readers suppose that that is exactly what poetry is: fancy trimmings. On the contrary, poetry is language brought to its most scorching, most succinct, most pellucid purity, like a Bunsen burner, where we want, not a bonfire, but a small prick of blue flame.[12]

It is because of the open-ended images of poetic forms that their power is exercised. All imagery forces us beyond containment. Words carefully crafted induce us to move beyond their literal meaning towards thinking in quite a different way, and so, potentially, of a quite different order of reality. Poetry allows a creative freedom in terms of 'constructing meaning' as opposed to be 'being told something'. The great poet Geoffrey Hill calls this poetry's 'democracy'. As readers of scripture we all too quickly jump to a single meaning whereas scripture derives much of its power from the fact that the images are multivalent, that is they allow our imaginations the possibility of moving in more than one direction. Language must be richer than our prejudices, and even in a clash or dissonance of words they can function sacramentally. Our faith is nothing without metaphor, without analogy, without sacramental shape and sound. Scriptural poetry liberates words from a hardened possession of definition in praise of a God beyond our imagining and yet intimate to our realities. Let's celebrate the fact!

The whole scriptural enterprise is that of trying to read the love between the lines. Nothing saddens me more than the thought of the poetic and radical richness, and the imaginative playfulness, of the Christian tradition being daily simmered down into a self-exonerating interpretation of selected parts, often narrowly centred on who's supposedly in and who's out in God's eyes. The Orkney poet Edwin Muir wrote about a form of Presbyterianism he had been brought up on:

> The Word made flesh here is made word again
> A word made word in flourish and arrogant crook.
> See there King Calvin with his iron pen,
> And God three angry letters in a book,
> And there the logical hook
> On which the Mystery is impaled and bent
> Into an ideological argument.[13]

We all need to watch ourselves, though. It is too easy in a world of constant chat and comment to develop low expectations of language, to see it purely as some helpful utensil to point to things or clarify reason with. If I suddenly appeared next to you now and said in a prim BBC voice, 'Here is the news', you would probably sit up and be expectant to hear truth coming your way as facts, things that have happened over the past 24 hours with some added commentary you will try to assess for accuracy. If, though, I said to you instead, in more hushed tones, 'Once upon a time', you would probably be equally expectant, maybe more so, and ready to hear truth coming now in a different form, in narrative or poem, and your heart and mind will work at different levels together to draw meaning from this encounter. We are used to tuning in to truth in lots of ways but often forget it:

It is difficult
To get the news from poems
Yet men die miserably every day
For lack
Of what is found there.[14]

The questions here for those of us with Christian faith are: When I go into church how are my ears tuned? When I sit down to study the scriptures, how then am I tuned in? When I take part in a liturgy, a Bible study, a retreat, how have I adjusted my hearing? Can I see the poetry that is called a psalm, a collect, a hymn, a eucharistic prayer? Can I hear the poetry of the worship song, the Bible reading, the sermon? These are important questions because if we come ready to 'hear the news' but are actually being asked to come and live in a poem, there is a problematic category error (*mythos* being encountered as *logos*, to be a bit classical about it) and this will lead to a lot of frustration at everything sounding a bit implausible – or very implausible. Religious faith is poetry plus, not science minus.

Think back to the Wendy Cope poem. On one level it is ridiculous to imagine you can ever sum up a woman's life in 107 words. You can have a good go, though, and when you do with an astute poetic sensibility the result can say much more than a 12-volume biography. We need both; but to read Cope's poem as you would that long biography would be a baffling project. Religious language, as it flickers with the living transcendence and immanence of God, has a similar vocation. We are not to 'hear the news' but to 'hear the good news' and, as Jesus knew, that requires both poetry in the speaker and 'ears to hear' in the rest of us.

The worse your art is the easier it is to talk about.
John Ashbery

It looks, then, as if poetry is the native language of faith. Why are poetry and faith inseparable, though? What is it that makes them so understanding of each other, so encouraging of each other?

As a Christian, I believe that God has given us all a gift. It is our being. God asks for a gift in return – our becoming, who we become with our being. Because our gift back to God is life-long and continually shifting and changing, it means that any language that is to be true to this spiritual adventure of being alive needs equally to resist closure, to protest at black and white conclusions and fixed meanings. To be a language of human growth and formation it needs to be a language of provocation with tricks of the light and complex, nuanced prompts that shift our terrain, that interrupt our snoring. Only this type of language will resemble the life of the soul in relationship and conversation with God, always furthering our boundaries into fresh wisdom and new being. The language that helps us become, develop and mature is rarely factually informative. It is, again as Jesus showed in his own teaching, parabolic and pushy as it forbids our comprehension to close down. I doubt that if Jesus had written a clear manifesto, mission statement or instructive text-book on the kingdom of God we would still be engaging excitedly with his vision today. His ceaselessly figurative preaching stops us, and our hope, becoming grounded. He never tells us what the kingdom is, only what it is like. 'A poem is never finished, only abandoned', noted Paul Valery. Poetry is the language that most truly reflects the life of the soul. It is not for nothing that the Psalms remain one of the most treasured parts of the Judeo-Christian tradition.

I am privileged to be a spiritual director to some incredible people. One of the questions we find ourselves asking from time to time is: Who do people become in my presence? When they are with me, who do they become? It is a question we can ask when in the presence of a poem too. Poems can be very helpful to two people in this soul-friendship as they unearth things that we know somewhere within us but have never yet said or even consciously recognized. When John F. Kennedy gave a eulogy to the American poet Robert Frost, reminding his listeners that art is never a form of propaganda but a form of truth, he said, 'When power corrupts, poetry cleanses'. And just as the person of faith brings herself before God in prayer, seeking the freshness that will illuminate her own reality so that it might be humbled by God's, so reading a good poem can be like standing in an empty room, having to confront yourself and the depths that you have learned to cover over or avoid. Poems and prayer make us think about lives that have never been ours because forces of habit have deprived us of them and they set us on course to be remade to fit our larger unspoken hopes and glimpses. Poetry may be fun or sad, complex or accessible, but it is always inseparable from possibility. The American poet Emily Dickinson captures this in one of her untitled poems:

I dwell in Possibility –
A fairer House than Prose –
More numerous of Windows –
Superior – for Doors –

Of Chambers as the Cedars –
Impregnable of eye –
And for an everlasting Roof
The Gambrels of the Sky –

Of Visitors – the fairest –
For Occupation – This –
The spreading wide my narrow Hands
To gather Paradise –[15]

I'm a Shropshire boy by birth and I love returning to what is one of the most beautiful counties of England. There are a lot of sheep in Shropshire and I joked once with an old shepherd that my boss in London had a shepherd's crook a bit like the one he was holding. I asked him if he used it to haul in the naughty stray lambs. 'No,' he said, 'that's not what this is good for. I'll tell you what I do with this crook. I stick it in the ground so deep that I can hold on to it and keep myself so still that eventually the sheep learn to trust me.' I've been dying to preach at a bishops' consecration service ever since! It seems, though, that as well as being a good model for a pastoral ministry, this story could be applied to how poetry differs from our day-to-day language. 'Let us be proud of the words that are given to us for nothing, not to teach anyone, not to confute anyone, not to prove anyone absurd, but to point beyond all objects into the silence where nothing can be said', advised Thomas Merton.[16] Instead of it being used to barter, argue and casually relate, poetry is the language that is more rooted in a deeper earth and which, with patience and attentiveness, we can learn to trust. We can have faith that it is leading us to places of refreshment even if we don't yet know where those might be. It is the language that takes on the spirit of self-postponement that can too easily take hold of a life.

A poet enchants for the purpose of disenchanting people.
W. H. Auden

To return to the partnership of poetry and faith: what is it that poets and people in search of God recognize in each other?

Poetry challenges first impressions. First impressions can be dangerous things,[17] because the thing about our first impressions of things, of people, or life itself, is that they are not first. Our first impressions arise out of our histories, our pasts, out of the ingredients of the particular person we have become. Our past takes in a deep breath of air in our first impressions to show us that it is still alive and kicking. A first impression may well be an insight – but more often of us who have it rather than the observed. A first impression is a moment of self-revelation. Jane Austen's novel, *Pride and Prejudice*, was originally going to be called *First Impressions*, and you can see why. Our first impressions are made up of our pride and prejudices and all that we have trained to disfigure the truth to sustain our own composure. Quite often a first impression uses the past to shield out the present and so the very art of psychoanalysis, for instance, is to unsettle first impressions and what we make of them. Because they are self-revealing they also have the potential to be tools for self-revision. After all, nothing is less self-evident than the self.

Both poetry and faith work to challenge the sleepwalking life of those who only believe in their first impressions, those seduced by the quickly passing, the gut instinct or the immediate defensive response. To live in a world of first impressions, teach the scriptures, is a half-life. The haunting question of God to the first human beings in Eden echoes still: Where are you? Where are you hiding? What from? How has your fear made you blind?

In the stories of the Gospels, Jesus opens eyes and helps people to see the world redefined. What he does so often is see where the hard little full-stop is in a life and transform it into a comma. He sees where a person internally closed down, where others may have stifled their self-value or hope, and he opens up a new chapter for them by helping them hear a new and fresh message of their value, vocation and dignity. Poetry, like the other arts, no matter how dark their subject, is in some way an invitation to fall in love with life again but a little deeper. The full-stops of first impressions are given a little curly tail and become commas into a world as yet undiscovered, breaking through things that we are too good at. The theatre critic Benedict Nightingale argues that playwrights and actors are there to help us all 'listen, speak and think less thinly'. He defines the theatre as a 'gymnasium for underused imaginations'.[18] This could be a description for poetry, but what about putting it up on the church noticeboard? 'Welcome to St James' church – a gymnasium for underused imagination'. Just a thought.

Attentiveness, said Malebranche, is the natural prayer of the soul. Poetry is a form of attention, a literal coming to our senses, a turning aside from convention and memory. Our attentiveness will make us more alive by the time we die. We are freed of first impressions as we properly attend patiently on what is before us. In poetry, with this initiation of attention, seeing is meaning. This is more than important because of all the aggressive danger that fantasy fuels in us. Poetry can instil a peace as we come to see, in an incarnational way, how the material and the spiritual are indivisible. Poetry and faith are both arts of attention.

Rowan Williams has written:

> . . . one of the tests of actual faith, as opposed to bad religion, is whether it *stops you ignoring things*. Faith is most fully itself and most fully life-giving when it opens your eyes and uncovers for you a world larger than you thought – and, of course, therefore, a world that's a bit more alarming than you ever thought. The test of true faith is how much more it lets you see, and how much it stops you denying, resisting, ignoring aspects of what is real.[19]

Again, the same could be said of poetry.

Christian faith teaches that the One whom we are to love most is the one whom we can never fully possess. It means that our faith's language will be inevitably infused with desire, ache and search. The One we long for most finally eludes us. This is why Advent is the most poetic of the Church's seasons. Faith's pulse is found in this evocative longing. It weakens when we think we somehow have captured God or contain God. This is when certainty more than doubt becomes the opposite of faith. A faith-language will be always open enough for a God who has more truth to teach us, who 'speaks', not 'spake'. It will be a language that finally reads us more than we read it, helping us to listen to our life. 'The whole life of the good Christian', wrote St Augustine, 'is a holy longing. What you long for, as yet you do not see . . . by withholding of the vision God extends the longing, through longing he extends the soul, by extending it he makes room in it . . . So let us long, because we are to be filled . . . That is our life, to be exercised by longing.'[20]

Christian faith also teaches that in Christ we have a body-language of God, an expression of God that reveals the nature of who God is, but who, again, breaks free from our places of death and containment. The doctrine of the Church has developed so we understand God as Trinity: beyond us, beside us, within us. But always faith asks us to deepen, not resolve these sacred mysteries – to perform them, sing them, pray them, play them and not take the colour out of the covenant rainbow by prim logical summaries or banal bumper-sticker theology. Christians should be poets in residence and their worship should be a poetry in play because, at the end of the day, we are not seeking *relevance* but *resonance* – not the transient ideas of today that can convince for a time but the truths that address the deepest longings of a human life and a fragile world. Poetry, like God, with an immense intimacy and intimate immensity, is our faith's pulse. All other languages we learn in other lands.

The Irish poet Seamus Heaney once commented on the passage in St John's Gospel where the scribes and Pharisees bring a woman who has been caught in the act of adultery to him and ask whether they should obey the Mosaic law and stone her. Jesus replies saying that the one without sin should be the first to throw, and then, the Gospel tells us, he stooped and wrote on the ground. Heaney finds in that silent writing an allegory for poetry:

> The drawing of those characters is like poetry, a break with the usual life but not an absconding from it. Poetry, like the writing, is arbitrary and marks time in every possible sense of that phrase. It does not say to the accusing crowd or to the helpless accused, 'Now a solution will take place', it does not propose to be instrumental or effective. Instead, in the rift between what is going to happen and whatever we would wish to happen, poetry holds attention for a space, functions not as a distraction but as pure concentration, a focus where our power to concentrate is concentrated back on ourselves. This is what gives poetry its governing power.[21]

The poet Jane Hirshfield has argued that every good poem begins in a language awake to its own connections and therefore is dependent on concentration.[22] The dictionary definition of this word 'concentration' moves in three directions. It can mean 'to direct toward a common centre', and for a poem this is what pulls it together from disparate parts and makes a poem's only possible definition the poem itself. 'Concentration' can also mean 'to focus one's attention', to face outward and seek the feeling of clarity that a poem can bring to rinse clean and ground both the poem and the world. 'Concentration' can also mean 'to increase in strength and density' and, continues Hirshfield, a good poem will oppose the laziness and entropy of 'ordinary mind' as it alters our inner being. She writes:

> Concentration is one translation of *dhyana*, the Sanskrit term – source of the Chinese *chan* and Japanese *zen* – that describes the one-pointed mind of meditation. In the western word's etymology, we find a related concept, *kentron*: the Greek word for the sharp point at the centre, from a verb meaning 'to prick'. When you go to concentration's centre, you are pricked, which should mean you wake up – exactly what a good poem helps you do.[23]

Again, faith can claim similar qualities as poetry as it directs us to a common centre, the divine source and inspiration of all that is. It helps focus our attention on all lives, objects and connections as being gifts and on the subsequent need to be schooled in our relationships to each other and to our fragile planet. It also increases our density, working within us in ways that enlarge the heart and mind. Poetry and faith are both disciplines in concentration in all aspects of that word's meaning. They are both means into an exploration, an adventure of soul, without limits and in search of truth, world, self, and, therefore, of God.

Reality is not simply there, it must be sought for and won.
Paul Celan

In one of the best recent introductions to poetry[24] Glyn Maxwell writes his two first chapters on 'White' and 'Black'. He argues that poetry needs two things: nothing and something. That is, it first needs the whiteness, a blank sheet of paper, a white screen, ice plain, a dizzying light, nothing. Then it needs the black ink or pixels, the poet scoring lines into the silence like words on an iced window or drumming fingers in the dark. Poets work with these two materials: one is black and the other is white. Call them sound and silence, life and death, hot and cold, love and loss. To a novelist, a journalist or a blogger the whiteness, the white sheet, is nothing, just a *tabula rasa* waiting to be filled. But to a poet it's half of everything. If you don't know how to use it, you are writing prose. There can be no cheap spillage in poetry as it works, in Maxwell's view, to coherently express the presence of a human creature. The spaces matter. The gaps, silences, unknowns, coldness, blanks, are part of our human shape and so must be part of the poetic form.

At one point he asks his readers to write down on a piece of paper the lines of love written by a man several centuries ago: 'Shall I compare thee to a summer's day?' As you do so, you can imagine the 'quality of space' from which those words first came – 'warm, sunlit, infused with joy and serenity'. Now, he says, as you write those words down today:

> Feel the power of the line you thought of – passing through you – into the pen, into the keys. Again, pretend you thought of it and look, now it's in your handwriting, or the font you named it in. But this happened to someone once, in our country, with hedgerows in the distance and a sparrow wittering on. Bear in mind again the actual time and space poetry claws from us, as you see those words appear. This deed should start to suggest to you also – and it's the slowing down that allows this – the unearthly weirdness of what you're doing. What on earth *are* you doing? This is where white goes black, where person becomes poem, where the ears of time prick up . . .[25]

It's a noticeable word to use, 'unearthly', but not surprising in the light of what we've seen so far here. The act of poetic creativity links time and present, body and spirit, space and matter, light and shadow. This forging together of black and white ironically leads to the least 'black and white' conclusions but instead starts a process within of recognitions, associative freedoms, and yet uncertain fragmentary glimpses of a life and world you once thought you knew and understood. Poetry is more of a threshold than a path, and the continuous creativity of encountering it is in itself a transcendent immanence, 'unearthly', a strangeness that feels like home, maybe even a reflection of the divine in our midst.

A poem should be more interesting than anything that can be said about it.
W. H. Auden

I have tried briefly to make the point that poetry is more than an esoteric entertainment. It should be pleasurable as well as transformative, of course. Wordsworth mentions the word 'pleasure' 42 times in his *Preface to Lyrical Ballads*. What we have to learn quickly, though, is that it is the struggle of poetry that is part of its pleasing and welcome work. As in life, it is the difficult and hard moments that have most potential even though at the time it can feel anything but. Jane Hirshfield has said that for her a good poem has been like spotting a beautiful bird in the thicket and jungle of her life. Just for a second she has been made to stop in all the overgrown chaos and see the colour of the world as it is. I have argued that, exactly because of this, poetry is the language of religious faith, and those of us in the Christian tradition need to reclaim this unapologetically at a time when a shallow literalism is on the prowl. I have tried to show that poetry and faith reflect parts of each other and, even if not married in everyone's mind, should at least be on friendly terms as they seek to deepen and not resolve the meanings, mysteries and mayhem of the world and the rumour of God that encircles it, infuses it.

Poetry is like fish. If it's fresh, it's good. If it's stale, it's bad. And if you're unsure, try it out on the cat.
Osbert Sitwell

So, enough from me and over to the poets themselves. Poems follow. They are written by people of different heritages and environments, gay and straight, some past and some contemporary and from different parts of the world. Some of the poets believe in God, some don't and others aren't sure. I have chosen the poems because I like them – pure and simple. I have not always chosen the 'best' poems by each writer. Some of the poems are well known and some are not. I write a few thoughts after each one. I do this with some trepidation because to make explicit in prose what is implicit in the poem can work against the whole poetic vocation. I hope I leave enough unsaid. What I do say is not an insightful literary criticism nor is it a theological commentary. It is, rather, a brief introduction to the poet and some immediate thoughts and feelings that began to ripple out towards my shore when I encounter each poem's 'splash of words'. Some of those ripples are conscious of God, others are not. I believe, however, that God is in the ripples nevertheless and that just because I don't bring God overtly into the script here all the time, like an actor reluctantly brought on stage to take a bow, does not mean that God is absent in the world of which the poem speaks – quite the opposite in fact. Sometimes we need to be silent about God so that the God of our thinking can be revised and enlarged by the force of the waves. I don't believe that theology always needs a self-consciously theological vocabulary to express itself. Often it doesn't need any vocabulary at all but art, music, dance, design, science, justice, challenge, love, stillness. A reader might finish a chapter and ask, 'But where is God here?' My reply would be, 'But where is God not?'

I have spent the past three years travelling around here and there encouraging various groups and churches to engage with poems more. You might decide to look at one a day for a month or gather occasionally with friends to go through a couple of them together to see what each poem does to you and whether, like me, you cannot shake off the unignorable intuition that lies at the heart of everything written here, that God is in this world as poetry is in the poem.

Paternoster
(for A.B.J.)

Jen Hadfield (b. 1978)

Paternoster. Paternoster.
Hallowed be dy mane.
Dy kingdom come.
Dy draftwork be done.
Still plough the day
And give out daily bray
Though heart stiffen in the harness.
Then sleep hang harness with bearbells
And trot on bravely into sleep
Where the black and the bay
The sorrel and the grey
And foals and bearded wheat
Are waiting.
It is on earth as it is in heaven.
Drought, wildfire,
Wild asparagus, yellow flowers
On the flowering cactus.
Give our daily wheat, wet
Whiskers in the sonorous bucket.
Knead my heart, hardened daily.
Heal the hoofprint in my heart.
Give us our oats at bedtime
And in the night half-sleeping.
Paternoster. Paternoster.
Hallowed be dy hot mash.

Jen Hadfield, the youngest person to have won the T. S. Eliot Prize for poetry, lives on the Shetland Isle of Burra. The subjects of her poems are often local to her homeland, and so are the words that she can use to pour light on, and through, the people, animals and landscapes that make her feel 'connected and protected'.[1] Her poems root themselves around the alien but evocative vocabulary of the Scots and Shetland dialects, and we discover words like 'glid' (sunshine between showers), 'snuskit' (in a sulky frame of mind), 'glinder' (to peer through half-shut eyes) and 'blashey-wadder' (wet and unsettled weather). Hadfield has said that in the Shetlands 'some words are so local that they don't occur ten minutes down the road'.[2] When I read Hadfield's poems I'm reminded of Kenneth Koch's observation that 'each word has a little music of its own' which, he continues, 'poetry arranges so it can be heard'.[3]

'Paternoster' comes from Hadfield's second collection of poetry, *Nigh-No-Place*.[4] It is a collection of outward-looking poems, with a plucky pulse, that interrogate and bless the natural world with gratitude. In her exchange with nature we become aware that this world might have vital messages to surrender to the human soul or, in the words of the philosopher Bertrand Russell, that 'the world is full of magical things patiently waiting for our wits to grow sharper'. This makes for an exhilarating and expectant journey for her readers. You can almost feel the wind in your hair and the salt on your lips as you listen in, poised and willing for a fresher understanding of life. In 'Daed-traa', for instance, she writes, 'I go to the rockpool at the slack of tide/ to mind me what my poetry's for'. She observes that the rockpool '. . . has its ventricles, just like us –/ pumping brine, like bull's blood, a syrupy flow' as well as its own language of a 'holy hiccup' and 'Its minute's silence'. The natural systems of life spark associations with our own human living and, by this connection, we are given a sense of presence in the world, almost a reassurance that the world is trustworthy. Like the landscape she inhabits, there is a surefooted mystery to much of her imagery as she brings the familiar startlingly close in ways that first dislocate, but then resuscitate our perception. She has referred to her work as a type of 'ecopoetics'. Hadfield used to work in a fish-gutting factory. She is not romantic about nature. Its primal and uncontained forces are felt too strongly by her for that. There is, rather, a draw to the slow exposure of the raw elements of the world where she finds herself pushed into her own element in the process. She has said that her poetic outlook is 'being honest about the present tense that you live in and looking as accurately and intently as possible at one place'.

The person of faith might well discern a sacramental approach in her work. Her poems on love, memory, language, place and movement frequently channel themselves through the natural world, and the startling metaphors she employs to reset our compass in our environment stay with us. Hadfield compels us into sensing that a life is not lived if it passes by our natural habitat. It is made to pass through it, to become attentive to what she calls in one poem its 'realistic mysteries'.[5] Jane Hirshfield has written: 'Poetry's fertility lives in the marriage of said and unsaid, of languaged self and unlanguaged other, of the knowable and the gravitational pull of what lies beyond knowing'.[6] The truth of this observation lies at the heart of Hadfield's skill. Her recent collection of poems is called *Byssus*, named after the beard of a mussel, the tough fibres which anchor it to the seabed. The similar fibres of her strong but flexible language make the moveable seasons and cycles of nature its deep homeland.

She has said in interviews that the sense of the sacred is something she returns to again and again in her work. In *Nigh-No-Place* she instils a sense of heaven and earth being each other's natural home where each gratefully breathes the other in. Because she takes herself to such isolated places in her life, having a 'hunger for big skies', Hadfield's poems don't seem to want to communicate with us who read, so much as give voice to an impulse of wild gratitude, even bliss, that rises in her when she breathes in her landscape, whether it be her own Shetland or Canada where she has travelled. Some of her poems consequently have the feel of a liturgical litany or psalm, linking powerfully with her occasional, almost reverential repetition of sound as an initiator of a poem's internal rhythm. Many of her images are also funny and self-deprecating, such as when she notes how

'I crackled in my waterproof/ like a roasting rack of lamb'[7] or compares 'Badlands light' to 'the underwear you gave me:/ pilled and balding, porridge-white'.[8] When it comes to description, it is as if, in the words of the poet Susan Mitchell, 'the world is wily, and doesn't want/ to be held for long',[9] but poets such as Hadfield are able to hold it a little longer than most.

'Paternoster' is, to my mind, one of her most beautiful poems. It is a prayer of a draughthorse in which she reworks the texture and rhythm of the Lord's Prayer through the horse's heart. You can listen to the poet reading it on the Poetry Archive website.[10] If you want a glimpse of the beauty of a prayerful, intimate litany from a tired but hopeful heart, then I recommend you listen to it as well as read it. Hadfield's poems are mesmeric and are meant, as are all poems, to be heard.

In this poem the horse is weary but reverent, his (or her) voice solitary but accepting. There is a heaviness to his day that reaches his soul and he prays that his heart might be kneaded by God so that it might rise and take its true shape. Like many of us, he half-sleeps and realizes that it is in the night when his hungers are most evident. All that drifts up into the mind in the dark speaks of who we are and where we need nourishment. The buckets we rely on for this are too often hollow and noisy.

At night our hidden selves come out to play in our dreams and restlessness. The horse prays for oats as he enters the darkness *half-sleeping*. His subconscious life needs nurturing by God as much as his conscious one. He cannot be defined by his work alone. We sense he is looking for intimacy, connection and play. He is not a proper horse without them. How easy it would be to pray for his wants, to be stronger or more decorated and esteemed, rather than for his needs. The horse can see who he is in danger of becoming if he can only feel the harness on him. His yoke is not easy and his burden not light. He needs *Paternoster*, Our Father, to comfort and be strengthened by, so that, as the poem says, he can both *still plough the day/ and give out daily bray.*

At the end this horse is not too tired to dream. In the spirit of the heavenly banquet, he tells God that *hot mash* is hallowed and will always be received by him as a warm, beautiful gift at close of day. Hope stretches our minds creatively beyond our particular plough. The horse has work to do. He does not shirk it. He does, however, see with clarity that the soul shaped only by what we do is a half-soul. He places himself before his creator, munching his oats, and recalls his being, now, in the present moment. The present is aptly named: it is the primary gift. A life can be haunted by what it never was and only retrieved by placing it into the hands of God for the future. The ancient Assyrian people had a word for prayer that was the same word they used for unclenching a fist. Here, there is a similar intimacy being voiced – a soul opening, in the vocative, praying behind the doors of a closed stable, the harness off, laying its life and burdens and hopes before its loving creator.

The French philosopher Voltaire once observed that 'If God has created us in his image, we have returned him the compliment'. Does the draughthorse imagine God to be horse-like? *Hallowed be dy mane*, he prays. What else would God be like for him? Surely not a human? Humans are busy, ungrateful beings, 'distracted from distraction by distraction', as T. S. Eliot puts it. No, God understands what it is to be a draughthorse from within. Only he could *Heal the hoofprint in my heart,* the pressured imprint of daily labour that affects his spontaneity and joy of those things that are *on earth as it is in heaven.*

So many of Hadfield's poems in *Nigh-No-Place* explore the dislocations of being in 'no-place' and leave us asking what it means to be 'at home' in a natural world that has become unnatural to us. 'Paternoster' takes up these themes within the inner life, showing us an animal resting in a relationship of complete trust with its creator, a home-place, a stable of the heart with plenty of wheat for the whiskers, from where all journeys yet to come will set out. As we overhear the horse at prayer we glimpse that God can be the intimate friend in whom all our loose ends find their home, their stable.

Procedure

Jo Shapcott (b. 1953)

This tea, this cup of tea, made of leaves,
made of the leaves of herbs and absolute

almond blossom, this tea, is the interpreter
of almond, liquid touchstone which lets us
scent its true taste at last and with a bump,

in my case, takes me back to the yellow time
of trouble with bloodtests, and cellular
madness, and my presence required

on the slab for surgery, and all that mess
I don't want to comb through here because
it seems, honestly, a trifle now that steam

and scent and strength and steep and infusion
say thank you thank you thank you for the then, and now

Life is a hospital where all the patients want to change beds,
said the French poet Baudelaire. We distract ourselves from our
mortality by ambitions and competitions, knowing intellectually
that we will die one day but not quite emotionally believing it. It
was while university professor Jo Shapcott was at her busiest –
travelling, teaching and completing commissions – that she was
diagnosed with breast cancer. The landscape of her life changed
fundamentally:

The body has always been a subject for me. It is the stage for the high drama of our lives, from birth to death and everything in between. When you observe your own body under physical change like that, there's a new kind of urgency. I had a lumpectomy, my lympth glands out, chemo and radiotherapy. You go through several different stages, so you don't know how ill you are for a while, and the verdict keeps getting worse and worse, until you can actually take action, start treatment.[1]

The collection of 45 poems from which 'Procedure' comes is called *On Mutability*. 'Mutable' means subject to change or alteration and, as is typical of Shapcott's poetry, the interior changes of the mind and heart are inseparable from the external changes of the human body and the natural world. The writer Virginia Woolf, in an essay of 1926 called 'On Being Ill',[2] talks about the amount of time you spend on your back when you are sick so that the horizontal view is suddenly more typical than the vertical view and so, open to the sky, life is seen from an alternative perspective and 'undiscovered countries' are disclosed. The title of this poem hints at this suffering potential: 'procedure' can refer to a medical treatment but it can also mean the way of proceeding, moving on, going forward. In both meanings of the word, possible transformation is in the air.

On Mutability was published in 2010 and was Shapcott's first collection of poetry for 12 years. It made the headlines by winning a Costa Book of the Year award and the judges praised the poems: 'Fizzing with variety, they are a paean to creativity and make the reader feel that what matters to us all is imagination, humanity and a smile'. Shapcott's poetry is a rich mixture of the accessible with the obscure, the practical with the cerebral. She is bold, investigative, poised. She has a particular interest in science – noting how poetic it is by being reliant on analogy and metaphor – and the passion of her curiosity is fearless. *On Mutability* includes exploration of the City of London, physics, neuroscience and even killing a scorpion. The presiding spirit of the book is the work of the artist Helen Chadwick, whose 1986 exhibition had the same title. It is in many ways a series of meditations on mortality but the poems often have an agile wit and, because change is the focus, they avoid being overly grim and instead have moments of joy, even of ecstasy. 'Procedure' is a good example of this.

The poet holds a cup of tea. The *leaves* are mentioned twice in the first short stanza, the double meaning here of the herbal infusion and of leaving a place preparing the ground of the work. We sense the distillation and self-scrutiny that the tea comes to symbolize: *interpreter, touchstone, true taste, bump* all alert us to an authentic process of discerning the genuine and real in times that are difficult to read. Her protracted illness is captured fleetingly and without self-pity: *yellow time, bloodtests, cellular madness, slab, mess.* She doesn't want to *comb through* these things, though, because the perspective that has broken through is so startlingly fresh and energized that they seem *a trifle.* The word *honestly*, held in place by two commas, stands out in the poem as honesty always does as it calls our attention back to those things we fail to read between the lines of life we choose to inscribe in black and white. In fact, there is not one full-stop in the entire poem. Not even at the end. The ecstasy, out-of-timeness, with which the poem resonates has no end. The poet is proceeding still. This poem is an antidote to the deathly full-stop that closes down and completes. The 14 commas of the work remind us of what happens when an interruption, such as cancer, occurs and that may in one stroke transform the full-stops of our life into a comma, celebrating more of our life's chapter yet to discover. Shapcott does not take us down a path of dissolution even in the darkest hours. In our emotional autobiography, what happens to us, Shapcott has said, is never the most interesting thing – that will always be, 'What does it mean?'

The final stanza is heady and almost gratefully overtaken by all the senses of the moment: *scent and strength and steep and infusion.* Her response is *thank you thank you thank you.* Again, no full-stops. Just an outpouring of a heart humbled and strengthened by all that it has undergone and is now being enlarged by. This response of gratitude, so closely tied to a cup, makes the poem almost eucharistic. The ordinary cup of tea we all take for granted is here sacramentally understood as a vehicle for the grace that can only be met with vulnerable human thanks and amazement. The result is a transfiguration of the heart and a transformation of the mind. Although two-thirds of the poems in the collection are written in the first person, there is no self-aggrandizement but rather an acknowledgement, as one poem reasserts, 'So this is me'. Unusually with poems about illness, nothing is in the passive case. There is no screaming of victimhood. Instead we sense a person well on the journey to another landscape. 'There is another world and it is in this one', noted the French poet Paul Eluard.

Shapcott has said that at the edges of change there is 'twinkling green'. For the person of Christian faith our being, with its shifts and losses, is a gift from God. The mystic Meister Eckhart wrote: 'If the only prayer you ever said in your whole life was "Thank you", that would suffice'. A life shaped on thankfulness is a life poised to become more of a fragile but beautiful gift. The poem ends with *now*. The grateful, graced life is attentive to the present. The poems in *Of Mutability* achieve what the Christian seeks to achieve in life: the exposure of all illusions but without becoming disillusioned.

Jo Shapcott is well now and working hard on her next collection. In a recent interview she said that publishing *On Mutability* 'cleared a block in my head' and that her new book she thinks of being 'The Book of Life, because the poems all seem to be about things that are teeming'. The interviewer, maybe with 'Procedure' in mind, asked her if she still feels the euphoria she did at the end of her treatment. 'I do,' she said. 'All these years later, it hasn't gone away.'

Don't give me the whole truth

Olav H. Hauge (1908–94)

Don't give me the whole truth,
don't give me the sea for my thirst,
don't give me the sky when I ask for light,
but give me a glint, a dewy wisp, a mote
as the birds bear water-drops from their bathing
and the wind a grain of salt.

Olav Hauge was a Norwegian poet and translator. He lived in
Ulvik on the Hardangerfjord in a simple home with handmade
chairs, bowls and wooden bookcases stacked with poetry from
around the world. He was a solitary figure living in three acres of
ground and surviving on the proceeds from his 70 apple trees. He
translated international poetry into Norwegian and was a learned
man, modest and self-contained. He married at the age of 65 and
enjoyed his companionship with his wife for over twenty years
until, in 1994, he was discovered dead, peacefully sitting in his
reading chair.

This poem-prayer is translated, as many of his poems are, by
Robin Fulton. Like much of his native Norwegian landscape
there is a wild beauty to enjoy in Hauge's poetry and there is also
a bleakness, human breath made visible in the cold indifferent
terrain. Influenced by classical Chinese poetry, Hauge's poems are
often short, graceful and distilled. He composed in various poetic
forms, often short, such as sonnets and Haiku-like structures. He
wrote in his native western Norwegian dialect, giving an earthi-
ness to the original text, fortified by concrete vocabulary and

simple imagery. The result is an artistic simplicity which, some wonder, might have less to it than meets the eye. For admirers, however, Hauge's plain style is deceptive and gives a rich flavour that lingers in the mind and clarifies the presence of the world.

Here in this poem, Hauge prays that he will be given only enough in life to keep him going. He doesn't want all that there is. Like birds who carry off only a few drops of water from the stream or wind that takes only a grain of salt from the ocean, he doesn't want to possess everything or understand it completely. Instead, he asks for glints, epiphanies, droplet recognitions that feed us enough to keep us exploring but not enough to make us feel we have arrived. It is the prayer of a pilgrim.

The imagery within the poem is elemental – *sea, sky, birds* and *wind* – and you sense a person here alone with the natural world as company. Reflection in such solitude has perhaps made him sense that the easy answers are never the ones worth having. He seems to imply that we can be seduced by our need for clarity, our desire to be 'right', by that unattractive preening side to us that longs to be full of impressive knowledge to swank about with. Our brains can go to our heads. In reply, the hardened landscape is never impressed. From its distance, it leaves us standing alone without comfort with the wind teasing us, making us topple over.

The Judeo-Christian scriptures are full of reminders that we are limited beings who cannot ever understand God or the totality of the universe. Our absolute systems of thought and belief only make us look absurd if we take them too seriously for, with God, all is as yet unfinished and undisclosed. Prayers that are fashioned out of a conviction that God agrees with our take on things are pale imitations of what prayer is. Prayer invites us to stop gripping, to become dependent, to rinse out our eyes so that when the momentary miracle comes we can say 'Thank you', not 'I told you so'. Like St Kevin who prayed with his hands open so still that a blackbird nested in them, Hauge here implies that whereas a possessive accumulation of facts gives a disproportionate sense of our knowledge and control of life, a receptive modesty gives birth to a wisdom capable of feeling the rhythms of the world and attending to them in awe and thankfulness.

I'm reminded at this point of the 'Pie of Knowledge'. This is an attempt to describe our knowledge of things in relation to all the knowledge in the universe by making a pie chart, like a sliced cake, and cutting it into sections. The first slice of the Pie of Knowledge is made up of *those things that you know you know*. This might be, for example, the plot of Jane Austen's *Sense and Sensibility*, the name of your dog, or how to make pancakes. Then there are the *things you know you don't know*. This may be a larger slice and may include nuclear physics, the mating rituals of the horsefly, the names of the stars, or the rules of polo. The third slice contains *the things you know but have forgotten*. Again, this may include how old the Queen was when she came to the throne, your grandchild's phone number, how chocolate is made, and who the author of this book is. The fourth slice of the pie is very interesting: *the things you don't know you don't know*. I can't give you examples here because that would mean I knew. The last slice is *the things you think you know but really don't* – your family or friends might be better able to identify these for you but they include the symbolism in Tolstoy's *War and Peace*, why my neighbour is like he is, the causes of inner-city poverty or what it was like to have been in Auschwitz.

Which would your biggest slice of the cake be? For all human beings the largest slice will be those things *you don't know you don't know*. This slice probably makes up 99.9 per cent of the cake for most of us. The total knowledge of our universe is so vast that the sum of all human knowledge is infinitesimally small by comparison. Leadership and management trainers use this Pie because they know that people who have a large slice of the 'I think I know it all' piece can be people who make hasty and ill-advised decisions based on ignorance, and it is vital, so their training goes, that everybody knows that there is a slice, a very large slice, containing the things we don't know we don't know and to act accordingly in our transactions.

For believers in God, the Pie of Knowledge is very pertinent. When we approach the Mystery of God we come face to face with our ignorance. Wise theologians such as Thomas Aquinas even try to burn their theology from time to time. It might well be that eternity will be spent being shown all those things we didn't know we didn't know as well as the things we thought we did but had got badly wrong. This is why at its best Anglican theology, the resource from which I try to make some sense of God's being in the universe, has never tried to over-define God or his mysteries. Instead of offering a dogmatic dotted line to sign, it has instead preferred to offer people a Prayer Book to see if they'd like to join in. So badly do we misunderstand ourselves, never mind anything else, that St Theresa commented that more tears are spilt over prayers that are answered than those that aren't.

Christian faith has learned that God does not make himself into a convenient and understandable bit of information, facts of knowledge packaged for human consumption. There is no divine text, email or blog that relays to us everything about him. How could this be done anyway? Instead of giving us information, or complete comprehension, he gives us his presence. His eternal Word is not published or stored, according to St John. It is, rather, made into human being and is living in relationship with us. He dwells among us. In fact, in the Greek, John implies that God tabernacles with us; that is, he pitches his tent next to ours, sets up camp alongside us – not so that we can know him fully, pin him down like a dead butterfly and pride ourselves in what we know and others don't, but so we can relate to him, begin to understand him through prayer, learn how to love him, begin to trust and sit with him, like sitting in the sunlight, to be changed by him – to have a relationship that grows and develops. This is a living knowledge, like that with someone we love and want to understand better. It knows setbacks and hurts, it demands some changes in us if we are to learn more, love better.

The God to whom we relate may not be fully understood. In fact, at times we want to take him on and shout at him. God is never fully understood but is always present, always in relationship no matter how shadowed. He seeks from us not cleverness but connection, and this always demands of us the ability to receive more. To this end, as Christians we should learn to question more, to question as a ritual, as an exploration of grace rather than as a search for certainty.

In a competitive world that prides itself on information and where the first person to draw a breath is declared the listener, Hauge's prayer puts us back in proportion. It recalls the words of Henri Nouwen: 'My deepest vocation is to be a witness to the glimpses of God I have been allowed to catch'.

At Hauge's funeral his body was taken up the mountain to its resting place in a horse-drawn cart. Trotting next to its mother all the way, and beside the coffin, was the horse's foal, dancing and energetically alive as the mourners made their way uphill. It is an image that seems appropriate for a poet who saw the cyclical nature of the world as its glory and perceived that it is only the unencumbered childlike soul that can celebrate the sacrament of the present moment. Hauge lived all his life in the place where he was born and yet his soul was a very seasoned traveller. As Marcel Proust came to appreciate, 'the real voyage of discovery consists not in seeking new landscapes but in having new eyes'.

North Haven

Elizabeth Bishop (1911–79)

In memoriam: Robert Lowell

I can make out the rigging of a schooner
a mile off; I can count
the new cones on the spruce. It is so still
the pale bay wears a milky skin, the sky
no clouds, except for one long, carded horse's-tail.

The islands haven't shifted since last summer,
even if I like to pretend they have
– drifting, in a dreamy sort of way,
a little north, a little south or sidewise,
and that they're free within the blue frontiers of bay.

This month, our favorite one is full of flowers:
Buttercups, Red Clover, Purple Vetch,
Hawkweed still burning, Daisies pied, Eyebright,
the Fragrant Bedstraw's incandescent stars,
and more, returned, to paint the meadows with delight.

The Goldfinches are back, or others like them,
and the White-throated Sparrow's five-note song,
pleading and pleading, brings tears to the eyes.
Nature repeats herself, or almost does:
repeat, repeat, repeat; revise, revise, revise.

Years ago, you told me it was here
(in 1932?) you first "discovered *girls*"
and learned to sail, and learned to kiss.
You had "such fun", you said, that classic summer.
("Fun" – it always seemed to leave you at a loss . . .)

You left North Haven, anchored in its rock,
afloat in mystic blue . . . And now – you've left
for good. You can't derange, or re-arrange,
your poems again. (But the Sparrows can their song.)
The words won't change again. Sad friend, you cannot change.

Although she published only 101 poems in her lifetime, Elizabeth
Bishop is now considered by many to be one of the best American
poets of the twentieth century. Known for her apparently object-
ive, serene observations of the physical world, there is, underneath
the controlled perfectionism of her style, a discernible pain, even
a struggle to grieve and belong. In apparently neutralized descrip-
tion, Bishop is implying to us but not imploring us.

Bishop's father died when she was only a year old and her
mother suffered mental illness as a result, eventually being placed
in an institution when Bishop was five. She never saw her mother
again. She was brought up by both sets of grandparents, for a
while living in Nova Scotia, before going on to study and travel
widely. Independently wealthy, eventually she settled for a while
in Key West, Florida, and later in Brazil where she lived with
her partner the architect and political activist Lota de Mercedo
Soares. Lota took her own life in 1967 and Bishop moved to New
York, San Francisco and Massachusetts, where eventually she
took a teaching job at Harvard. It is not difficult to see why loss,
emotional hurt and the search for 'home' have been identified by
readers of her work as being embedded beneath her almost beguil-
ing composure. She writes as if in flight from something. She liked
to live near the sea and said she was like the sandpiper, running
along the edges of different countries looking for something. On
many levels it was hard for her to move inland.

One of the best descriptions of Bishop's style I have come across was published by Ernie Hilbert in Random House's online magazine *Bold Type*:

> Bishop's poetics is one distinguished by tranquil observation, craft-like accuracy, care for the small things of the world, a miniaturist's discretion and attention. Unlike the pert and woolly poetry that came to dominate American literature by the second half of her life, her poems are balanced like Alexander Calder mobiles, turning so subtly as to seem almost still at first, every element, every weight of meaning and song, poised flawlessly against the next.

'North Haven' was written after the death in 1977 of her best friend and fellow poet Robert Lowell. You would not know that it is an elegy for someone dear to her from the first four stanzas. It begins with what Bishop is famous for, that detached and solitary observance of the natural world. She records a boat on the water, new cones on spruce trees, a single cloud in the sky. Often, to look at this outer world, for Bishop, was a way of avoiding looking at the inner one, the fractured feelings and losses of her past as they clung on inside her.

What Elizabeth Bishop said she admired in her favourite poet, George Herbert, was the fact that 'he wrote about the most fantastic things imaginable in perfectly simple everyday language'. 'That', she continued, 'is what I have always tried to do.'[1] She admired his 'absolute naturalness of tone'. A poet who lives in emotional exile, with a distant and unsettled sense of homeland, will inevitably find a 'naturalness of tone' a desirable quality as it helps us fit in wherever we find ourselves to be. You don't draw attention to yourself but keep camouflaged, spying but rarely spied.

In 'North Haven', however, a poem written only a year or so before her own death, the poem shifts from her observation of the wildlife on the small island where she spent summers in her later years, to that of her friend, their shared times together, and all that has come to an end by his unexpected fatal heart attack.

One senses that his death has attacked her heart too, though as you expect with Bishop, her feelings are kept under reins, in cool poetic form, controlled and even masked. When she writes that he has *left/ for good* we know that it is exactly not 'for good' and that Bishop is grieving. This loss, as losses and farewells always do, stirs up deep memories of all the others in her past – not least her mother and her lover.

The poem begins pleasurably. The poet has returned to a much loved place, and with the word *can* used twice in the first two lines, she reveals her own life and capability there, capturing all that passes before her with her tuned senses. She allows us to know she was on the island last summer and we get a half-concealed glimpse of another person or persons with her there at some point as she refers to *our favorite*. She lists the flowers with a sense of gratitude, it seems, and evokes in their names the colours that *paint the meadows with delight*. *Daisies pied* is a description from Shakespeare's 'A Winter's Tale'.

The fourth stanza brings the beginnings of the shadow. We are told that the goldfinches have returned to the island – but they may not be the same ones as were seen last year. Is she referring to them being different species or to the actual birds of last year not being there? Goldfinches die too. The sparrow's song is *pleading and pleading* and *brings tears to the eyes*. The poet seems on the verge of crying. It is, perhaps, the first momentary glimpse within. She is not a poet of self-expression but her coiled self is present in her poems, guarded but insistent. Her island, her life and its friendships are not, she learns, impervious to change. The last line of each stanza is a hexameter, following usual pentameters, as if there is something more to come, unexpectedly disturbing the rhythms – like the end to life itself.

Robert Lowell was well known for revising and amending his poems. In one of his own sonnets he wrote that God 'loved to tinker'[2] and tinkering with his own poems was for him a creative, energizing act. Many of his letters to Bishop contained thoughts and suggestions about their work and how it might be bettered. Bishop juxtaposes at the end of verse four the work of cyclical nature (*repeat*) and the work of a restless poet (*revise*) so that the italicized line almost sounds like birdsong itself. It is a surprising marriage of two verbs but alerts us to the way in which nature's give and take includes also the ones who observe it and who work hard to capture it on paper.

The fifth stanza begins *Years ago*, as if there is no repetition in a human life but a linear path where memories have to work hard and be revised (*in 1932?*). This is the verse when Lowell enters, addressed, and so is given back life for a few moments. We get a photo shot, as it were, of the island being used for parties and young romance. Things are *learned* there and *fun* makes a doubtful appearance. Lowell came to the island summer after summer to spend time with Bishop but the temporary departures of shared time are now over and he leaves *for good*.

The literary critic Helen Vendler argues that 'every elegy must contain at least one moment in which the actual death of the lost person "happens over again", is enacted rather than merely reported'.[3] She writes of this poem:

> By introducing the passage of time in the first-stanza phrase 'last summer'; by giving a hint of another person in the second-stanza adjective 'our'; by allowing hearing, in the bird stanza, to join sight; and finally by her fourth-stanza admission of tears and the human self-correction of revision, Bishop prepares her speaker to acknowledge the ever-present absence of Lowell. He is at last permitted actual entrance to the poem as a 'living person' when the speaker recalls his mention (in the past tense) of their island. The speaker herself, musing in recollection . . . quietly restores herself too to full emotional personhood. She had begun as an Emersonian 'transparent eyeball'; now she is a mourner ending her Lowell stanza with the human word 'loss'.[4]

The hardened pain at the end of the poem is that Bishop recognizes that Lowell will never again be able to revise his words. Bishop shifts the reference in the last stanza from Lowell (*you've left*) to the words he wrote that now *won't change again*. He slips from view and she puts him at rest: *Sad friend, you cannot change*. Or is she the sad friend who cannot change her dislocating bereavement? Friendship is the relationship where all our fragility can find a surer ground. When it is taken away we begin to fragment a little. Many of her poems refer to those nearby as fleeting presences, temporarily glimpsed.

The Irish writer Colm Toibin has written a beautifully insightful book on Bishop and her work.[5] He says of her that 'she began with the idea that little is known and that much is puzzling'[6] and that therefore to make a true statement in poetry required of her a hushed and solitary concentration. He notes that, as in the work of the poet Thom Gunn, contrary to the expectations of a confessional age, grief is masked by reason, nourishment is not sought by laying emotions out on the table: 'puzzled by the world's strategies they began to invent their own'.[7] He argues that she buried what mattered to her most in her tone rather than confronting it and it is this tone that lifts the best poems to 'a realm beyond their own occasion'.[8] Toibin reflects:

These poems by Bishop are full of resigned tones and half-resigned undertones, but there is always something else there in the space between the words, something that is controlled but not fully, so that the chaos or the panic held in check is all the more apparent because it is consigned to the shadows.[9]

Love (III)

George Herbert (1593–1633)

Love bade me welcome: yet my soul drew back,
    Guiltie of dust and sinne.
But quick-ey'd Love, observing me grow slack
    From my first entrance in,
Drew nearer to me, sweetly questioning,
    If I lack'd any thing.

A guest, I answer'd, worthy to be here:
    Love said, You shall be he.
I the unkinde, ungratefull? Ah my deare,
    I cannot look on thee.
Love took my hand, and smiling did reply,
    Who made the eyes but I?

Truth Lord, but I have marr'd them: let my shame
    Go where it doth deserve.
And know you not, says Love, who bore the blame?
    My deare, then I will serve.
You must sit down, says Love, and taste my meat:
    So I did sit and eat.

The philosopher and activist Simone Weil famously thought this
to be 'the most beautiful poem in the world'. It is certainly one
of George Herbert's masterpieces. It is carefully structured with
triple stanzas, a trinitarian form, with each stanza containing
a rhyming quatrain completed by a couplet. It is the dramatic

dialogue, the polite point and counterpoint, of a man in conversation with God that is so affecting. Even though the poem has a refined and quiet tone to it, restrained but seductive, it reaches deep into the nature of human beings and of our creator. The absence of modern quotation marks gives the whole a seamless quality. This is an interrogation into the being of Love that is a natural part of, not separate from, the relationship we have with God. For Herbert, it is quite all right to debate with God. God is big enough to take anything that might come up.

George Herbert had a privileged upbringing and was an obvious candidate for high public office and a career at Court. For a time he 'lost himself in a humble way' and this eventually led him to seek ordination in the Church of England. He served the parish of Fugglestone-with-Bemerton, outside Salisbury, for three years before his death at the age of 39. When he was dying Herbert sent a collection of his handwritten English poems, which had never been published in his lifetime, to Nicholas Ferrar at Little Gidding with a note: 'If he think', wrote Herbert, 'it may turn to the advantage of any dejected poor soul, let it be made public; if not, let him burn it'. We should be very grateful that Ferrar did not go anywhere near the fireplace.

A decade after Herbert's death his brother Edward wrote of him: 'His life was most holy and exemplary, in so much that about Salisbury . . . he was little less than sainted. He was not exempt from passion and choler, being infirmities to which all our race is subject, but that excepted, without reproach in his actions'.

Over my years of reading Herbert I have come to see him as the poet who most expresses our relationship with God as a friendship. I'm not talking about friendship in terms of the 600 'Friends' that some have on Facebook, but rather the one or two people who have changed our life for good and maybe at some cost to us both. Thinking about these friends can dare us to reflect, as I think did Herbert, that our life with God is a friendship that asks of us a mutual freedom. Friendship deepens as honesty deepens. We cannot put the other on a pedestal. We must try to prise off the mask that has begun to eat into our face. We need to be brave in hearing what we don't like or saying what we have never dared. Friendship requires courage enough to stop skating so quickly over our own thin ice in case we disappear through the cracks. Instead, we face the fact that we need support and connection and that we have much to give as well.

It was T. S. Eliot who said in an essay on Herbert that the greatest difficulty for a poet is to distinguish between what one really feels and what one would like to feel. The same could be said of people of faith. We can often use religious language, even pastoral language, to distance ourselves from where we actually are. The script and persona of a priest, for instance, can sometimes lead us into being manicured middle-distance relaters and very ill at ease with intimacy. And here is where Herbert begins to speak to us about the transformative nature of friendship with God. At the close of his poem 'Jordan (II)', for instance:

> But while I bustled, I might hear a friend
> Whisper, *How wide is all this long pretence!*
> *There is in love a sweetness ready penned:*
> *Copy out only that, and save expense.*

In the presence of a true friend we become very different people from those we often spend the day being, and Herbert is clear that self-scrutiny is called for in the presence of his truest friend and God. He knows that if a friendship with God and with himself is to be authentic then it needs to be open.

Whereas John Donne, the influential poet and friend of Herbert's family, similarly wrestled with God, he was in many ways more removed, maybe more fearful of God, knowing that his salvation lay partly in his own hands. In Herbert we feel a security and confidence in God his friend. 'In this love, more than in bed, I rest', he writes. You sense that whatever happens or is said, all will be well between them. Herbert never once talks of hell-fire or damnation. The wrestle in Herbert is speaking the truth of how life is and feels. As he writes: 'Dare to be true. Nothing can need a lie: a fault which needs it most, grows two thereby'. There is an audacious familiarity in his relationship with God, and his struggle is to find the sweetness of love in all our daily difficulties, knowing that his divine friend will not condemn the wit or punch with which he expresses himself when he can't find it or when it's all too much. Because God is his friend, you sense in Herbert's words that salvation is secure, forgiveness is unconditional, grace is irresistible. The intimacy with God we find in Herbert comes from a confidence in the inviolability of their relationship. The underlying unity of devotion means he can adore and be impudent, be hostile and angry, and can also love and be speechless as one who sees how much he is treasured. Nothing he can do or say can separate him from God, as St Paul also came to believe. Indeed, in his poem 'The Holdfast', he comes to a clear perception:

> I stood amazed at this,
> Much troubled, till I heard a friend express,
> That all things were more ours by being his.

In 'Love (III)', we see this relationship beautifully expressed and fed by biblical imagery, including the parable of the wedding feast, when the guests fail to turn up (Matthew 22.1–14) and Psalm 23.4 and Luke 12.37 where God prepares a table for his people. In Luke's telling of Christ's parable of the feast to which the invited guests don't come, we read: 'A certain man made a great supper, and bade many' (Luke 14.16). From the very first line of Herbert's poem we hear the bounce and eagerness of Love in the short syllables of *Love bade me welcome* and the contrast with the long and heavy syllables of *my soul drew back*. Similarly *quick-ey'd Love* is sprightly in comparison to *grow slack*. The tone of the dialogue is set straight away. A universal tone is created by Herbert by using the word 'Love' instead of God or Christ, making the person of faith recall that love is the only metaphor for God that should be pursued relentlessly. It also helps the doubter to get beyond the loaded word 'God' that may have so many shadows attached to it because, sadly, it can be a weaponized word, carrying projections and used abusively. How this poem would change if the word 'God' replaced 'Love' is a telling question.

Love draws nearer. He sees how the man is pulling away. He also *sweetly* questions him. Love asks three questions in the poem, while the man asks only one. At a time when many see religion as a project to answer questions this is helpfully corrective. Love, instead of answering questions, questions our answers but only in an invitation to come closer.

The man in the poem says he is not worthy because he is *unkinde, ungratefull.* He cannot look at Love in the eye. He asks that his shame *go where it doth deserve.* Love reaches out and touches him, takes him by the hand and then cracks a pun: *Who made the eyes but I?* Again, this is God as friend, not tyrant. His eyes are sensitive and full of tenderness. Love is smiling as he speaks and reminds the man that Love has borne all the blame already. The man is *guiltie of dust and sinne* and the dust from humanity's long road since its divine creation lies heavy on us, but just as Simon Peter protests his unworthiness and Christ washes his feet in reply, so here Love prepares a meal and asks the man to stop beating himself up and to eat and enjoy what is set before him. Love has carried the blame for Herbert's unworthiness and the only thing asked of Herbert now is that he sits down and enjoys nourishment. The master becomes the servant. The poem ends with six very short equally stressed words conveying a poignant surrender to the words and the loving body-language of God which have brought a peace to his inner conflicts against all the odds: *So I did sit and eat.* The last lines of a Herbert poem so often transform, even subvert, everything that has gone before them. You sense in them that God might do the same to a human life as it draws to its close, such is the power of his love. Words of the Song of Solomon must certainly have been in Herbert's mind: 'He brought me to the banqueting house, and his banner over me was love' (2.4).

So many voices today come at us from every side telling us that we are small, fat, ugly, stupid, poor and not of any value unless we dance to the tune of the culture's advertisers. We internalize these voices, believing ourselves to be valueless but often lash out at others to hide it. Here we find the gospel encapsulated in a few intimately charged lines: don't listen to the noisy bullying voices because only one matters – the voice that comes from heaven telling you who you really are, that you are loved and wanted and for always. The gospel asks us to live up to this voice and not to live down to the others. The last line, in a typical Herbert monosyllabic resolution, shows us that the banquet begins when the man finally listens to Love and sits with him, no doubt to continue a conversation where they can now, at last, look into each other's eye.

Most of us think there is something that God must hate about us. Herbert in this magnificent poem shows that, quite the contrary, God loves us just the way we are but that he loves us so much he doesn't want us to stay like that. The human self is always a little suspect in Herbert's poetry. Grace is needed to resolve, amend and complete it, shaping it into a soul rather than just a self.

I was brought up by my grandparents. As a boy I knew that my grandfather had flown in the Royal Air Force in the Second World War and he was a bit of a hero to me but he never spoke about his experiences, except one day mentioning 'Dresden' and weeping. He has since died but a few years ago I was asked to preach in the reconstructed Frauenkirche in Dresden. He was very much in my mind. On the way to the railway station at the end of my visit the taxi driver asked me why I was in Dresden and I told him I had always wanted to come. 'Why?' he asked. I took a deep breath. 'Because my grandfather was a navigator of a Lancaster bomber and I know he flew here on 14 February 1945 as part of the bombing raid and he could never talk about it.' The man was quiet and then said, 'Ah, that was the night my mother was killed.' He pulled the car over and turned the engine off. He then turned round to me, put out his arm towards me and said, 'And now we shake hands.'

At the end of many of Herbert's poems the last few lines completely upturn all that you have been reading so far with fresh surprise. His poems reveal that God is loyal to the future, just as we are invited to be. In 'Love (III)' Herbert says that he has *marr'd* his own eyes. Marring is the opposite of mending, which we see *Love* do in the poem in every question, statement and gesture. That man in Dresden whose name I shall never know took the risk of the outstretched arm, just as God does to us, and as God did to Herbert, and only in that courageous desire to connect – in the face of all that could have come between us from the past – is a friendship and a future possible. *Love took my hand. Smiling.*

When Herbert collected his poems together for his friend to look at, he was careful as to the order in which he placed them. He placed this poem right at the end. The message was clear – for the person of faith 'Love' must be the last word.

Tripping Over Joy

Hafiz (c. 1320–89)
trans. Daniel Ladinsky

What is the difference
Between your experience of Existence
And that of a saint?

The saint knows
That the spiritual path
Is a sublime chess game with God

And that the Beloved
Has just made such a Fantastic Move

That the saint is now continually
Tripping over Joy
And bursting out in Laughter
And saying, 'I Surrender!'

Whereas, my dear,
I am afraid you still think

You have a thousand serious moves.

Hafiz, or Shams-ud-din Muhammad, is one of the most loved and admired Persian poets. Little is known of his life. Probably born around 1320 and dying 70 years later, he lived at about the same time as the great early English poet Geoffrey Chaucer. He spent most of his life in the cultured garden city of Shiraz. Born into a poor family, he worked to pay for tuition and was educated in the disciplines of the day. Medieval Persia took poetry seriously and Hafiz would have immersed himself as a student in the works of the great poets. He would have studied theology carefully too. 'Hafiz' means 'memorizer' and is a title given to a person who knows the entire Quran by heart.

It seems that Hafiz had poetic talent and he quickly gained a name for himself at court and around the city. Some of his poems, however, were considered heretical and he went through periods of his life when he fell out of favour, even going into exile at one stage. A more tolerant regime welcomed him home and he served as a respected teacher and writer again until his death. For hundreds of years his burial place was a pilgrimage site. It was Goethe who mainly introduced Hafiz's poems to the West and Ralph Waldo Emerson famously translated them into English. Others began to admire his verse including such diverse figures as Queen Victoria, Nietzsche, Lorca and Brahms, who put lines of Hafiz into compositions. Even Sherlock Holmes quotes Hafiz from time to time. He remains one of the most popular poets in Iran, with 12 October being celebrated as Hafiz Day.

Hafiz was a Sufi master and his *Divan* (collected poems) is a classic in the literature of Sufism, celebrated for perfectly express-ing the human experience of divine love. Sufism is a mystical, meditative and poetic tradition of Islam. The stories told about Hafiz witness to his desire, with the help of his own life teacher Muhammad Attar, to distil his Self so that the deeper dimensions of divine and human love might be welcomed, understood and expressed in his life. God, the Beloved, is the one in whom we are lost or consumed as the moth is taken by the flame to which it is drawn. He learns that you cannot 'master' love but only serve as its vessel. Love is the sole spiritual imperative, the ultimate intoxicant, the only law of the authentic soul. The stories and poems reveal the frustrations and despairs on this path. The dis-tillation is painful. Hafiz also mocks and plays with those who, in their 'orthodoxy', condemn intoxication in the divine and insist on correct behaviour and naively take their own preaching as truth. It is impossible to be proud of your own purity because as soon as you are proud you are no longer pure. Following the fixity of the law's letter we miss the flame of God's spirit and become blind to what matters.

Hafiz is said to have written a poem a day for his teacher, many of them being set to music. He used a popular form of love song, the *ghazal*, to explore every step in his growing wonder at the enormity and power of love whether it is immersed in the creation, in a courtly romance, his homely relationship with his wife or protective embrace of his son. In all this exuberance and richness, God does not remain aloof but is found right in the centre of every form love takes, reflecting in his own essence what love itself knows within – beauty, longing, freshness, grief, waiting, ecstasy. Each word and image is imbued with mystical overtones of the sacred. 'Good poetry makes the universe reveal a secret', he writes.

Ghazals can be a bit puzzling to the Westerner. Frequent perplexing images appear in them and the poems often seem to go nowhere: not much setting of the scene at the beginning, no action, little by way of a resolution. Hafiz said that a poet is someone who can pour Light into a spoon. Light is often disorienting if you've got used to the darkness. 'Tripping Over Joy' is, perhaps, a little easier to enjoy.

The writer and raconteur Frank Muir used to say that his definition of a saint is 'dead sinner: dig up and edited'. We can have idealized views about saints, as some sort of superhuman 'A' team of humanity. Hafiz begins his poem asking how your existence might differ from that of a saint. We might immediately begin to think about our failures, our lack of courage, our failure to be serious about or committed to the spiritual life, our wasted time and hardly existing prayer life. Hafiz takes us a different way, though. He tells us that the spiritual path is a *sublime chess game with God* and that the saint knows this. Chess, of course, is a remarkably simple but extraordinarily complex game at the same time. It engages both players with immense concentration as you try to work out the future moves of your fellow-player to see which kingdom will take over the other.

Vladimir Kramnik, the Russian chess grandmaster, once said that 'in chess one cannot control everything. Sometimes a game takes an unexpected turn, in which beauty begins to emerge. Both players are always instrumental in this'. Hafiz says that in the spiritual life the Beloved, God, has always just made a *Fantastic Move* and when we understand this, looking up out of our lost strategic manoeuvres, we simply burst into a laughter of delight, seeing his move has defeated any thought of future defence, and we shout out, *'I Surrender!'* It is as beautiful an image of grace as any I have come across. It is an image of the resurrection too. Hafiz sees, though, that not everyone has yet understood and that some are so committed to their religious game that they are convinced that their *thousand serious moves*, their pious devotions to win God over or their righteous thoughts that win his favour, will bring control of the board. They believe that God and life are both to be controlled somehow by our significant gravity. Hafiz gently tries to show that the game is always God's, no matter how serious a player we think we are. Joy comes in accepting the fact and, in an expression used of George Herbert, becoming 'lost in a humble way'. Usually with God, and each other, when we are on our best behaviour we are never at our best. In another poem Hafiz writes:

Pulling out the chair
Beneath your mind
And watching you fall upon God –

What else is there
For Hafiz to do
That is any fun in this world!

At a party once, so it is said, the rock star Mick Jagger said to the jazz singer George Melly, who was staring at Jagger's face, 'No, George, these aren't wrinkles on my face – these are laughter lines'. To which Melly replied: 'Mick, nothing's that funny'. It is a strange and sad fact that it is easier to detect the wrinkles than the laughter lines in the Church. Strange because at the heart of the Christian community's faith is the acknowledgement that it is not our faithfulness towards God that is the last word but God's fidelity towards us, a fidelity that is deathless. This interruption into our earnest games of self-justification makes the disciples, according to the Gospel of John (chapters 20 and 21), run from tombs, have a picnic on a beach and renew their vows of love, and share peace even in the presence of significant questions. Throughout Christian history poems and liturgies have tried to be playful about Easter, revealing laughter to be the truest way of celebrating the resurrection.

Like humour itself, resurrection breaks into our foibles, recognizes who we are, and instils an otherness, a break, that offers change and newness. As one hymn puts it: 'Hail Easter bright! Ye heavens laugh and sing!' There is even evidence that in medieval Bavarian church services it was considered proper for the preacher to get the congregation laughing on Easter Day by doing a sort of saucy routine of jokes. At Pentecost, too, a wooden dove would be lowered over the congregation to symbolize the Holy Spirit among them, only for children in the rafters to then pour buckets of water down onto them so as to remind them that God isn't wooden – his loving Spirit is more of a reckless drenching. The truest theological allusions are often in tune with the stem of that word 'allusion' – 'ludere': to be playful, dallying or touch lightly upon. But if you ever doubt that Hafiz is right in thinking that we get paralysed by a view that to be 'more spiritual' we should somehow be more serious, then just ask yourself when you last saw a picture or depiction of Jesus Christ laughing.

In Persian, Hafiz is sometimes referred to as 'the tongue of the Invisible' because his poems appear to be love songs from God to his treasured world. Hafiz scorns mediocrity, compromise and hypocrisy as the things that deflect the love of God in all his passionate exuberance and indiscriminate search for a love in return:

What is this precious love and laughter
Budding in our hearts?
It is the glorious sound
Of a soul waking up![1]

Prayer Before Birth

Louis MacNeice (1907–63)

I am not yet born; O hear me.
Let not the bloodsucking bat or the rat or the stoat or the
   club-footed ghoul come near me.

I am not yet born; console me.
I fear that the human race may with tall walls wall me,
   with strong drugs dope me, with wise lies lure me,
      on black racks rack me, in blood-baths roll me.

I am not yet born; provide me
With water to dandle me, grass to grow for me, trees to talk
   to me, sky to sing to me, birds and a white light
      in the back of my mind to guide me.

I am not yet born; forgive me
for the sins that in me the world shall commit, my words
   when they speak me, my thoughts when they think me,
      my treason engendered by traitors beyond me,
         my life when they murder by means of my
            hands, my death when they live me.

I am not yet born; rehearse me
in the parts I must play and the cues I must take when
   old men lecture me, bureaucrats hector me, mountains
      frown at me, lovers laugh at me, the white
         waves call me to folly and the desert calls
            me to doom and the beggar refuses
               my gift and my children curse me.

I am not yet born; O hear me.
Let not the man who is beast or who thinks he is God
   come near me.

I am not yet born; O fill me
With strength against those who would freeze my
   humanity, would dragoon me into a lethal automaton,
     would make me a cog in a machine, a thing with
       one face, a thing, and against all those
         who would dissipate my entirety, would
           blow me like thistledown hither and
             thither or hither and thither
              like water held in the
               hands would spill me.

Let them not make me a stone and let them not spill me.
Otherwise kill me.

The English poet of the First World War period Wilfred Owen
once said that 'All a poet can do today is warn. That is why the true
Poets must be truthful'.[1] Louis MacNeice, writing 'Prayer Before
Birth' some years later during the Second World War, agreed with
Owen. In fact, this poem powerfully embodies Owen's plea for
honesty and forewarning.

MacNeice was born in Belfast, to a father who was to become a
Church of Ireland bishop and a mother who, suffering depression,
entered a nursing home when he was six years old and whom he
never saw again due to her death shortly afterwards from tuber-
culosis. His sister commented that his last memory of his mother
walking up and down the garden path in tears haunted him for
the rest of his life, much of that life spent as a scriptwriter and
producer at the BBC. Some think MacNeice blamed his mother's
illness on his own difficult birth. He was later to write a poem
about his childhood and the loss of his mother in *Autobiography*.
It is written with a nursery-rhyme simplicity, a wakeful child
making a song out of his own abandonment in the dark. It has an
obsessive refrain, not of reassurance but of wounded ultimatum:

In my childhood trees were green
And there was plenty to be seen.

Come back early or never come.

My father made the walls resound,
He wore his collar the wrong way round.

Come back early or never come.

My mother wore a yellow dress;
Gently, gently, gentleness.

Come back early or never come.

When I was five the black dreams came;
Nothing after was quite the same.

Come back early or never come.

The dark was talking to the dead;
The lamp was dark beside my bed.

Come back early or never come.

When I woke they did not care;
Nobody, nobody was there.

Come back early or never come.

When my silent terror cried,
Nobody, nobody replied.

Come back early or never come.

I got up; the chilly sun
Saw me walk away alone.

Come back early or never come.

There is an almost liturgical feel to this poem suspended between nostalgia and anxiety, a remnant rhythm from his young days in church perhaps. The contrast between the refrain and the metric pattern of the couplets underpins the shifts in emotion and understanding that the poem contains. Beneath the simplistic surface ease of expression in the form of the poem there lies a darker, unsure, lip-biting loss of security and innocence. The reference to his father, and his clerical collar, reveals the sermonizing boom of a distant parent whose 'conspiracy with God', he admitted, made him frightened. We feel the intimacy with his mother in the third stanza but we see her and the comfort she brings taken away, never to be seen again. The painful parallel structures of *Nobody, nobody was there* and *Nobody, nobody replied* lead us to that *chilly sun* and the *walk away alone*.

MacNeice's childhood naturally had a shaping effect on the person he became in adult life. He was a detached outsider, sceptical of God, fixed systems and abstractions, an acute observer. '*With* but not strictly *of* the company', as his work colleague Bob Pocock put it.[2] Like many liberal individualists in a world threatened by fascism, communism and the lies that war generates on every side, MacNeice was able to see that his personal values, such as he could fathom them, were becoming less relevant and in jeopardy. He was, however, doubtful of any 'armchair reformists', what are often today called 'virtue signallers', marching with the poor but eating with the rich.

In 1944 he published 'Prayer Before Birth' in which the poet takes on the persona of an unborn child. It is a poem to read out loud so you can fully grasp the assonance of images such as *tall walls*, *wise lies* and *black racks*. Although it is free verse with lines and verses of varying lengths and rhyme patterns, the high level of repetition of sentence structure and the use of the word *me* as the last word of the first and last line of each stanza gives a strong rhythmic backbone to the whole. I often think the strength of MacNeice's poetry lies in his rhythms more than in his imagery. Each stanza, except the last, is a single sentence and, again, there is almost a crazed 'litany' feel to the poem, an anguished plea from the other side of the womb. The repeated *O* cry, as well as the statement *I am not yet born*, alongside the frequent alliter-ation, give it a religious formality as it evokes God or the powers of the universe.

This is a protest poem, not only against war but against the raw animal in nature and in humanity. In the first stanza where the unborn child asks to be heard, he prays that the nocturnal *bloodsucking bat*, *rat* and *stoat* don't come near. The child needs consoling because of fears that the human race also will, with deadly drugs and clever lies, *wall him* in, *dope* him, *lure*, *rack* and *roll* him in blood. Innocent nature is juxtaposed with such violence and bloodlust as he asks for *water*, *grass*, *trees*, *sky*, *birds* and *light* to guide him. The child seems to know the power that human life will have over him once he is born and asks for forgiveness for when the world, rather than himself and his conscience, speaks through him. He can see the opposition he will face from *old men* lecturing him and *bureaucrats* hectoring, *lovers* laughing at him and even his *children* cursing him. Then there is a very direct reference to those European dictators who were in full flow as the poem was written: *let not the man who is beast or who thinks he is God/ come near me*. He wants no part in a collaboration with totalitarian regimes that thrive on fear and regimentation but realizes that being humane is, as it were, not for beginners. It requires resilience, courage and an inner compass of steel. The poem is full of imperatives as the child calls for help.

Finally, the child prays that he will be filled with strength and be able to stand up against all those people, systems and ideologies that would simmer down human life by categorizing it, make it an automaton or lost in the crowd, all those things that *would freeze my humanity*. At the end he asks that the world will not harden him into an unfeeling animal or *spill* him like something easily wasted and expendable. If this is going to happen, he ends eerily, then *kill me*.

Whether MacNeice's view of humanity is too dark and negative is debatable, although the times in which he wrote surely allowed him to see the real consequences of our potential for evil. It is one of the hard lessons of Christian faith that just as standing in a garage doesn't make you a car, so sitting in a church doesn't make you a Christian. It is the transformation of the heart and mind, and the translation of that change into our behaviour, that the gospel invites us to. This means that from time to time, in sometimes small and sometimes courageous ways, we have to take a stand and confront what is unjust. As the former concentration camp prisoner Elie Wiesel said in his Nobel Peace Prize acceptance speech in 1986, 'We must always take sides. Neutrality helps the oppressor, never the victim. Silence encourages the tormentor, never the tormented'. This has sometimes been called 'speaking truth to power' but it is not as simple as that because often those who have the power already know the truth but are choosing to ignore it or reframe it. So often the powerful, including those who write the political scripts we hear or adverts we read, have hypnotized the culture so that one of the vocations of the Church is to carefully scrutinize what everyone is getting so excited about at a certain time or what everybody just takes for granted as 'common sense'.

Christian 'witness' often has the reputation for being pushy and know-it-all. In the Bible, however, the ones who end up speaking for God and God's justice are usually pretty unsure of themselves. Moses was a murderer and stammered, Jeremiah was melancholic at best, Jonah ran off and Isaiah was convinced he was utterly unworthy. Many Christians are introverts, at home in the inner landscape and not naturally keen to put their neck out. We cannot escape the call, though, to confront what is corrupt. This may be an injustice at work or the need to speak up for someone who is voiceless. Christians need to make our fears our agenda because it is fear that so often stops us from witnessing to what is right and good. Fear of the bully, of our reputation, of upsetting someone, of being isolated – these are all genuine anxieties and need to be recognized by us first if justice is ever to win the day. Christianity is a religion whose spirituality is a gradual learning of speaking up for others.

MacNeice was very aware of the fears and doubts that can challenge our principles so deeply we are paralysed into inaction. In a short poem called 'The Springboard' we find a man poised high above London on a springboard, prepared to sacrifice himself but uncertain what the gain would be:

> If it would mend the world, that would be worth while
> But he, quite rightly, long had ceased to believe
> In any Utopia or in Peace-upon-Earth;

It is only those who, like Martin Luther King Jr, 'have a dream' and relentlessly journey towards it taking the fears with them who can admit that courage is still being afraid but doing it anyway. I was very moved and humbled to hear Jeffrey John, the Dean of St Albans, say on the radio:

> I have a memory from my schooldays that still haunts me. One year we had a boy in our class – I'll call him David. He was a pathetic kid, weedy and rather effeminate. And his life was hell. Children can be incredibly cruel to anyone who's different, and David was a brilliant target. He was beaten up, he got his lunch thrown away, he got called girls' names, and he always sat on his own. I can hardly think of the misery that kid must have gone through. Now I never beat him up, I never called him names; the fact it was happening used to churn my stomach. But I never said or did a thing to help him. Because of course I was terrified that if I did, they'd turn on me too, and I'd get the same treatment. And of course that's how it works, in so many bad situations in the world – and yes, in the Church too. We know what's happening is wrong, but we keep our heads down, and hope someone else will do the martyr bit and face down the bullies with the truth.[3]

There is a way of being human that does not allow fear to be the last word. Those we admire most are usually those who live with this integrity where belief and behaviour coincide. Jesus was constantly being criticized and was eventually executed for interrupting the unchallenged narratives of the powerful with the truth and dignity of the vulnerable and overlooked. To follow him means to do the same in our day and in our own way. As a

Franciscan blessing invokes: 'May God bless us with discomfort at easy answers, half truths, and superficial relationships. May God bless us with anger at injustice, oppression and exploitation. May God bless us with enough foolishness to believe that we can make a difference in this world, doing in his name what others claim cannot be done'.

To read a poem such as 'Prayer Before Birth' helps us see just what forces, conscious and unconscious, can be at work in us and the world at large. It can help us recall that human beings have a will, and that if they don't stand for something they may fall for anything – and that when this happens we are not just asleep but spiritually dead.

MacNeice died at the age of 56. After a funeral at St John's Wood church in London his remains were taken back to Ireland and placed with those of his mother.

Song VIII

W. H. Auden (1907–73)

At last the secret is out, as it always must come in the end,
The delicious story is ripe to tell to the intimate friend;
Over the tea-cups and in the square the tongue has its desire;
Still waters run deep, my dear, there's never smoke without fire.

Behind the corpse in the reservoir, behind the ghost on the links,
Behind the lady who dances and the man who madly drinks,
Under the look of fatigue, the attack of migraine and the sigh
There is always another story, there is more than meets the eye.

For the clear voice suddenly singing, high up in the convent wall,
The scent of the elder bushes, the sporting prints in the hall,
The croquet matches in summer, the handshake, the cough,
    the kiss,
There is always a wicked secret, a private reason for this.

Auden is probably my favourite poet. Strangely, it is his face that is more famous than his poems to many. It became craggy by creasing very deeply in later life and has been compared over the years to a dry riverbed, an elephant's hide in the mud and, in his own words, a wedding cake that has been left out in the rain. Cecil Beaton captured this transition in Auden from youth to age in some very memorable photographs. Then some of his love poetry had a surge of popularity after the actor John Hannah read his 'Funeral Blues' in the film *Four Weddings and a Funeral* (1994). 'Funeral Blues' is actually a cabaret song written by Auden for a play he jointly wrote with his friend Christopher Isherwood, *The Ascent of F6*, the music for which was composed by Benjamin Britten. His poem 'September 1, 1939' was also read publicly at memorials following the events of 9/11. This is actually a poem that Auden later discarded from collections he put together because he felt it was dishonest and not true to the feelings and beliefs he had when he wrote it. He was a poet for whom, when it came to language, truth was always at stake and self-scrutiny of the first order was essential.

Auden's literary executor and biographer, Edward Mendelson, has stated rather boldly that 'Auden was the first poet writing in English who felt at home in the twentieth century'. What he means, I think, is that Auden relished the ideas and work of the novelists, historians, theologians, philosophers, psychologists, anthropologists and political scientists of his day. He had no great romance about the past or hatred of the future. He was very much in the present as a poet. Everything is life-size in Auden's work. He was the first English poet to be influenced by psychoanalytical theories, such as those of Freud, and by Marxist theories too. To read Auden is to be immersed in a poetic encyclopaedia of the twentieth century, a creative engagement with the history, emotions, thinking and beliefs of that incredible but fractured century. The American National Book Committee, which awarded him the National Medal for Literature in 1967, concluded that Auden had 'illuminated our lives and times with grace, wit and vitality. His work, branded by the moral and ideological fires of our age, breathes with eloquence, perception and intellectual power'.

He was certainly quick to establish his own distinctive poetic voice as a young man. Tersely omitting definite articles, forging a compressed syntax and inverting word orders, for instance, give the breathless sense that there is time to write only the words that matter most, making some of his phrasing sound as if someone has literally translated a German sentence into English: 'In month of August to a cottage coming' (from '1929'). As he developed, he became more versatile and inventive, always keen to understand the workings of the world, the nature of feeling and the moral and spiritual truths that might ultimately order the patterns of human existence. In the words of Mendelson: 'He welcomed into his poetry all the disordered conditions of his time, all its variety of language and event, even while he resisted the tendency characteristic of his time to perceive human beings as the product of collective, instinctive and archetypal forces, rather than as individuals who think, choose, and feel'.[1]

Auden published about 400 poems, including seven long poems (two of them book-length). His poetry ranges in style from obscure twentieth-century modernism to the lucid traditional forms such as ballads and limericks, from doggerel, haiku and villanelles to a 'Christmas Oratorio' and a baroque eclogue in Anglo-Saxon meters. The tone and content of his poems range from pop-song clichés to complex philosophical meditations, from the corns on his toes to atoms and stars, from contemporary crises to the evolution of society. Working your way through a collection of Auden's work is to feel as if you've landed in a poetic *Wunderkabinett* containing weird and wonderful insights into the human, whether alone or in collaboration. Some prefer his earlier work and some his middle to late work, written in America to where he controversially emigrated at the beginning of the Second World War. What is undisputed is that he was one of the most influential and admired Anglo-American poets of the last century. 'Whatever criticism we may make of Auden, he has been there before us and said it of himself, and more cleverly.'[2]

The poem I have chosen here is not Auden's best by any means but it is one I have been drawn to for many years. It also might come as a relief to those reading this book who are longing for a poem that rhymes! Like 'Funeral Blues', it was written as a song for the play *The Ascent of F6* and was first published in 1936. Auden characterized the 1930s as the 'Age of Anxiety' and this poem, though anxious about a love affair being discovered, is also an observation of human nature at large. It is a poem that exposes the telling details that don't quite tell. Auden believed that adults are basically children who have learned to hide their emotions – but not quite. In this song he shows that, ironically, it is our masks that expose us most. Our secrets do not like hiding and find inventive ways of drawing attention to themselves in ways beyond our control. A secret is not celibate. It longs for a partner – but there lies its danger. The possession of a secret is not as fun as sharing one.

The first two words *At last* show the inevitability, maybe relief, at the secret being *out*. The secret must always come *in the end*. It often also comes 'at the end' of a relationship or friendship, creating an end to something precious by the truth it spills out. The word *end* at the end of the first line is therefore ominous and uncomfortable. The poem then acknowledges that a secret, especially about others, can be *delicious* and *ripe* to tell people. Human beings are clever with their disguises. The writer Joseph Conrad thought that speech itself is one very subtle way we develop to conceal our real thoughts. We have to catch ourselves out, as it were, to get to 'what is not false' that lies very deep beyond our clichés and easy polite conversation. Auden shows that speech is now going to unearth things that are secretive for which *the tongue has its desire*. The two overused conversational proverbs about still waters and smoke intimate that we do mostly understand that people are more complex than they first appear but that we nevertheless try to sum them up with intrigue and gossip more than with compassion. No wonder we fear our secrets being exposed.

He then outlines in evocative images those parts of another's story that we get to see but which also hide the truth from us: Why is the man drinking? Why has that person got serious fatigue? *There is always another story, more than meets the eye.* We are even made to wonder why a woman is in a convent and why a person has sporting prints in the hall – with all that chase and panting, uniforms and whips! Over 80 per cent of our communication is done non-verbally through our bodies and so *the handshake, the cough, the kiss* are all revealing things about us that we can't see. Handshakes don't have to be Masonic to be telling a secret. Coughs can be choking up our fear or lies. Kisses can be a cover-up, over-exaggerated or cold, as in the case of Judas Iscariot.

The poem ends spelling out the basic thesis: *There is always a wicked secret, a private reason for this.* By using the word *wicked* he creates a sexual overtone to the secrets, though there are many other wicked secrets than sexual ones; and *private* fortifies the idea that when we are not being observed we have a different being, thoughts and fantasies that the public, should they see them, might condemn as shocking – though secretly everyone else also shares such a private world that lies submerged under the small cool top of the iceberg we allow to emerge above water.

Auden was very interested in psychology and his early work especially shows an interest in this role of repression in both art and human life. Reading this poem makes me very mindful of the work of Carl Jung, the great Swiss psychoanalyst and contemporary of Auden's who died in 1961. Jung believed that the human self as it grows up and learns to fit in, socialize and keep people happy (parents, siblings, schoolmates and teachers, work colleagues, bosses and so on), develops a 'persona', a mask, a social self or 'face' to present to the outer world like a shop window showing off all our best items. But this persona, says Jung, is that which in reality you are not but which you yourself – as well as others – think you are. As we fix this mask on us to be acceptable and fit in with all the expectations around us in day-to-day life, we have to repress and push down a whole heap of stuff – emotions, qualities, character traits and talents, sides to us, feelings – that are an essential part of who we are but which we don't want seen by others, or ourselves, because they don't go with the mask; or we are scared of them because at some time in our life they have been forbidden and we are ashamed of them. Guilt is when we have *done* something wrong. Shame is when we believe we *are* something wrong. Eventually we become a guarded version of our own nature.

It can be a very interesting exercise to ask yourself what forbidden things have been forced on you through your life by others or by yourself. These may include being forbidden to grow up or change, to be original, to be proud of yourself, to speak your own thoughts, to be alone, to be gay or bisexual, to express strong emotion, to enjoy your sexuality, to not know, to feel stupid, to distinguish yourself creatively, to live the life you dream about, to make mistakes, to have an intimate life, to show affection, to be loved or to love. I could go on and on. Our lives have all these 'Don't go there' signs and we push down the emotions, qualities and talents we have concluded are not acceptable. We push them into a big rubbish bag and it gets heavier and heavier. It is our untouchable within us – nobody must come near it, including us. It's dark, scary and out of view.

The more we invest in a certain image for ourselves, the more we push parts of us down out of sight, out of consciousness, and this forms what Jung called the 'shadow'. This shadow, or the rubbish bag, can be recognized and explored, often with help, and used for great creativity and wholeness – or it can be ignored. Its playground is our dream life. This is where it breaks free and takes some air, sending its messages to us because we aren't taking it seriously. This is why dreams have been thought to be sacred, because they are speaking out of the unseen depths, translating our intimate self to us because our social self has forgotten it. It can be why some people drink or take drugs, because layers of inhibition drop away and we start to see the other self that is really us – but of course we are not then in a state to integrate what emerges.

The thing about the shadow is that it will always out, whether in our subconscious acts, our projections onto others, or obsessions, unreasonable outbursts or somatic illness. Depression is its loudest voice. This shadow ticks away like a time-bomb in us. 'Whatever we ignore for the sake of ambition', says Jung, 'will always come back knife in hand to take its revenge.' So, the shadow embodies all the life in us, the emotions, the as yet undeveloped talents that have not been allowed expression. It is not only individuals, thought Jung, that have shadows but nations, communities, groups – and churches. Clergy, by the way, usually have very big shadows because of their often very manicured personas and their inability to publicly say or do what is thought to be inappropriate for a 'person of God'. Clergy, and all people in a public role, need to be aware of their shadow because a lot of damage can be done with it if not – to themselves and those they live among. If the shepherd is hungry, the danger is that the shepherd then eats the sheep.

Jung believed that human beings have an appointment to keep

with their shadow, usually around mid-life, the time when one sees that the image you've been working on in life doesn't add up to much and you need to make amendments. As the great mythologist Joseph Campbell once said, 'We spend the first 35 or 40 years of our existence climbing a tall ladder in order to finally reach the top of a building; then, once we're on the roof, we realize it's the wrong building'.

Day to day, one of the most dangerous parts of our shadow life is the projecting we do with it. This is where all the unloved parts of ourselves which we try in vain to remove from our lives project themselves onto others, forcing us to recognize them on their surface, as it were. Those we project onto either become fascinating or repulsive; they are either idealized or loathed depending on whether those things we are transferring onto them we feel are desirable or threatening. Such projection can be very harmful as relationships become distorted by it; we don't relate to the real person but to our created fairground mirror version of them. 'He hated what he did not have the courage to touch', says the recent biographer of E. M. Forster.[3] Projection in us or in nations can lead to frightening scapegoating.

When Jesus tells us to love our enemies, he asks us to love those who are often bearing the weight of our shadow. Indeed, the Gospels are full of stories of Jesus denouncing unhealthy projections, addressing those without sin to cast the first stone. To take back and assume responsibility for your projections will often turn enemies into neighbours. 'Love your enemy' means 'love your shadow'.

I'm conscious of the need for a spiritual exercise after reading Auden's poem – to take my shadow seriously. To start to see that it will mean such things as examining what I envy or dislike in others and acknowledging those very things in myself. It can mean listening to the criticism I launch off about people. So often this is nothing but unrecognized bits of autobiography. This helps prevent us blaming or envying others for what we have not done ourselves. By conversing honestly with our shadow we lift enormous projections of animosity or envy off others and life becomes freer and richer.

Other windows onto our shadow are such things as asking ourselves what we tend to avoid in conversations with people; asking what we think are our most flattering aspects of our social selves and then seeing what we have had to repress to achieve this; examining in what situations we become over-sensitive, defensive, nervous; or in what situations we feel inferior, embarrassed, panicky at the thought of someone seeing our weakness; being alert to what criticism irritates us, what compliments we can't take; we can ask what value our family most upheld and made the culture of home and then see what we had to keep hidden. We can analyse our dreams, so often full of dangerous animals and situations, fear and running away. Freud called sleeping the 'undressing of the mind'. We can be attentive to our fantasies and daydreams, our humour and our cruelty.

Often at moments of life transitions and conversions, radical changes, we try to forget the past and do a lot of repressing to live our new life full-on without looking back – usually to later pain, exhaustion or collapse. Conversion for the Christian is lifelong for this very reason. Our shadow is crying out in so many ways to be befriended. To do so will not make us perfect, but it will make us more integrated and less tortured. Acknowledging the drives of your shadow does not always mean obeying them, but owning them. To touch the untouchable within is a road of healing – the whole person, rubbish bag and all, being before God and yourself and those you love and meet each day.

'I'm afraid to tell you who I am, because, if I tell you who I am, you may not like who I am, and it's all that I have.' So, rather than risk being hurt, we don't tell others who we are and hide ourselves, but in hiding we are in danger of losing ourselves and becoming a non-self in our relationship to people. To such people Christ spoke, asked their name, touched, lifted up and took the snide comments from the sidelines. He came to the fractured, let down, ashamed, confused, hiding and self-loathing and never abandoned them to what they thought of themselves. What he teaches is that I am because he is. We tell him who we are, light and shadow, because he is the one who will still hold us after we have told him. Whatever road we have been on and are on, he comes too, and his faithfulness and belief in us encourage us to be us again. For the Christian, death is not the worst thing. Not living your life is the worst thing. We always need others to help us achieve that. So often our *ego* is the part of us that cleaves to the status quo even when it's not working.

Both Auden's grandfathers were Anglican clergy. His mother was a devout Anglican too. His very last poems are haikus that describe or take the form of prayer. His life, that is, had a rounded integrity of commitment to Christian faith. He recovered his faith in the early 1940s and his poems began to give voice to his spiritual interrogation of the world and himself, the motives we have for accepting or refusing the realities of the world. He knew that human redemption is a costly business for all involved. He wrote that 'the point of psychology is to prove the Gospel'. Sometimes our loudest voice is the emptiest, our most forceful beliefs are the most insecure, our most plausible self can be the most inauthentic. We need to hold back, sometimes, and interrogate ourselves as to what stage we are on and whose script we are playing. Truth is always at stake if there isn't some pause, some poetry:

For given Man, by birth, by education,
Imago Dei who forgot his station,
The self-made creature who himself unmakes,
The only creature ever made who fakes,
With no more nature in his loving smile
Than in his theories of a natural style,
What but tall tales, the luck of verbal playing,
Can trick his lying nature into saying
That love, or truth in any serious sense,
Like orthodoxy, is a reticence?[4]

Getting It Across

(for Caroline)

U. A. Fanthorpe (1929–2009)

'His disciples said unto him, Lo, now speakest thou plainly, and
speakest no proverb. Now are we sure that thou knowest all
things.'
St John 16.29–30

This is the hard thing.
Not being God, the Son of Man,
– I was born for that part –
But patiently incising on these yokel faces,
Mystified, bored and mortal,
The vital mnemonics they never remember.

There is enough of Man in my God
For me to construe their frowns. I feel
The jaw-cracking yawns they try to hide
When out I come with one of my old
Chestnuts. *Christ! Not that bloody*
Sower again, they are saying, or *God!*
Not the Prodigal bleeding Son.
Give us a new one, for Messiah's sake.

They know my unknowable parables as well
As each other's shaggy dog stories.
I say! I say! I say! There was this Samaritan,
This Philistine and this Roman . . . or

What did the high priest say
To the belly dancer? All they need
Is the cue for laughs. My sheep and goats,
Virgins, pigs, figtrees, loaves and lepers
Confuse them. Fishing, whether for fish or men,
Has unfitted them for analogy.

Yet these are my mouths. Through them only
Can I speak with Augustine, Aquinas, Martin, Paul,
Regius Professors of Divinity,
And you, and you.
How can I cram the sense of Heaven's kingdom
Into our pidgin-Aramaic quayside jargon?

I envy Moses, who could choose
The diuturnity of stone for waymarks
Between man and Me. He broke the tablets,
Of course. I too know the easy messages
Are the ones not worth transmitting;
But he could at least carve.
The prophets too, however luckless
Their lives and instructions, inscribed on wood,
Papyrus, walls, their jaundiced oracles.

I alone must write on flesh. Not even
The congenial face of my Baptist cousin,
My crooked affinity Judas, who understands,
Men who would give me accurately to the unborn
As if I were something simple, like bread.
But Pete, with his headband stuffed with fishhooks,
His gift for rushing in where angels wouldn't,
Tom, for whom metaphor is anathema,
And James and John, who want the room at the top –
These numskulls are my medium. I called them.

I am tattooing God on their makeshift lives.
My Keystone Cops of disciples, always,
Running absurdly away, or lying ineptly,

Cutting off ears and falling into the water,
These Sancho Panzas must tread my Quixote life,
Dying ridiculous and undignified,
Flayed and stoned and crucified upside down.
They are the dear, the human, the dense, for whom
My message is. That might, had I not touched them,
Have died decent respectable upright deaths in bed.

Ursula Askham (known as U. A.) Fanthorpe was the daughter of 'middle-class but honest parents' who, after boarding school, was the first in her family to go to university. Gaining a First in English from Oxford, she became a teacher at Cheltenham Ladies' College and eventually was made Head of Department. After 17 years of a successful teaching life and only in her late forties, she became what she called 'a middle-aged drop-out'. She resigned her academic post and became a low-paid receptionist in a hospital for nervous diseases. There in her 'glass dugout' and 'excruciatingly unimportant' she was able to freely observe and encounter people in all their fragility (as patients) and power (as doctors). She then began to write poetry as a way of 'bearing witness' to her experience and to many things that so often get pushed under the polite carpets of so-called civilized life. There was a disused caravan in the hospital grounds and in her 40-minute lunch break she locked herself away with pen and paper. Eventually she became a full-time and prolific writer, her new life as a poet being honoured years later by her being awarded the Queen's Gold Medal for Poetry.

Fanthorpe's poetry is characterized by its wit, subtle intelligence, compassion, historical resonances and Englishness. She champions the underdog and relishes the anachronism. Though often dealing with absences the tone remains buoyant. Her syntax is always elegant and it is the aptness of her vocabulary rather than the rhythms or music of her work that stands out. She very much agreed with the poet Robert Graves when he said that 'I should define a good poem as one that makes complete sense; and says all it has to say memorably and economically'. Her poems are accessible, clear and straight-talking. They are incisive but gentle.

Many of her poems reflect on Christian themes. Fanthorpe was a Quaker and her quiet but trusting faith is often discernible in her work.

'Getting It Across' sees the poet in the persona of Jesus, finding it difficult to communicate his message to his *mystified, bored and mortal* disciples. It is a monologue, a poetic form that Fanthorpe perfected for her readers. The second stanza sees those disciples disguising yawns as they hear Jesus repeat one of his parables. Of course, they may be like many regular churchgoers, getting so used to the words of Jesus that they need a new conversion. Fanthorpe here also reminds us that Jesus, as preacher, was inventive. He was a creative storyteller. Unless we enter his imaginative world the door remains shut to the kingdom of God. The third stanza refers to the disciples wanting *the cue for laughs*; again, so much religious life can shape itself as entertainment as it competes in a leisure-obsessed world for our attention. Even our hearts can have bad taste. The disciples have been *unfitted* for *analogy*. It's almost as if their discipleship has strangely divested them of the things any searcher for God needs most – analogy, parable, metaphor and allusion – as we dive into the richer plurality of meanings that the divine mystery opens up and lives within.

The fourth stanza reminds us, though, that we are all inescapably human and that sacred realities nestle in the heads, hearts and mouths of flawed and limited humans who too often back away from ambiguity and elusive meaning for a harder, fixed precision. Jesus' question resounds through every Christian heart in every generation: *How can I cram the sense of Heaven's kingdom/ Into our pidgin-Aramaic quayside jargon?* He is jealous of Moses who could carve on stone the commands of God, and of the Prophets as they screamed out their relentless uncompromising demand for change in readable forms. Jesus, as the body-language of God, must alone *write on flesh*, his word only translatable in living, breathing forms. These forms, his friends, are far from perfect. In fact that they are *numskulls, Keystone Cops, always,/ Running absurdly away, or lying ineptly,/ Cutting off ears and falling into the water*. The stories of the disciples found in the Gospels, especially those about Peter, are in mind here. They are *dense* and *human* but they are also *dear* and *for whom my message is*. They are also faithful at the end, loyal and loving as they die *ridiculous* and *undignified* deaths because of the man who so, for all their confusions and messing up, *touched* them into life.

So much talk today about martyrdom suggests it is something a person does to kill themselves for a cause and often taking other, innocent, people with them. This is the opposite of a Christian understanding where martyrdom is not a matter of what we might be prepared to kill for but of what we might be prepared to die for. It is something done alone, a courageous 'witness', which is what the word means, to that which centres your life and which, should it be taken from you, would bring your identity to an end anyway. We see by the end of the poem how Jesus tattooed God on *make-shift lives* and how his writing on ordinary lives makes them, by the end, extra-ordinary in what they are willing to sacrifice.

In another poem by Fanthorpe, 'The Wicked Fairy at the Manger', she outlines a life of Jesus himself that, in just a few lines, powerfully conveys his own sacrifice for the sake of the divine communication which must break in to the human flow of convention and compromise. The Wicked Fairy, after the shepherds and magi have given their presents, decides what to offer the baby Jesus in his manger and in his life ahead:

My gift for the child:

No wife, kids, home;
No money sense. Unemployable.
Friends, yes. But the wrong sort –
The workshy, women, wimps,
Petty infringers of the law, persons
With notifiable diseases,
Poll tax collectors, tarts;
The bottom rung.
His end?
I think we'll make it
Public, prolonged, painful.

Right, said the baby. That was roughly
What we had in mind.

Thinking about the integrity of human lives and how they often speak louder than words, makes me think about U. A. Fanthorpe herself. Of course, I admire her dramatic and brave decision to leave her teaching career for an uncertain but, in the end, fulfilling future. It is a perfect example of the wisdom that can force itself out in our mid-years if we permit it. What I also admire Fanthorpe for is her honesty and transparency about the life and love she shared with her partner Rosie Bailey for 44 years. Bailey was the great encourager of Fanthorpe's writing and was the wind beneath her wings as well as the protection from the cold. I remember seeing them read poems together once, as they often did at formal readings because many of Fanthorpe's poems require two voices, and sensing that if Bailey had not been on stage Fanthorpe herself would have been partly missing. There is a beautiful short book of the love poems[1] they wrote to each other at various moments in their life – often when the other was away somewhere – and in one that Fanthorpe wrote about Bailey, 'Atlas', she celebrates the sort of practical, 'maintenance' love that one often gives that holds up the whole world of the other, like Atlas:

There is a kind of love called maintenance
Which stores the WD40 and knows when to use it;

Which checks the insurance, and doesn't forget
The milkman; which remembers to plant bulbs;

Which answers letters; which knows the way
The money goes; which deals with dentists

And Road Fund Tax and meeting trains,
And postcards to the lonely; which upholds

The permanently rickety elaborate
Structures of living, which is Atlas.

And maintenance is the sensible side of love,
Which knows what time and weather are doing
To my brickwork; insulates my faulty wiring;
Laughs at my dryrotten jokes; remembers
My need for gloss and grouting; which keeps
My suspect edifice upright in air,
As Atlas did the sky.

Bailey once said that she and Fanthorpe never really 'came out' but were never really 'in' either. They lived through some very dark days for lesbian and gay people and yet their lifelong commitment and cherishing were what always mattered for them, a home-centred support of each other. As I write this, the Church of England is going through prolonged and agonized debates about LGBT people and their place within the community of faith. I am of the mind, and the relationship of Fanthorpe and Bailey proves it as so many gay relationships do, that where such love is, God is. LGBT men and women do not choose their sexuality. They discover it, and how painful or frightening that is depends on those around them as they face their truth.

I look forward to the day when the Church can see that any penalizing of women and men due to their sexuality, no matter what biblical rounds might be fired as warning shots, is discrimination and is therefore as evil as any discrimination that has similarly used God as a back-up to subvert the dignity of those in a minority. Until this is acknowledged and corrected, any talk of the Church being inclusive and 'for everyone' is a lie. I will celebrate the day when the Church will apologize for its past mistakes and come to recognize and celebrate the love of LGBT folk, a love both intimate and public, in church services. The idea that any prayers for them should be done in private, as is the current demand by bishops, is insulting to faithful people and to God. If God is being invoked, why would anyone ever do that in private? The poems of Bailey and Fanthorpe are a beautiful, timely reminder of the love the Church is missing out on until the day it wakes up and sees the thrillingly diverse creation of the God who loves us all equally. How great the day will be when the

Church might be able to say what Fanthorpe said about her life's work as a poet:

> I'm particularly involved with people who have no voice: the dead, the dispossessed, or the inarticulate in various ways. I'm not carrying on a campaign on their behalf but this is the theme I recognize as having a call on me: people at the edge of things.[2]

Do not go gentle into that good night

Dylan Thomas (1914–53)

Do not go gentle into that good night,
Old age should burn and rave at close of day;
Rage, rage against the dying of the light.

Though wise men at their end know dark is right,
Because their words had forked no lightning they
Do not go gentle into that good night.

Good men, the last wave by, crying how bright
Their frail deeds might have danced in a green bay,
Rage, rage against the dying of the light.

Wild men who caught and sang the sun in flight
And learn, too late, they grieved it on its way,
Do not go gentle into that good night.

Grave men, near death, who see with blinding sight
Blind eyes could blaze like meteors and be gay,
Rage, rage against the dying of the light.

And you, my father, there on the sad height,
Curse, bless, me now with your fierce tears, I pray.
Do not go gentle into that good night.
Rage, rage against the dying of the light.

To be asked to write about Dylan Thomas is like being asked to write about what it's like to be alive. There is no other writer whose work can exhilarate me like his – no one whose vision of this life can fill me with the same sense of awe and appetite, no one whose words can make my mouth water as much, or whose images demand such mouthing. The combustible mixture of sly parochialism and exotic sensuality, underpinned by a roiling pagan intelligence, has a vitality and immediacy that can hit you like a slap on a cold day.

These words were written by the actor Michael Sheen as he took up the role of ambassador for the Dylan Thomas Festival in 2014 to celebrate the 100th anniversary of Thomas' birth. Thomas is very much an actor's poet and you only need to listen to the recordings of Richard Burton or Anthony Hopkins reading his poems to see why. Thomas was immersed in the sound of words, their musicality and power to seduce the imagination. To listen to his poems, though many are difficult to understand, is to be transported into a dreamland of sounded imagery that is infused with both the warm disturbance of memory and the chill of a world that doesn't embrace us as we would like. Language is a physical sensation for him. Though many in his day would tune in to the radio or go to hear Thomas read his own work, it sounds too histrionic and contrived today; but for Thomas the words were not just poetry's script but its stage, the vocal arena for dramatic effects in the mind and heart.

Critics have sometimes made too much of his hypnotic incantatory style, charging him with verbal opportunism or sentimentality, implying there are too many flamboyant labels on empty luggage. Thomas used sensuous worldly imagery as a carrier of meaning, though, to explore human selfhood; there is an evident sacramentality to his approach that captures the inner graces of a carnivorous, carnival cosmos. There is an impulse for liberation expressed through imagery of sun, song, ascent and, later, grace, joy, glory. At his best Thomas is technically original and marvellously resonant. There is a moral energy to much of his later work in particular. His metaphors, images, phrasing and witty dexterity can cast a unique spell that has made him one of the most loved poets of Wales and Britain in recent years – a difficult poet with a popular audience, imperfect but outstanding. His poetic drama *Under Milk Wood* is as enjoyed today as ever, as we are drawn into the story of a day in the life of the inhabitants of the small Welsh seaside village of Llareggub (read it backwards) by its opening sentence: 'To begin at the beginning: It is spring, moonless night in the small town, starless and bible-black . . .'

Seamus Heaney, in a lecture on Thomas, quoted the poet Evan Boland on poetic tone:

> Poetic tone is more than the speaking voice in which the poem happens; much more. Its roots go deep into the history and sociology of the craft. Even today, for a poet, tone is not a matter of the aesthetic of any one poem. It grows more surely, and more painfully, from the ethics of the art. Its origins must always be in a suffered world rather than a conscious craft.[1]

Heaney argues that sometimes Thomas' language is too self-conscious in his bardic vocation and this robs the poems of an emotional staying power. He can be 'too obligingly suffused with radiance'. However, when Thomas writes 'in a suffered world rather than a conscious craft', when a veteran knowledge within his soul finds its natural home in his own exceptional expression, then he becomes the poet, says Heaney again, who will 'always be credible and continuing'.

'Do not go gentle' is a good example of Thomas at his most skilled as an emotionally in-tune voice of that 'suffered world'. The poem is a villanelle; that is, a 19-line poetic form consisting of five three-line stanzas followed by a four-line one in iambic pentameter. There are two refrains and two repeating rhymes, with the first and third line of the first stanza repeated alternately until the last stanza, which includes both repeated lines. The poet Anne Ridler once said that sometimes for the release of the deepest and most secret feeling, to use a very strict form such as the villanelle is a help to a poet, because you concentrate on the technical difficulties of mastering the form and allow the content of the poem a more subconscious and freer release. This is proved true in this remarkable poem, perhaps now one of the most famous villanelles in English.

This is a poem addressed to his father dying of cancer and with failing eyesight. Thomas wrote it when he was 37 and at a time when his relationship with his wife was beset with difficulties. It is an urgent poem, a plea to his father not to surrender to death and an affirmation of life for life's sake beyond all the hurts and disappointments it may contain.

The first stanza begs his father not to *go gentle*, not to be gentlemanly about death but to fight, be foolish even, and not accept the end that is that *good night* – meaning death, of course, but also being the last words of farewell we wish to someone at the end of a day. Thomas calls it a *good* night, though. His father was a very convinced atheist and did not believe there was anything on the other side of death for him. Thomas would tell how his father, so opposed to the idea of a personal God, would stand at the window and growl, 'It's raining, blast Him'. By using the phrase *good night* Thomas hints that, nevertheless, death will be a restful sleep; but still, old age should *rave at close of day*. This is a phrase we tend to use for when a shop or business finishes its work, when the day's duties have been done. He refers to the *dying of the light* and by its repetition through the villanelle, the word *dying* is relentless and, we realize, inevitable. We find it at the last line as we find it at last in every life.

Thomas then outlines how different types of people do, or should, *rage* against the ending of their lives. He appears to describe how wise men do, but with the others – *good, wild*, and *grave* – it is unclear whether he is being descriptive or prescriptive. Wise men, when they face their own death, see that all their words have *forked no lightning*; they haven't thrown any real light or been generative in any way. They *know dark is right*: that death must come but also that human understanding is limited and mortal. Death remains a mystery no matter how many doctorates you have. So, these wise men rage against their own past pride and revered intelligence and, almost in a penitence perhaps, want more time to begin again with a truer wisdom. Their wish will not be granted. Is there a suggestion in the use of *wise men* that all this is true of the religious as well, like the magi of that most famous faith journey of all?

Good men, continues Thomas, with *the last wave by* – that is, the last crash of the wave of life gone – cry (shout or weep?) *how bright/ Their frail deeds might have danced in a green bay*. Those who have been good see that their actions have been weak or indifferent and now wish that they had been more life-affirming, fertile and of consequence. If only they had had more willpower, more opportunity or more love of life. Again, the use of the word *wave* leads us to the sea near the green bay, but also to think of that *last wave* goodbye we make when someone leaves us.

Thomas then refers to wild men, of which he was one! He had became known in his later years for many things other than his poetry – drink, debts and adultery among them. Here he tells us that it is the wild men who *caught and sang the sun in flight*, harnessed life's energy and celebrated all its rays, but then learn *too late, they grieved it on its way*. Their behaviour was unthinking, reckless and injured people – including themselves. Life was grieved by their life, and seeing this they want more time to make amends and so rage against death too. Their songs to the sun have become laments. Just how do we live with our regrets and seek amendment when time is short?

Finally, Thomas speaks of grave men – a very obvious double meaning here. Serious people near death see with *blinding sight* what is obvious when you are blind to everything else. They are to blaze *like meteors* and be full of joy for as long as life still is. 'May I be alive when I die!' said the child psychologist Donald Winnicott, having spent a lifetime trying to explore what an integrated and authentic life might be.

The poem ends with Thomas directly addressing his father *there on the sad height*, looking down on his past life and now so near the edge of the cliff. Thomas begs him to *curse, bless, me now with your fierce tears*. Thomas wants his father to say good things or bad things to him, just as long as he stays alive. As long as there is curse and blessing there is still a relationship, he still has a father. I see this poem really as a love poem. It is a poem that expresses a love for his father and a deep fear of losing him. It reveals the poet and all of us who love and can't bear the reality of losing the one who means most. As we know, the last thing many elderly or ill people near death want to do is rage against it. Rather, they come to terms with it and even welcome it as an end to pain or life's exhaustion. It's an interesting exercise to compare Thomas' villanelle with a poem like 'Let Evening Come' by the American poet Jane Kenyon, who died at the age of 47 from leukaemia, as an exploration of what both poems are saying and what they are celebrating about life, relationship and hopes:

Let the light of late afternoon
shine through chinks in the barn, moving
up the bales as the sun moves down.

Let the cricket take up chafing
as a woman takes up her needles
and her yarn. Let evening come.

Let dew collect on the hoe abandoned
in long grass. Let the stars appear
and the moon disclose her silver horn.

Let the fox go back to its sandy den.
Let the wind die down. Let the shed
go black inside. Let evening come.

To the bottle in the ditch, to the scoop
in the oats, to air in the lung
let evening come.

Let it come, as it will, and don't
be afraid. God does not leave us
comfortless, so let evening come.

This poem has always struck me as a contemporary Nunc Dimittis, a hymn that still praises as the voice fades. It seems to me, though, that Thomas and Kenyon are not ultimately writing about the same things and that, as readers, both the love of the force and energy of life and our loved ones, as well as the hope that we can lie down in peace and take our rest having received our life as a true gift, are both resonant and to be found in most human hearts. In the Christian tradition we find death referred to both as our enemy (St Paul) and as our sister (St Francis).

Not conventionally pious by any means but often seen sitting at the back of church during services, Thomas inhabited the suburbs of the city of God. Shored up with Christian imagery and language, he was a person for whom 'communion' was an elusive and, perhaps, difficult notion. His religious convictions remain equally elusive but he was able to pen such beautiful exaltations as 'Vision and Prayer', which ends:

> I turn the corner of prayer and burn
> In a blessing of the sudden
> Sun. In the name of the damned
> I would turn back and run
> To the hidden land
> But the loud sun
> Christens down
> The sky.
> I
> Am found
> O let him
> Scald me and drown
> Me in his world's wound
> His lightning answers my
> Cry. My voice burns in his hand.
> Now I am lost in the blinding
> One. The sun roars at the prayer's end.

He is both found and lost. He once described his poetry as 'two sides of an unresolved argument'. When he wrote a 'Note' to his *Collected Poems* he ended it by saying: 'These poems with all their crudities, doubts and confusions, are written for the love of Man and in praise of God, and I'd be a damn fool if they weren't'. He died in New York at the age of 39.

Bird

Liz Berry (b. 1980)

When I became a bird, Lord, nothing could not stop me.

    The air feathered
                    as I knelt
by my open window for the charm –
                  black on gold,
              last star of the dawn.

Singing, they came:
                throstles, jenny wrens,
jack squalors swinging their anchors through the clouds.

      My heart beat like a wing.

I shed my nightdress to the drowning arms of the dark,
my shoes to the sun's widening mouth.

        Bared,
  I found my bones hollowing to slender pipes,
    my shoulder blades tufting down.
        I   spread   my flight-greedy arms
to watch my fingers jewelling like ten hummingbirds,
my feet callousing to knuckly claws.
      As my lips calcified to a hooked kiss

silence

then an exultation of larks filled the clouds
and, in my mother's voice, chorused:
Tek flight, chick, goo far fer the Winter.

So I left girlhood behind me like a blue egg
          and stepped off
    from the window ledge.

How light I was

as they lifted me up from Wren's Nest,
bore me over the edgelands of concrete and coal.

I saw my grandmother waving up from her fode,
       looped
  the infant school and factory,
      let the zephyrs carry me out to the coast.

Lunars I flew
      battered and tuneless

  the storms turned me inside out like a fury,
there wasn't one small part of my body didn't blart.
Until I felt it at last the rush of squall thrilling my wing
    and I knew my voice
was no longer words but song black upon black.

I raised my throat to the wind
       and this is what I sang . . .

Note: Black Country – standard.
charm – birdsong or dawn chorus; *throstle* – thrush; *jack squalor* – swallow;
fode – yard; *blart* – cry.

I first came across the work of Liz Berry at the Forward Prize
ceremony on London's South Bank. She read from her debut
collection *Black Country* and I was totally mesmerized by what

I was hearing. It was the extraordinary fusion of Berry's wild, playful and descriptive musicality with her equally bold and unapologetic West Midlands accent that bewitched me. Regional English accents don't always get much of a look-in with poetry, though the Scots dialect has been taken seriously as we saw in Jen Hadfield's work. Berry's poetry is a celebration of the rough, no-nonsense lyricism of a local dialect that is so often derided as dense and ugly. Berry shows its beauty. If you don't believe me, make sure you listen online to her reading her poems. One of the poems in *Black Country* is called 'Homing' and in it she speaks to a relative about the accent that she was forced to lock in a box under her bed by elocution lessons. She continues:

Clearing your house, the only thing
I wanted was that box, jimmied open
to let years of lost words spill out –
bibble, fettle, tay, wum,
vowels ferrous as nails, consonants

you could lick the coal from.

Berry's poetry is rooted in place. The old story is that Queen Victoria once passed through the industrial heart of England with its iron foundries and steel mills, submerged in smoke and fumes, and asked that the curtains of the train be closed so that she couldn't see 'this awful Black Country'. Berry brazenly opens them again and, with an assured maturity and fizzing fairytale inventiveness, helps us see the Black Country more as a black diamond, a 'gift from the underworld'.[1] She told the Poetry Society's Young Poets Network that for her to revisit the language, accent and terrain of her locality all confirmed that 'the stuff of poetry was glinting out of the muck'. This might be one of the best descriptions of incarnation that I have heard.

One of the noticeable things about *Black Country* is its constant use of religious reference. There are poem titles such as 'The Patron Saint of School Girls' and 'The Assumption' with its picture of 'Christ the Lamb'; the cattle are lowing in 'Owl',

'Carmella' is 'Our Lady of the Hairdressers' and several of the poems refer to 'Lord', whether as a divine reality or a reference for human hope it is not always clear. Her poem 'The First Path', in which a bruised and lost dog is found by someone and picked up and carried home, is a beautiful work that has resonances of the stories Jesus told of the Good Samaritan and the Prodigal Son where God, and those who reflect God's compassion, search for the battered and unlovely:

> When you found me there was nothing beautiful about me.
> I wasn't even human
> > just a mongrel
> kicked out into the snow on Maundy Thursday
> when all the world was sorrow,

The poems ends almost sounding like a contemporary psalm of gratitude for grace:

> > > You touched me then,
> > When I was nothing but dirt,
> took off your glove and laid your palm upon my throat,
> slipped the loop of the rope,
> > > lifted me
> into your arms and carried me home
> > > > > along the first path.

> In the banks the foxes barked *alleluia alleluia.*

> The blizzard tumbled upon us like confetti
> and I, little bitch, blue bruise,
> saw myself in your eyes:
> > > > a bride.

With its direct appeal in the centre of the poem, 'Lord help me', there is a sense of this being a twenty-first-century take on George Herbert's 'Love (III)': the unworthy being assured of their true place in God's eyes, a bride to love.

One might think that a collection of poems about the Black Country, with its closed pits and hardened history, would be under the force of gravity, everything pulled down and left in the grit. Berry's poems, though, endlessly reverse such a heaviness with a startling upward pull, with searches and escapes, charms of promise and transformation, metaphoric journeys and fruitful tensions between the real and imagined. This is never truer than in the opening poem of *Black Country* called 'Bird'.

As you take a quick glance at the form of the poem you can see immediately that it is, indeed, as free as a bird. This helps us into the subject as we are launched into a magical metamorphosis. The first line takes us into the poetic spell being cast: *When I became a bird, Lord, nothing could not stop me.* It's easy to overlook that 'not', as it is to pass over why the poem is addressed to God or 'Lord'. The excitement of this narrative of transformation is being relayed to God as if this is something he would want to know about – and celebrate. Or is 'Lord' just there as a redundant emphasis? The speaker kneels by an open window, her heart beats like a wing, her nightdress which covers up our naked self is shed like a skin *to the drowning arms of the dark.* Her body then begins to take the shape of a bird, her feet *callousing to knuckly claws* and her lips becoming a beak: *calcified to a hooked kiss.* The larks chorus her mother's heartfelt plea to her young life: *Tek flight, chick, goo far fer the winter.* She leaves girlhood behind *like a blue egg* and steps off the ledge and flies, looking down on her old life – her grandmother waving from her backyard, her infant school and factory. Storms turn her inside out and batter her but then she feels

the rush of squall thrilling my wing
          and I knew my voice
was no longer words but song   black upon black.

I raised my throat to the wind
                    and this is what I sang . . .

The theme of a life escaping its imprisonments and frustrations like a bird in the fresh air is, of course, a common one. 'The Caged Bird' by Maya Angelou famously notes that even imprisoned birds sing of freedom. Birds are often used metaphorically for spiritual liberation and transition. In the Christian tradition, the dove has particularly been important in symbolizing creativity, God's energy and promise, such as in Noah's ark, and confirmation of a new vocation and path – as at Jesus' baptism. Not only do birds fly free but their warmth also hatches new existence: new lives which break through hard shells. Christian iconography has used particular birds to speak of faith. The pelican, which legend has it fed its young on its own heart, quickly became a picture of the sacrificial love of God. The eagle represented Christ as the only creature who could look at the sun, the majesty of the Godhead. The swallow as it hid in the mud during winter represented Christ's incarnation and, as it returned in spring, his resurrection. The theme of this poem – a young person discovering her own identity, a readiness to soar and find her voice – is one of spiritual growth and fresh living. It is a poem that sustains itself on a wing and a prayer.

In early 2015 the United States Postal Service issued a stamp in honour of Maya Angelou with, unfortunately, a quotation attributed to her that is actually a saying of Joan Walsh Anglund: 'A bird doesn't sing because it has an answer. It sings because it has a song.' 'Bird' ends in a way that makes us lean in to hear what comes next:

> I raised my throat to the wind
>> And this is what I sang . . .

We don't get to hear what she sang, though. We often don't even get time to hear what we sing ourselves or what we should be singing in life. The dots that end the poem almost hand over the script to us as readers to see what we would place there if we too could take off out of our current lives and learn what it means to be free and ourselves.

If I had to choose one song to be with me on a desert island it would be Nina Simone singing 'I Wish I Knew How it Would Feel to be Free'. The lyrics are:

I wish I knew how it would feel to be free
I wish I could break all the chains holding me
I wish I could say all the things that I should
say 'em loud, say 'em clear for the whole round world to hear.

I wish I could share all the love that's in my heart
remove all the bars that keep us apart
I wish you could know what it means to be me
Then you'd see and agree that every man should be free.

I wish I could give all I'm longing to give
I wish I could live like I'm longing to live
I wish that I could do all the things that I can do
though I'm way overdue I'd be starting anew.

Well I wish I could be like a bird in the sky
how sweet it would be if I found I could fly
Oh I'd soar to the sun and look down at the sea
and I'd sing cos I'd know how it feels to be free.

This song of civil rights, liberty and the need to rise against oppression, not least within ourselves, is certainly one worth singing. It's not unlike the first sermon Jesus gave (Luke 4.18–19), the song to which he tuned his life and work, as it were, where he sees that he and his followers must speak to the poor, heal the broken-hearted, make people see again and liberate captives and the bruised.

A former Dean of Westminster Abbey, and a supportive friend to me in my younger days, was Michael Mayne. In one of his books, he centres his thoughts on the idea of the 'enduring melody' of his life, the *cantus firmus*. For most of the Middle Ages church music consisted of the so-called Gregorian chant – one line of melody attached to the words of prayer – and until the ninth century that melody was left unclothed. That plainsong melody is the *cantus firmus*, the 'fixed song'. By the twelfth century it was found that two or more melodies could be combined, and the *cantus firmus* became the basis of a polyphonic composition. Gradually the traditional plainsong began to be given to the singers of the middle voice, that is the tenors (from the Latin *tenere*, to hold), literally the holders of the fixed song, while the lower and higher voices surrounded it with developing counterpoint.

The saints and friends of God who inspire us are those who try to tune their lives, their words, their busyness, their quiet times and prayers, to that fixed song, the *cantus firmus* of Jesus Christ – himself the song of God sung to us. There is so much other noise in the now that clamours for our attention, the noise and disharmony that reduce us into being frantic and distant, liers, hoarders, moaners, leaving us empty and exhausted. The Christian faith is an invitation to listen more deeply to that enduring melody, the song that holds the world itself, and to which the human heart is most truly itself when tuned.

What makes Liz Berry's poem most remarkable is the fertile way in which her imagination sees the physical transformation of the subject into a physical bird but, in this creaturely material, she also sees an inner life being born. One of her poems, 'Birmingham Roller', is named after a special type of pigeon that breaks off from the crowd to freefall and tumble before making its way back to its mates:

Little acrobat of the terraces,
we'm winged when we gaze at you

jimmucking the breeze, somersaulting through
the white-breathed prayer of January

Berry has commented in interviews that this pigeon symbolizes the Black Country – a grey and unnoticeable existence which, if you keep your eye on it, hides a great talent and surprise under its wing. Berry's poems make us wonder if that is not true of life itself.

Raptor

R. S. Thomas (1913–2000)

You have made God small
setting him astride
a pipette or a retort
studying the bubbles,
absorbed in an experiment
that will come to nothing.

I think of him rather
as an enormous owl
abroad in the shadows,
brushing me sometimes
with his wing so the blood
in my veins freezes, able

to find his way from one
soul to another because
he can see in the dark.
I have heard him crooning
to himself, so that almost
I could believe in angels,

those feathered overtones
in love's rafters, I have heard
him scream, too, fastening
his talons in his great
adversary, or in some lesser
denizen, maybe, like you or me.

I started reading the poems of R. S. Thomas at the age of 18 and, without being too dramatic, they have been life-vests that have kept me bobbing in the sea, keeping my head just above water, ever since. I want to do something a little different here then. I want to write something more personal – about how Thomas has weaved in and out of my life and my Christian faith for nearly 30 years and to do so with reference to 'Raptor' which appeared in 1995 in a collection called *No Truce with the Furies*. My copy at home, signed by Thomas on the one occasion I met him, is one of my most treasured possessions.

There are messages around that if you take the Christian faith seriously you must either be intellectually very limited or an emotional wreck; and so, the narrative goes, if as a religious person you refer to the past you belong there; if you refer to the Bible you must be a fundamentalist; if you wear a cross you must be litigious or have a martyr complex. I don't know how or when we became so spiritually illiterate – this mental contagion so doubtful that Christian spirituality might actually inform the mind, might deepen the human heart, and might even have civic resources to contribute – but the sound-bite world seems to be pretty sure that the world would be a better place without God-talk poking its nose in.

In this cultural darkness, it is difficult to feel our way through as people of faith, to find a language for the soul and a way of communicating that's plausible and trustworthy. It is a challenge to keep the rumour of God alive in a way that is magnetic to mystery rather than dismissive; there is also clearly a lot of bad religion around, which makes you totally understand what all the sceptics and atheists are all on about. Speaking for my own faith, it's almost as if we as a Church are living down to people's expectations sometimes, remarkably adept at discrediting ourselves by finding small opportunities to be mean when there are large opportunities to be generous. So, even when you have serious people looking for paths of authentic spirituality at the moment, they don't often think the Church is on their map because, ironically, the Church appears too secular, too much like what we are trying to escape from: the bureaucracy, the compromises, the self-righteous distance, the structures and strictures, the clichéd language and so on.

The medieval mystic Meister Eckhart once said that God is like a person hiding in the dark who occasionally coughs and gives himself away. There's a lot of darkness we're trying to grope through at the moment, both outside and inside the Church, if I can put it like that, and we long for a cough, just a little cough, to keep trust part of our faith in God, rather than just argument, ritual and politics. One of those coughs for me has been the poetry of R. S. Thomas.

They say that the definition of a politician is someone who, when he or she sees light at the end of the tunnel, orders more tunnel. They may not be alone. Of commentary, analysis, sermons and scholarship on the priest and poet R. S. Thomas there seems to be no end – always more to dig and develop. And this is surely because he is one of the finest Welsh poets of the last century, as well as one of the finest religious poets, and because his subject matter is often evocative and enigmatic in equal measure. This, coupled with an expanding mythology regarding the contradictions of his personality as much as any perceived in his thinking, and we find a poet whose body of work invites an engagement from a whole variety of readers across the board.

What I want to try in response to this poem is to unravel something of a threefold relationship of about 30 years standing. That relationship or conversation is one that has been taking place between me, God and R. S. Thomas.

I first came across the work of Thomas while at Kings College London studying for my theology degree. It was an important discovery at a time when what I was learning was beginning to uproot some of my personal beliefs and I wasn't sure how to connect my head and heart. A few years later I was training for ministry and had, in the middle of my time there, a period of extreme doubt about God, not least working on an HIV/AIDS ward seeing men of my own age die, and anger at the Church for its many dishonesties, hypocrisies and lack of prophetic edge. All romance in my spirituality dried up and, hardened and sceptical, I decided to leave training. I packed a bag and went to visit a friend who was working in India. With not much room in that bag I packed only one book (quite heavy it was too) – the poems of R. S. Thomas.

Two things happened to me in those six weeks in India. I suddenly realized how big the world is and how laughable it is to imagine that anyone or any group can somehow claim the monopoly on truth when so much is as yet unknown, unexplored. Becoming a visitor in a totally different culture also makes you into something of a stranger to yourself, and I became aware of that vast unexplored territory inside that I had been calling 'me'. At the same time, the poems I carried around with me – getting brushed with spices, sweat and bashed about next to chickens on the bus – those poems were teaching me something about the breadth and depth of God, should there be such a reality, in relation to this huge world and hidden self. The poems had a real magnetism of mystery to them and somehow seemed to place a compass back in my hand that said, 'Start again, start afresh'. Looking back, I see now that so much was having to be re-learned in order to live, contours were being pushed wider, habits of thought unpicked – all growing pains. Thanks to a patient principal, I returned to college to see whether God and I had a future. R. S. Thomas came too. New poems were devoured. Trips were made to go and hear him and, just once, I met and had the chance to talk with him.

Jumping ahead, I finished training and was ordained in 1993. I have been fortunate to serve in fascinating ministries. Suffice it to say that the doubts have often returned and still do, in different guises and sometimes very dark and helpless, and the anger at the Church, as an institution, comes and goes as regularly as clockwork. I have got older, read more, thought more, loved and lost – as we all have. And two things have stayed constant: God and R. S. Thomas. For no matter how much I have fought with God, dismissed 'him' (I don't consider 'God' to be a boy's name), thought him cruel – the relationship with him has always been there. I can't shake him off. And no matter how much I have scratched my head over his poems, some days thought him too romantic, some days too bleak – my relationship with the work of Thomas has never diminished either.

As I write this bit of autobiography I am also aware of the context in which I have tried to live out my ordained life: the culture that affects today's Church, today's public arena, today's priorities. What takes place on the outside affects the inside. So as a priest and pastor, what has been the air that I breathe? And what air is affecting, without us knowing sometimes, our Christian communities? I want to explore something of this in a slightly odd way. I want to imagine that the Greek gods are alive today, and that four of them are especially alive and kicking. By looking at these gods we might begin to see the influence that they are having on me and, I think, on many of us, and then how this might begin to shape our language and thinking in a God-search. This will reveal, I hope, why Thomas is vitally important in such times.

The first god alive and well today is called 'Gloss', the goddess of beauty and surfaces – a fickle being, incarnated in paper and adverts, a god so big she makes us all feel small and ugly. We are drawn by her siren voice but her perfection is impossible even for those who anoint themselves with her many sensuous creams and labels. She is cunning too – she makes humans confuse their wants for their needs, and this leads to many tears. She teaches that life is survival of the fittest – fit for what she never reveals. She makes objects into people and people into objects so in her adverts you can never work out if the man is having an affair with the woman or with the car. Any church under the spell of Gloss will always be in danger, as Archbishop Robert Runcie liked to quote, of becoming a swimming pool – with all the noise coming from the shallow end. Its theology will have all the integrity of a bumper-sticker. Read it, agree and honk – or just drive by.

'Obese' is the god of gathering, of acquiring, who is never satisfied: happiness for him is having what you want, not wanting what you have; and he always wants more, even when bloated. Although people say he is seen on earth at the moment in the form of bankers, in fact he is found in the hearts of all those of us who have forgotten that the best things in life are never things, and that there is always a price to be paid when everything has a price. He is related to that great god who makes us buy things we don't need called Ikea (mainly worshipped on a Saturday). Together they magic us into spending money we don't have on things we don't want in order to impress people we don't like.

'Instantaneous' is the goddess of now. She cannot wait. She must have fast cars, fast food, fast money, fast death. She is blind, never having the time to stop and see anything. She often gets into a mess, too, because she never has the patience to listen to anyone else. She beckons people to live full lives but strangely leaves them feeling empty. She is afraid of people meeting face to face in case they discover the joys of wasting time together, and so she invents screens and devices that trick us into thinking we are communicating but which actually add to our loneliness and sense of isolation. She seduces with fast clarity and easy answers, and so hates ambiguity, poetry, faith. She invented what R. S. Thomas often called 'The Machine' – but she doesn't know this because she would never waste time reading him.

And finally there is 'Punch', the god of violence and division. If hate can be escalated he'll have a go – if they don't agree with you, lash out. If they're different, slap them down. If they're not in the majority, don't invite them. When in doubt, just punch them. Now obviously Punch is the creator of some computer games, street gangs, film directors and state leaders. Religious leaders are often drawn to his clarifying power too. But also, Punch can be a subtle god and can hide in the consensus of the middle classes, and his punch can be made not of a fist but of plausible, respectable, articulate words. Punch can be very charming as he drives around in his bandwagon. He can make you feel better. And he loves to play a little trick – he likes to make people yawn whenever the conversation turns to human rights and responsibilities, refugees, the poor, the environment, the planet's survival and equality for everyone on it – in fact, anything that Christians believe are close to God's heart.

As I have grown up and tried to become adult, with mixed results, these four gods have had me and many of my colleagues and friends under their power. Moments have come along in our lives, however, when we have seen it and caught ourselves in the mirror and regretted what we have become. We recognize that we have quite a lot to live with but not a great deal to live for. A character played by Maggie Smith in a recent play noted that the obituary of our generation will be, 'We left no loft unconverted'.

Seeing ourselves as we have become has made some city folk flee to the countryside to be distilled. Others have given more time to children or to friendships. Some have sought out opportunities for doing good or reading or being creative or meditating. And some have asked questions about God, about whether reality is ultimately trustworthy and how we might, if so, begin to let our roots which are so thirsty drink from deeper pools. R. S. Thomas once wrote in the *Times Literary Supplement*: 'Is this not also a mechanised and impersonal age, an analytic and clinical one; an age in which under the hard gloss of affluence there can be detected the murmuring of the starved heart and the uneasy spirit?'[1] All this has led to so many of my generation telling me as a priest that they are spiritual, but not religious. Some will go further: they say that they are atheist but value spirituality. What they find intriguing or frustrating or disappointing is that as people who believe they value the dignity of the human soul, the Church is not on their map of spiritual adventure. It is a frustrating irony: spiritually hungry people find the Church too secular. As an 'ambassador' for the Church I often feel that people are looking to me to somehow raise their low expectations; or I can often sense their resentment towards me as someone who appears to peddle spring-like fantasies in a wintry world.

What matters to me, then, as a priest is the quality of the language of our conversations, the language with which we begin to try and dive into fresher, deeper waters, avoiding the tyranny of cliché and deaf answers. How do we ask people to be patient with language, as they might be with a painting, waiting to let it change you rather than use it for one's own agenda? As I look for a way to find that language for today's soul, for my soul, for a people for whom so much of the grammar of Christian faith is just not there, I have turned to Thomas. For here is someone who has given voice to the difficulties of the God-search, who has exposed both the richness and poverty of our words, a man whose own distillation seems quite progressed – as Seamus Heaney said of Thomas, he appears as 'a loner taking on the universe, a kind of Clint Eastwood of the spirit'.[2] As I review the longings and questionings of my generation and as I review my own flickering communion with God, with the romance long past and the relationship under way but faltering, I find that Thomas' poems speak honestly:

> They laid this stone trap
> for him, enticing him with candles,
> as though he would come like some huge moth
> out of the darkness to beat there.
> Ah, he had burned himself
> before in the human flame
> and escaped, leaving the reason
> torn. He will not come any more
> to our lure. Why, then, do I kneel still
> striking my prayers on a stone
> heart? Is it in hope one
> of them will ignite yet and throw
> on its illuminated walls the shadow
> of someone greater than I can understand?[3]

What is very important to me is that the one who offers me a poetry in which to explore the relationship to God is also unflinchingly up-front about his own rebellion and reverence, about his devotion but also the overwhelming derelictions of pursuing God. I remember interviewing a woman offering herself for ordination. 'Why?' I asked. 'I suppose I want to help people have that relationship with God that I only wish I had myself,' she replied. This is how it feels but the task is as urgent as it was when the French worker priest in the 1960s was asked why he had got ordained in a time of secular fundamentalism and totalitarian commercialism. 'I was ordained', he said, 'in order to stop the rumour of God disappearing from the face of the earth.' These two responses, to use a Thomas word, form the 'counterpoint' of a priestly ministry for me today.

Thomas' insights on our situation as regards belief are razor sharp. Much of what I have described as the erosion of faith and the paralysis of doubt is, of course, not new. The reasons may have changed somewhat, but we can still read a poem like Matthew Arnold's 'Dover Beach', probably written in 1851, and understand. Arnold famously reflects on the ebb of the sea and this leads him to think that:

> The Sea of Faith
> was once, too, at the full, and round earth's shore lay like the
>   folds of a bright girdle furled.
> But now I only hear
> its melancholy, long, withdrawing roar,
> retreating, to the breath
> of the night-wind, down the vast edges drear
> and naked shingles of the world.[4]

Arnold wants us, in his words, to 'witness the discouragement'. Thomas wrote a poem indebted to 'Dover Beach' called 'Tidal':

> The waves run up the shore
> and fall back. I run
> up the approaches of God
> and fall back. The breakers return
> reaching a little further,
> gnawing away at the mainland.
> They have done this thousands
> of years, exposing little by little
> the rock under the soil's face.
> I must imitate them only
> in my return to the assault,
> not in their violence. Dashing
> my prayers at him will achieve
> little other than the exposure
> of the rock under his surface.
> My returns must be made
> on my knees. Let despair be known
> as my ebb-tide; but let prayer
> have its springs, too, brimming

disarming him; discovering somewhere
among his fissures deposits of mercy
where trust may take root and grow.[5]

In Thomas' poem there is both ebb *and* flow. Thomas metaphoric-
ally compares his relationship to God to tidal rhythm and a fitful,
fleeting contact with him. This poem does not have the same defin-
itive, pervasive despondency of Arnold's, for we hear the words,
'spring', 'brim' and 'surprise' and reference to a discovering of
'deposits of mercy'. There is erosion but there may be discovery
in the rock-face yet. Such a positioning is important for we have
a diminished way in which we try to speak of God at the moment
– either as a Dawkins dismisser or in the other corner a believer
in an inerrant religious authority, be it person or text. We are so
often being asked to side with one of two fundamentalisms. But
many of us are poised somewhere in the balance – uncomfortable,
difficult to articulate but the place of integrity for us – unafraid to
reason, unashamed to adore – thinking critically and trying to live
faithfully. Thomas allows us to roam freely in this space and, by
so doing, gives us a fresher air to breathe and clears an approach
often far too hidden today.

We find this space offered us too in Thomas' 'The Other', where
listening to the sea's swell rising and falling 'the thought comes of
that other being who is awake too',[6] on whom prayers break for
days, years and eternity; and also in 'The Moon in Lleyn' where
we read:

> . . . the tide laps
> at the Bible; the bell fetches
> no people to the brittle miracle
> of the bread. The sand is waiting
> for the running back of the grains
> in the wall into its blond
> glass. Religion is over, and
> what will emerge from the body
> of the new moon, no one
> can say.

But a voice sounds
in my ear: Why so fast,
mortal? These very seas
are baptized. The parish
has a saint's name time cannot
unfrock. In cities that
have outgrown their promise people
are becoming pilgrims
again, if not to this place,
then to the recreation of it
in their own spirits. You must remain
kneeling. Even as this moon
making its way through the earth's
cumbersome shadow, prayer, too,
has its phases.[7]

The sense one receives from these and many other poems is that our ignorance, though blunt, is a kind of knowledge; we do not know what it is or how to interpret it but, to use his words, 'the meaning is in the waiting'.[8]

Thomas opens up a space in which our doubt, scepticism and ignorance are allowed to break on a shore, somehow, and to reveal another form of comprehension that reaches beyond the usual categories of right and wrong, real and unreal, true and false. It is a space that is both comfort and challenge. It is a place where meaning is forged in mystery, where we are grasped by that for which we wait. He is engaged, in his phrases, in an 'interrogation of silence', 'an experimenting with an Amen', a nailing of his questions one by one 'to an untenanted cross'. Thomas writes of what he knows and never asks for pity.

In 63 BCE the Romans stormed the Jerusalem Temple and were astonished, we are told, to find the Holy of Holies empty, with no statues and no object of worship. No gods, not even Gloss. This shock of absence is worth thinking about – and you are made to by Thomas time and time again. Endless mystics and holy teachers have advised we do. The Eastern tradition of apophasis means leaping towards the mystery, not just empty theology but the opening up of an encounter, a revelation that is unthinkable, unseeable. This is God giving us just enough to seek him and never enough to fully find him. To do more would inhibit our freedom and limit his holiness. 'The sensation of silence', wrote John Updike, 'cannot be helped: a loud and evident God would be a bully, an insecure tyrant, an all-crushing datum instead of, as he is, a bottomless encouragement to our faltering and frightened being.'[9] It is true that as we try to articulate God we discover his elusiveness, his receding before us. As Thomas says, 'language falsifies'.

We relate to God only in the context of nearness and distance, for if we ever think we possess him we will stop desiring him. 'Such a fast God', says Thomas, 'always before us and leaving as we arrive.'[10] It is as if we know there is a God because he keeps disappearing. Our longing is the necessary constant. Desire is the heartbeat of faith. Faith is a love of the hidden, a pursuit in relationship, a search for the visibility of the invisible. 'We want God's voice to be clear but it is not. It is as deep as night, with a dark clarity, like an x-ray. It reaches our bones.'[11] Waiting for God is a theme Thomas is known for:

Kneeling:
Moments of great calm,
kneeling before an altar
of wood in a stone church
in summer, waiting for the God
to speak; the air a staircase
For silence; the sun's light
ringing me, as though I acted
a great rôle. And the audiences
still; all that close throng
of spirits waiting, as I,
for the message.
Prompt me, God;
but not yet. When I speak,
though it be you who speak
through me, something is lost.
The meaning is in the waiting.

This absence is different from that felt by the many searchers I have been referring to. Their sense of absence of God is more likely to have arrived because of the disenchantment of the world by scientific explanation and by a culture that carries on as if God isn't; or it might have come about because of a failure to understand what it might mean to say God acts in this world – 'OK, he may exist but what does he do all day?' and 'If he can act, why doesn't he intervene at times of evil and pointless suffering?'

So, there is an absence for those who have begun to love the divine and understand the pains of relationship, the necessity of presence and absence in such a dynamic; and there is the absence of God felt by those for whom the talk about God doesn't make any sense. This last sense of absence is more akin to that of loss, bereavement perhaps. It is interesting to ask whether there are those for whom there has never been any sense of religious aware-ness ever, people for whom the word 'absent' cannot be compared with any understanding of presence at all.

For Thomas, shadows point the way. He tries to articulate God only to discover God's elusiveness, his receding before the poet. In his collection *Frequencies*, it is the eel-like God who slips out of your hands into the dark depths that Thomas attempts to express. Poem after poem is marked with a passage about this divine absence – 'God not there where he could have been, or was a little while before, or who might come if we are patient, or who has left just a small sign of his presence but one which gives no further assurance he will ever be apprehended again'.[12] 'We never catch him at work,' he writes elsewhere, 'but can only say,/ coming suddenly upon an amendment,/ that here he has been.'[13]

Pascal once stated that if there were no obscurity we would not be sensible of our corruption, and if there were no light we would not hope for a remedy; thus God, in fairness and to our advan-tage, remains partly hidden and partly revealed. As indeed we all do to each other.

Thomas develops poetry, often around the image of Christ, in which effort gives way to grace, a perception of receiving. It is when we acknowledge that we don't have the answers, and when we stop driving in a proud gear, that sight is granted. The more opinions you have, the less you see:

> I think that maybe
> I will be a little surer
> of being a little nearer
> that's all. Eternity
> is in the understanding
> that that little is more than enough.[14]

Poetry tries to find the music in the words that describe an intuition. Poetry captures, not explains, as statements of faith refer rather than describe. We worship a God who does not reveal propositionally but in collage, and we are called to reflect this God by resisting closure, raising expectations, opening up a generosity of spirit not a meanness of pious restriction.

Homo sapiens sapiens: The name defines a species that wants to know but a counter-thirst exists in us too, for something beyond knowledge and definition. Words such as mystery, camouflage, silence, stillness, shadow, distance, opacity, withdrawal, namelessness, erasure, cryptic, enigma, darkness, absence all suggest disclosure to the spiritual pilgrim. Frightening, tormenting, but still disclosing. Such is God in Thomas' work.

In the poem 'Raptor' God has been made small by the serious experiments of our limited minds. Our understanding and language will never pull off some great final discovery. Our theological chemistry *will come to nothing*. Thomas says he thinks of God *as an enormous owl* who is *abroad in the shadows*. Abroad can mean on different shores than our own but also stresses the word 'broad', expansive and uncontained. This God brushes him with his wing, touches him in flight, and Thomas' blood *freezes*. He's stopped in his unthinking track. The odd is put back into God. God *can see in the dark*: what we encounter as blinding, threatening and frightening is God's flightpath, as he finds his ways to souls. But Thomas says that he has also heard this owl *crooning/ to himself* and screaming as his talons reach into his *great adversary* or into us. The night owl swoops down to claw evil or indifference but at great cost and all alone.

In a traditional Hasidic story a man tortured by doubt travels a
great distance hoping to ask a famous teacher his question. At first
the teacher's disciples will not allow the stranger into the study
house, but one day he finds a way to slip in and approaches the
rabbi: 'Venerable Rabbi, forgive me for disturbing you but I have
travelled many weeks and waited many days for the chance to ask
you a question that has troubled me all my adult life.' 'What is
your question?' the teacher responds. The man asks, 'What is the
essence of truth?' The Rabbi looks at his visitor for a moment,
rises from his chair and slaps him hard. Then he withdraws again
to his books. Shocked, the questioner retreats to a pub across the
way and complains of his mistreatment. One of the rabbi's dis-
ciples, overhearing, takes pity and explains: 'The Rabbi's slap was
given you in great kindness, to teach you this: never surrender a
good question for a mere answer.' I can't help feel that Thomas'
poetry is similarly given in kindness.

R. S. Thomas was a poet of counterpoint, a poet in which sounds
of two possible readings meet, where two distinct melodies create
a texture. The readings are those of God's absence and his pres-
ence, his silence and his resonance, his shadow and his brightness;
the texture is that of a faith that may just be sustainable in our
twenty-first century. His poems rub up against each other, and
that uneasy collision of voices reciprocates in the turmoil of the
reader as we face the pleasant lies and burnt-out words that have
eaten into us as well as the gnawing feeling that we don't quite
believe our unbelief. Thomas undresses the mind in his simple,
sometimes harsh, unsentimental clarity.

We are far from being an atheist culture: indeed, there is a
hunger for the sacred that persists, even intensifies, in an era when
knowledge is exploding. This hunger I believe is rooted in some-
thing more fundamental than intellectual confusion. Regardless
of religious orthodoxies, it seems that people cannot brush aside
the sense that there are things that matter and that this mattering
is not a mere question of knowledge and social convention. It
implies an orientation of one's life towards what lies outside it, a
recognition of values that transcend the individual and even the
culture, a sense as if one was being invited to respond and to

receive. It is for me a profound sense, a humbling but glorious sense for which I shall always be grateful to R. S. Thomas, from early days together in India to the present – and, I guess, to the end of my life.

Colin Meir in *British Poetry since 1970: A Critical Survey* writes that Thomas believed that

> one of the important functions of poetry is to embody religious truth, and since for him as poet that truth is not easily won, his poems record the struggle with marked honesty and integrity, thereby providing the context for the necessarily infrequent moments of faith and vision which are expressed with a clarity and gravity rarely matched by any of his contemporaries.[15]

I am deeply thankful to, and thankful for, R. S. Thomas – priest and poet.

The Journey

Mary Oliver (b. 1935)

One day you finally knew
what you had to do, and began,
though the voices around you
kept shouting
their bad advice –
though the whole house
began to tremble
and you felt the old tug
at your ankles.
"Mend my life!"
each voice cried.
But you didn't stop.
You knew what you had to do,
though the wind pried
with its stiff fingers
at the very foundations –
though their melancholy
was terrible.
It was already late
enough, and a wild night,
and the road full of fallen
branches and stones.
But little by little,
as you left their voices behind,
the stars began to burn
through the sheets of clouds,
and there was a new voice,

which you slowly
recognized as your own,
that kept you company
as you strode deeper and deeper
into the world,
determined to do
the only thing you could do –
determined to save
the only life you could save.

When I introduce groups of people to poetry at conferences or
retreats I always try to set aside time for individuals to come and
talk in case they want to follow up anything they have personally
encountered – the ripples heading out after the splash. I'm always
struck by the way very different poems affect people, touching
something at their particular time in life and coming as a relief or
a shock – or both. I have found that the poems of Mary Oliver
particularly strike chords and I have spent quite a few hours
listening to a variety of people of very different ages exploring
how Oliver's words have prompted some necessary shift towards
honesty in them – usually with a box of tissues nearby. Her
poems are also frequently read at public occasions, such as when
Vice-President Joe Biden read Oliver's 'Wild Geese' at the 9/11
memorial in New York. Why are these poems both so intimately
moving and publicly poised?

Until her very recent move to Florida, Oliver lived most of her
adult life in and around Provincetown on the extreme tip of Cape
Cod, Massachusetts. This setting is the heartland of her work and
she is best known for her poignant observation of the natural
world's quiet occurrences. She begins each day with a long walk
to woods, ponds and harbours with her notebook in her hand –
scribbling, watching, learning – and then uses her notes as she
shapes the poems.

Oliver says that she tries to 'listen convivially to the world' and
it is this focused attention to her environment and the great 'family
of things' that marks out her writing. She attends to nature, from

grasshoppers to humpback whales, from the marshlands to the ocean, but never in a sentimental or simplistic way; although she is quite clear that 'attention without feeling is only a report' and that for poetic attention you always need an empathy. The clarity and fresh intensity of her poems is born and nurtured in her complete wonder at what is around her and of which she finds herself a part. She wants to help us feel at home in a world that looks dramatically different through ecologically informed eyes. 'Mary Oliver's poetry is fine and deep,' commented the poet Stanley Kunitz, 'it reads like a blessing. Her special gift is to connect us with our sources in the natural world, its beauties and terrors and mysteries and consolations.'[1]

Undoubtedly, one of the reasons for the popularity of Oliver's poetry is this re-call of the human back to an awareness of the natural world at a time when it has become frighteningly evident as to what our indifference towards it has, and is, doing. The minute and intricate focus on one small bird or animal in her work raises the alarm to a global creation in peril but also reveals that there is only a very thin membrane between human beings and what we call the 'animal'. When we don't see or attend to nature we are equally not seeing or attending to ourselves. We diminish ourselves, leave ourselves parched as well as our planet, by our distractions and desire to build things – from walled 'communities' and money's babel towers to personal reputations in what the Australian poet Les Murray has termed 'the Kingdom of Flaunt'.[2] Kunitz's comment about an Oliver poem reading like a blessing is insightful, we sense an invitation to a more complete wholeness by her invocation of the elemental, beautiful and unchangeable reality of the cycles of life.

Another reason Oliver is popular is because her work has an unapologetically 'spiritual' quality to it without being formally religious or dogmatic. 'Spirituality' is an increasingly vague term but popularly tends today to refer to religious experience without religious language. Oliver in a recent interview said that she thought to become 'spiritual' you became kinder, more people-oriented, more willing to grow old and more investigative. In much of her work there is reference, also, to prayer, the sacred, death and rebirth, light and darkness, alienation and reconciliation, but in a language that may sound to many traditionalist religious believers as airy, animistic or some literary propaganda for the Green Party. There is no doubt that many turn to her for 'the sustaining truths and feelings that conventional religion and modern society seem unable to provide'.[3] She has referred to her work as 'praise poems' for unawakened hearts[4] and celebrates that energy that is the white fire of a great mystery.[5] We live, she prompts us to remember, in a world of presences where we should be willing to be dazzled and put aside the world of facts that can weigh us down. It can be argued that Oliver is in fact attending to that other 'book of God' we know as nature, just as scholars read the Bible. This is not foreign to the Christian tradition, as St Augustine reminds us: 'Some people, in order to discover God, read books. But there is a great book: the very appearance of created things. Look above you! Look below you! Note it. Read it. God, whom you want to discover, never wrote that book with ink. Instead He set before your eyes the things that He had made. Can you ask for a louder voice than that?'[6]

Certainly Oliver has reminded me constantly that as creatures of God ourselves we are part of, not apart from, the created world and that there is a voice of integrity to be heard when we more consciously participate in, even celebrate, our natural environment rather than alienate ourselves from it. She has a deeper sense of the sacredness of the earth than many religious institutions seem to have, though their words endlessly speak of this sanctity, and there is a haunting and exciting invitation to her work: we sense we will ignore it at our loss. In a wonderful collection entitled *A Thousand Mornings* there is a poem called 'I Happened to be Standing' where she gives expression to many people's confusion as to what prayer might be, how it 'works' and whether it is meant to change the world or ourselves, and she does so in words that radiate the essence of prayer itself: gratitude, humility and a soul trying to focus:

I don't know where prayers go,
    or what they do.

Do cats pray, while they sleep
    half-asleep in the sun?
Does the opossum pray as it
    crosses the street?
The sunflowers? The old black oak
    growing older every year?
I know I can walk through the world,
    along the shore or under the trees,
with my mind filled with things
    of little importance, in full
self-attendance. A condition I can't really
    call being alive.
Is a prayer a gift, or a petition,
    or does it matter?
The sunflowers blaze, maybe that's their way.
Maybe the cats are sound asleep. Maybe not.

While I was thinking this I happened to be standing
just outside my door, with my notebook open,
which is the way I begin every morning.
Then a wren in the privet began to sing.
He was positively drenched in enthusiasm,
I don't know why. And yet, why not.
I wouldn't persuade you from whatever you believe
or whatever you don't. That's your business.
But I thought, of the wren's singing, what could this be
    if it isn't a prayer?
So I just listened, my pen in the air.[7]

Another reason I believe Mary Oliver's work is popular is that her later poems began to include an 'I', the emergence of a self-reflective voice that self-scrutinizes in the light of what the poem has been describing. Oliver does this in such a way that we never feel that her poems have been ruptured by some ego demanding centre-stage in the poetry, but so that the 'I' also becomes 'us' the readers. Her question to herself becomes our question. Her poems are an annunciation. We are addressed directly by many of them and are left slightly shaken by our inability to answer quickly what are so obviously urgent and x-ray interrogations into our being and will. Uncomfortable as it can be, we like to be addressed in this way and to be reminded that there are decisions to be made about our life. A good example would be her much-loved poem 'The Summer Day' which begins by asking who made the world, the swan and the black bear, and then continues by wondering what prayer is and stating that attention to the world is how 'to be idle and blessed'. It ends with the bald directness of a doctor in a surgery asking what we intend to do with our one precious life.

This single but universal voice of reflection and inquiry carries us through the poem I have chosen here called 'The Journey', first published in 1986.

The short lines and one stanza of this poem give it a sense of purpose and movement as we are pulled by its magnetic urgency. It is a poem of transformation, necessary change and of the heart finally making a decision to be true to itself. You can cluster the final words of the lines to get an echo of the poem's message: *knew, began, you – tug, ankles, life! – cried, stop, do – late, night, fallen – voice, slowly, own – deeper, world – do, do, save, save.*

One day the poem begins. There is always a day when finally everything becomes clear, when thoughts and feelings that have been stored, hidden, ruminated over and painfully percolated at last come to the mind and heart as being true and it is obvious that you need to change your life, job, relationship, or whatever, in some way – to be authentic. Quite often some loss or pain triggers the recognition. As the status quo is challenged by this, however, people advise us not to be foolish, selfish or rash. We are surrounded by voices that make demands on us: *Mend my life!* they say. That is, these voices speak for themselves and not for us. They want their own lives to remain unchanged or repaired, or maybe they want their own worldview or power base unchallenged, and don't have our own integrity and fulfilment at their heart. The pressure to conform is always deceptively strong and often is for someone else's benefit.

I remember when I decided to 'come out' in a talk I was giving at the Greenbelt Festival. I knew I had to do it if my talk was to be honest. It was a frightening prospect to address about a thousand people I didn't know, and I knew it would have consequences. When I told an English bishop what I planned to do I asked him if it was a problem for him. 'Not for *me*,' he said, implying that it would be for others, for my future, for . . . well, he never said. He just left me with the anxiety of what might come. He was not shouting bad advice but was certainly intimidating the truth, and honesty, by unnamed fears to preserve the status quo: *their melancholy/ was terrible*. On the other hand, when I told an American bishop his response was, 'Oh Mark! That's wonderful! No matter what happens it's always best to live in the light. So many will be grateful to you!' I was reminded of the distinction that Martin Luther King Jr made between negative peace and positive peace. A negative peace is the absence of tension. A positive peace is the presence of justice.

But you didn't stop./ You knew what you had to do, Oliver continues. Once we know what has to be done, there is no going back. Our focus becomes loyalty to the future, not the past, and the full-stop in our life that has changed to a comma now demands of us more on the page. I can't help but think that all those who encountered Christ in the Gospels and the ways in which he subverted their self-understanding, distilling it off from how others looked at them and telling them to listen to God's love for them instead, would all be able to read this poem with a very deep understanding.

It was already late, writes Oliver. It is *a wild night* with the road full of *fallen/ branches and stones*. Truth is wild. It is uncontainable and will always out. It disrupts everything we do to cover it up and when it emerges there is the sense that we've been a bit late catching up with it. Then *there was a new voice/ which you slowly/ recognized as your own*, and this authentic 'you' keeps you company, the poem says, it isn't alien or estranged from you. At last who you are, what you are, what you say and believe, all begin to travel together. You can now step over the stones and branches that have fallen because you're in better company. You have become your own friend at last. All this could sound self-obsessed and almost unsocial but Oliver is clear that the transformation is made so that we can stride *deeper and deeper/ into the world* and relate more openly, approaching difficulties and challenges with a fresh sense of who I am, what is important and what isn't.

On aeroplanes parents are told, in an emergency, to put their own mask on before putting their children's on. It sounds the wrong way round and yet we cannot feed unless we have been fed. We save *the only life you could save* so that we might be stronger in soul to help others in their lives. Our truth-transformations, sometimes small, sometimes big, do not make us less vulnerable, less doubting or more perfect. They just make us more us and, hopefully, a little more transparent so the world knows what it's dealing with when it meets us. As I write I think of the seamstress Rosa Parks in Alabama refusing to surrender her bus seat in 1955 to a white passenger. She knew her truth and what she had to do. There were plenty of voices shouting bad advice to her. Was she being selfish or was she trailing the way for the end of segregation and a more just and equal society? She and her action that day went *deeper and deeper/ into the world*. Oliver's poem is clear: no one else should live your life for you. Living – it's your call.

Oliver's voice, which queries who we have become and what we are going to do about it, is not some existential angst-driven demand as to how to survive life, nor is it some systematic moral enquiry as to the nature of the good life. It is a natural voice with a natural question in a natural world, a wondering as to how my human life might try to match the gift we are part of. On a day when she goes out on a little boat in the afternoon light she writes:

All through our gliding journey, on this day as on so many others, a little song runs through my mind. I say a song because it passes musically, but it is really just words, a thought that is neither strange nor complex. In fact, how strange it would be *not* to think it – not to have such music inside one's head and body, on such an afternoon. What does it mean, say the words, that the earth is so beautiful? And what shall I do about it? What is the gift that I should bring to the world? What is the life that I should live?[8]

Prayer

Carol Ann Duffy (b. 1955)

Some days, although we cannot pray, a prayer
utters itself. So, a woman will lift
her head from the sieve of her hands and stare
at the minims sung by a tree, a sudden gift.

Some nights, although we are faithless, the truth
enters our hearts, that small familiar pain;
then a man will stand stock-still, hearing his youth
in the distant Latin chanting of a train.

Pray for us now. Grade I piano scales
console the lodger looking out across
a Midlands town. Then dusk, and someone calls
a child's name as though they named their loss.

Darkness outside. Inside, the radio's prayer –
Rockall. Malin. Dogger. Finisterre.

Carol Ann Duffy is a well-known and popular poet. Since 2009
she has been Britain's Poet Laureate, the first woman to hold this
office. She once said in an interview, 'I like to use simple words
but in a complicated way',[1] and this mixture of accessibility with
imaginative challenge has placed her work on the school syllabus
since 1994. She was born in Glasgow but at the age of six moved
with her Roman Catholic family to Stafford. Her poems often
reflect a close familiarity with the Catholic faith that she later laid
aside, and 'Prayer' is one of them.

One of the many strengths for which Duffy is admired is her ability to be a poetic ventriloquist, able to take on the voice and perspective of a hugely varied collection of individuals from all times and places. She often does this in the form of dramatic monologues, and so a collection such as *The World's Wife* sees her adopting the views of the women who have been the lovers of the 'great men' of the world. Many of these men she recalled from the tales and myths she learned as a child. A phrase such as 'the world and his wife' reminds us that the world is casually thought to be 'his', male, and that women stereotypically just marry the real people of influence and never are them themselves. In a daringly funny and insightful way she places together monologues of women's voices that together create a choir of the forgotten, talented, overlooked and intellectually capable women who have borne but survived the costs of men's vanities and hubris. A short and very amusing example is 'Mrs Darwin':

7 April 1852.

Went to the Zoo.
I said to Him –
Something about that Chimpanzee over there reminds me
of you.[2]

Her *Feminine Gospels* (2002) similarly seeks to express the experience of women, frequently focusing on the marginalized and dispossessed, but through mainly narrative poems. In what way this experience is 'good news', as the title of the book suggests, is for the reader to reflect on. The collection is dedicated to her four brothers.

Duffy is also respected for her love poetry. Her 'Rapture', for instance, continues the long tradition of shaping a sequence of love poems, from the falling in love to the falling apart, and makes them so contemporary to the modern heart that they can be disturbingly poignant. In 'Text', the speaker, anxiously looking for messages from the lover, is described secretly tending 'the mobile now/ like an injured bird'. The final poem in the collection takes lines from Robert Browning as its epigraph: 'That's the wise thrush; he sings each song twice over,/ Lest you should think he never could recapture/ That first fine careless rapture!' Even though the lover is gone, what was shared together can be voiced and recaptured. The song can be sung twice.

Her work is brave in its repetition and use of word-play, strong in assonance and lyricism. Some critics think she can be over-sentimental or even guilty of cliché in some of her word choice and imagery. I think rather that she returns us to the words we have forgotten through our blind and lazy use so that we can see their original power and draw, connecting us to the channels of feeling and truth they open up. It is as if she gives clichés one last chance to prove themselves before we throw them away – and she makes them deliver.

'Prayer' is the last poem in one of her darker collections called *Mean Time*. Damaged relationships, harsh political climates and an indifferent cosmos all feature. The title of the book entices. Is time mean, pinched and cruel, does its passing just create hurt? Or, are we in the meantime here, that is, waiting for something more significant to happen? Or, to go back to our maths lessons, is time 'mean' in the sense of the average, levelling us all out equally as we inevitably submit to its power to end each life? All of us spend our days marked out by Greenwich Mean Time, all our encounters, thoughts, even breathing itself are measured by reference to this mean time. We write and speak with verbs that indicate whether things are, in this matrix, past, present or yet to be. It seems we mean nothing without time, yet time will make us mean nothing ultimately.

'Prayer' is a sonnet, a poetic form that Duffy has said, at reading events, can 'enter us as prayers can'. She speaks of the concentrated and contemplative communication in the brevity of its shape, calling it the 'little black dress of poetry'. 'Prayer' has been lauded as both a secular version of a religious prayer in an irreligious age and, on the other hand maybe, 'an odd and loving refusal of the secular'.[3] However we want to see it, it seems to celebrate Wordsworth's belief that poetry should be something that 'cherishes our daily lives'. It is wistful but strong, with a measured cadence that gives a sense that a busy and distracted life is being distilled or excavated for its treasure.

The first four lines (or 'quatrain') begin *Some days*, and we are cast immediately into the changing seas of time. Although *we cannot pray* (lack of belief? pain? distraction?) a prayer *utters itself*. So a woman lifts her head from *the sieve of her hands* and stares *at the minims sung by a tree*. This is *a sudden gift*. What are the minims here? Are they birds in a tree or the sound of the wind through branches and leaves? A minim has two beats, like a heart, and it appears to be the music of a sound that comes as a blessing to the heart of a careworn woman. It also has a resonance of 'minimum' and the least we live with. Both the moment of epiphany and the 'prayer' uttered are gifts. Prayer is not a banging on the table that demands attention but an opening of an attitude, letting our grip go on a life, that we may receive, hold, extend better. The story of St Kevin already referred to relays the same truth. His hands were so still and open as he prayed to God that a blackbird nested in them and brooded her young. Such an openness to gift always, this says, hatches fresh and unexpected life. 'Prayer', said Martin Luther, 'is not overcoming God's reluctance but laying hold of his willingness.'

From *some days* we then have at the beginning of the second quatrain *some nights*. Although *we are faithless*, the *truth/ enters our hearts, that small familiar pain*. Faithless can have two meanings. We can be without faith or we can be unfaithful towards a loved one. For the Christian, we recognize here the belief that, although humanity is faithless in both senses, God's truth comes as an offering and enters our life in a human form. Christ is both familiar alongside us and a judgement as he sees us for who we really are. We inflict the pain back to him in revenge. Nevertheless, this can be read equally as a statement about human beings being imperfect and yet the recipients of truth and beauty such as can make a man stand *stock-still* and hear *his youth in the distant Latin chanting of a train*. Did he decline Latin verbs as a boy? Is he declining, refusing those verbs I mentioned earlier of past and future and simply finding himself momentarily in the present now? This is very much how prayer functions, as it asks of us what our past is doing now. The train is distant, as is his past, and the image of liturgical *chanting* keeps us very much in this context of contemplation and wonder.

The third quatrain begins *Pray for us now*. This is part of the prayer known as 'Hail Mary' which includes the phrases 'full of grace', 'the Lord is with you', 'blessed are you'. All these seem to be true of those of whom the poem speaks. The Hail Mary ends asking that the mother of the Lord will 'pray for us sinners now and at the hour of our death'. Moments of epiphany in this sonnet make the mortal journey bearable, even gifted in its limited span. Again, it is sound that consoles the next individual, a lodger in a Midlands town, with Grade I piano scales. We are all lodgers in this world and all we own falls away in time. *Then dusk, and someone calls/ a child's name as though they named their loss.* All the people we have been with here have been brought back to their childhood, it seems, the more innocent time when we see the world as a place to be wondered at and embraced as fully as we can before we are called back home.

The concluding couplet is haunting. We have moved from days to nights to dusk, and now darkness falls *outside*. The speaker refers to *the radio's prayer* inside and we are given four names that are mentioned frequently in the shipping forecast issued by the Met Office and broadcast on BBC Radio. If you happen to hear it you are probably unable to sleep because it is broadcast in the very early hours of the day. *Rockall, Malin, Dogger* and *Finisterre* are all sea areas. The first three of these names have two syllables each and the last continues longer, takes us further, with three. They are heard on the radio by most people with total incomprehension – and yet there is a beauty to the forecast, a consolation and poetry, as these mystical unknown places out in the beyond are brought into our own night. For this reason the poet Imtiaz Dharker requested a recording of the shipping forecast as one of her desert island discs on the BBC radio programme.[4] As the sea's places are spoken, in a repetitive litany, we sense that ships are being guided to safe harbour. They are coming home, the lost souls, even through the night's wild weather.

A poem that alerts us to the comfort of sounds in a life of lost childhoods and lost loves will, of course, be full of sensitivity to the noises of its own words. Go back to the poem and say it slowly. Hear the vowels and soft consonants, the 's' of the third quatrain, and then if you say *Finisterre* out loud you'll discover, like the word 'prayer', it involves you gently expiring air at the end. This is called 'aspiration' and gives a timelessness to the word as it is breathed out with no discernible finality. Indeed, Finisterre means 'end of the earth'.

To the Harbormaster

Frank O'Hara (1926–66)

I wanted to be sure to reach you;
though my ship was on the way it got caught
in some moorings. I am always tying up
and then deciding to depart. In storms and
at sunset, with the metallic coils of the tide
around my fathomless arms, I am unable
to understand the forms of my vanity
or I am hard alee with my Polish rudder
in my hand and the sun sinking. To
you I offer my hull and the tattered cordage
of my will. The terrible channels where
the wind drives me against the brown lips
of the reeds are not all behind me. Yet
I trust the sanity of my vessel; and
if it sinks, it may well be in answer
to the reasoning of the eternal voices,
the waves which have kept me from reaching you.

Frank O'Hara was born in Baltimore and grew up in Grafton,
Massachusetts. After serving in the US Navy during the Second
World War and studying at Harvard, he became very much part
of New York's literary and artistic life during the 1950s and
1960s. He is at heart a city poet, and his poems, often dashed
off in bars, are infused with the energy of the Manhattan parties,
galleries and tabloids of the time. His poems have a very personal
tone and record the immediacy of his life, sociability, wit and

exuberance. O'Hara, said Allen Ginsberg, 'taught me to really see New York for the first time. It was like having Catullus change your view of the Forum in Rome'.[1]

A poet friend once wrote to O'Hara in gratitude for his poems:

> Your passion always makes me feel like a cloud the wind detaches at last from a mountain so I can finally go sailing over all those valleys with their crazy farms and towns . . . I always start bouncing up and down in my chair when I read a poem of yours . . . where you seem to say, 'I know you won't think this is much of a subject for a poem but I just can't help it: I feel like this.'[2]

This is an insightful review. O'Hara used conversations, notes and inventive, sometimes surrealistic forms to make his poems a sort of diary of his life in New York. To read his word montages is to discover a language in love with itself, breathless, urbane, an interplay between autobiography and detachment, intimacy and abstraction. Although many of O'Hara's poems might not be immortally resonant because of the time-bound 'I did this, I did that' nature of them, they remain beguiling because his overriding aim was to ensure that 'what is happening to me, allowing for lies and exaggerations which I try to avoid, goes into my poems'.[3]

When O'Hara was 40 he was struck down by a jeep on the beach at Fire Island and he died shortly afterwards. At his funeral in Green River Cemetery in Long Island his friend and fellow poet John Ashbery broke down trying to read the last lines of this poem 'To the Harbormaster'.

O'Hara once commented that 'my quietness has a number of naked selves', and 'To the Harbormaster' shows a more melancholic, self-reflective and exposed side of him. It is a love poem, a poem of desire and of the pain lived in not possessing. It takes one of O'Hara's favourite literary metaphors, the boat on the sea, and creates a not-quite sonnet with an irregular metrical scheme that doesn't scan well and has few full stops. The form it takes, like the boat's voyage he refers to, is choppy, halting, rocky.

O'Hara was gay and the poem was addressed to the painter Larry Rivers. Many of O'Hara's poems are addressed person to person, having an intimacy but with the windows left open, as it were, so we can hear what's going on. The first line states that the poet *wanted to be sure to reach you* and immediately the tension is set up between what he wants and what is to be. This is a poem that recognizes human imperfections and the insurmountable distance that can come between people because of forces, inner and outer, beyond our control. The poet with courageous honesty and acceptance, which saves the poem from a wistful sentimentality, sees that he is an unreliable lover. The cycles of life, the weakness of the will, the distractions of vanity and the loss of an emotional compass in the heart – these all work their strength against the union he desires. What he longs for evades him. The poem has a sadness, then, but also a nerve. The clarity of the speaker's voice is calm amid the uncertainties and frustrations of what takes hold of us. The heart can be its own worst enemy, O'Hara seems to say, but it is a heart nevertheless and it tries to make its way towards you – but I know how the story will end.

'To the Harbormaster' is the first poem in a collection called *Meditations in an Emergency*. In a busy life such as we live in Western cities like New York, perhaps the only time we get to meditate is at times of emergency. The title, though, seems to be a play on the priest and poet John Donne's 'Devotions upon Emergent Occasions' (1624) where Donne pursues the idea that sickness can be sent by God. 'It's well known that God and I don't get along together,'[4] said O'Hara, and in one way this is simply a romantic poem addressed to a lover. However, in the same way that the erotic love poems of the biblical Song of Songs have been allegorized and understood to be evocative of our desire for God, this poem has a spiritual charge to it that a person of faith can sense quickly.

The poem has no need of a 'spiritual interpretation'. It is a vessel of humanity, as disturbing as it is reassuring. It is possible, though, without too much godly romance, to read the poem as a prayer. God, the harbour of love to whom all our journeys are drawn as we are put off course by the things we don't want to do or be, is the one we reach out to. The disciples of Jesus had their relationship with him forged and moulded on boats at sea, and when I revisit this poem I often imagine Peter addressing Christ. Peter had been called to follow Jesus by his boat. He was to see Christ calm a storm and, a man who knew about water, he asked to be washed all over so he could be fully immersed in his commitment to him. He was, though, the one whose denial of his friend was so predictable and painful. He then had to live with his betrayal, and I often wonder, when the risen Christ appears to the disciples when they are back in their boats and Peter jumps into the sea, whether he was trying to get away! Perhaps his shame was too much to bear. When they are all together again on the beach, next to the water, Jesus teaches Peter that it is not his own faithfulness that matters but Christ's fidelity to him. The resurrection appearances are in the old haunted places of where the disciples and Jesus had spent their time. He called them, taught them, trained them and ate with them in these places. In resurrection he appears in these places once more to show how even though they failed and ran away, even told lies about knowing him, he is still with them where he always was with them, still needs them and loves them always. The gospel is the assurance of God's fidelity towards us, not ours towards him.

If we did pray Frank O'Hara's poem to heaven, I wonder what the answer might be?

Wedding

Alice Oswald (b. 1966)

From time to time our love is like a sail
and when the sail begins to alternate
from tack to tack, it's like a swallowtail
and when the swallow flies it's like a coat;
and if the coat is yours, it has a tear
like a wide mouth and when the mouth begins
to draw the wind, it's like a trumpeter
and when the trumpet blows, it blows like millions . . .
and this, my love, when millions come and go
beyond the need of us, is like a trick;
and when the trick begins, it's like a toe
tiptoeing on a rope, which is like luck;
and when the luck begins, it's like a wedding,
which is like love, which is like everything.

The novelist Jeanette Winterson has said of Alice Oswald that she 'is the real thing – a true poet of great power and capacity. She writes about the natural world and our relationship to it, reminding us that there is such a thing as a world we didn't make, and one that we badly need, for sanity's sake'.[1] There is no doubt that Oswald is one of the finest poets working in England today. This poem, 'Wedding', comes from her first collection of poetry, *The Thing in the Gap-Stone Stile*, published in 1996 and introducing us to her love of gardening, ecology and the natural world. We discover poems with titles such as 'Pruning in Frost', 'The Glass House', 'A Wood Coming into Leaf', 'The Apple Shed' and

'Gardeners at the Resurrection'. Many of the poems plough the depths of nature and bring its spiritual freshness to the top and into startling view.

Since then her work has generally shaped into book-length projects such as the polyphonic *Dart* (2010) which is a magical exploration of the environment and community along the River Dart in her native Devon. *A Sleepwalk on the Severn* (2009) was commissioned for the Festival of the Severn, and with memorable images such as the darkening sky with 'a few stars creeping out like cress' and the 'muscular unsolid unstillness of the moon' she embodies in the narrative a truth of poetry that 'It's not so much what you see as what you are seeped in'. Similarly hypnotic and imaginative imagery was highly praised by the critics' reading of her recent *Memorial* (2011), a reworking of Homer's *Illiad*. Trained as a classicist and with an interest in the oral tradition of poetry, you can almost hear the crackle of the camp fire in the background as the story is told. The ancient world valued a poet's capacity for *enargeia*, or evocative vividness, and this is Oswald's gift.

'Wedding' is a love sonnet, a procession of transformations that capture the life of love, as George Herbert's sonnet 'Prayer' lays out a collage of images for the life of prayer. The opening words *From time to time* introduce us to the theme of passing moments. The phrase can imply occasional periods (such as in 'I meet him from time to time') or, taken more literally, evokes an eternal sense of existence from the beginning of time to the end of time. Love is both particular and universal. The immediate *sail* invokes a voyage out of harbour that *begins to alternate* and yet stays its course. We then begin a series of images for love that start 'it's like . . .'. Love's language is always metaphoric. It seeks its expression constantly through our lives with a passionate and restless fear that it won't be understood and our vulnerable energy remain unrecognized somehow. A *swallowtail* is a butterfly, symbolic of fragile beauty in sunny times as the *swallow flies*. A *coat* brings to mind cooler periods and *a tear* can be read two ways – as a wound in fabric or as something we weep. Both *the wind* and *blows* keep a sense of the sail remaining upright even through these changing seasons. Love then returns in the heart of the poem and, though *millions come and go* its pulse and purpose lie deep in the speaker and the one addressed as *my love*.

Though the millions live *beyond the need of us* it is clear that the lovers have an inseparable need of each other and this is *like a trick* and *a toe/ tiptoeing on a rope* and *like luck*. *Begins* is repeated, creating a context of regeneration, rebirth even, and a shift into yet another new form for the relationship's constancy. This quickening blend of risk and new beginnings, precariousness and grateful surprise at what is, all make for the foundational final two lines. We feel the strength, resolution and heart's homecoming: *it's like a wedding,/ which is like love, which is like everything*. *Love* is what stands here between *wedding* and *everything*.

We shouldn't miss out on the sounds in the poem. It can help to read it aloud and enjoy the repetitions but also hear how the opening repeated word *time* has 'I' very much in its centre. The journey begins with more 'I' in it than might be needed but ends with a replacing of that early persistent 'I' with the rapture of *love* and *everything*.

One of the most privileged parts of ordained ministry for me is presiding at wedding services. There is a great deal of cynicism about relationships in popular culture at the moment and to the jaundiced everything starts to look yellow, but a marriage is a place where the human will comes back into view. We see that we can make decisions that change the course of our lives, that we can say to another person, 'I do, I will, I love you'. A church is a good place in which to celebrate a marriage. Christian faith is ultimately a celebration of human dignity, not depravity, and a human life can be dignified by the commitment of the love of one for another. The words spoken at a service are themselves poetic: 'to have and to hold from this day forward'; 'for better, for worse'; 'for richer, for poorer'; 'in sickness and in health'. There is something about a wedding that gets us to the very essentials of our being alive and of the threads that can hold our fragility together. It is one of the moments when I believe the rumour of God is at its loudest and most convincing, when we see that for a human self to be most itself it mustn't be selfish. It is the time when we see the potential of a heart to beat for two instead of one. It is, then, also a moment that needs as much affection, practical support and honesty from those who love the couple and live alongside them. Although mistakes can be made, and some relationships can draw to a close for many later reasons too, still there are marriages that would have learned to begin new chapters in their story if the wisdom of Oswald's poem had been patiently taken to heart.

The former Poet Laureate, Andrew Motion, has said of 'Wedding':

> The rush and change of the poem is its own point, and makes us think first and foremost about transformations. About the changes that love creates, and the changes that art creates as it takes hold of familiar experience, shines it up, and passes it back to us as something deeper and refreshed.[2]

In an early poem by Oswald called 'Prayer' the gardener-poet reflects, 'Here I work in the hollow of God's hand/ with Time bent round into my reach'. At the end of the poem the prayer is voiced:

> And all I ask is this – and you can see
> how far the soul, when it goes under flesh,
> is not a soul, is small and creaturish –
> that every day the sun comes silently
> to set my hands to work and that the moon
> turns and returns to meet me when it's done.

Oswald's work is alive with the turns and returns of nature's cycles and seasons and in 'Wedding' she shows how the human heart imitates them in the awakenings and patterns of love shared. As she put it in one interview, she does not claim to be 'a nature poet, though I do write about the special nature of what happens to exist'.[3]

Missing God

Dennis O'Driscoll (1954–2012)

His grace is no longer called for
before meals: farmed fish multiply
without His intercession.
Bread production rises through
disease-resistant grains devised
scientifically to mitigate His faults.

Yet, though we rebelled against Him
like adolescents, uplifted to see
an oppressive father banished –
a bearded hermit – to the desert,
we confess to missing Him at times.

Miss Him during the civil wedding
when, at the blossomy altar
of the registrar's desk, we wait in vain
to be fed a line containing words
like 'everlasting' and 'divine'.

Miss Him when the TV scientist
explains the cosmos through equations,
leaving our planet to revolve on its axis
aimlessly, a wheel skidding in snow.

Miss Him when the radio catches a snatch
of plainchant from some echoey priory;
when the gospel choir raises its collective voice
to ask *Shall We Gather at the River?*

or the forces of the oratorio converge
on *I Know That My Redeemer Liveth*
and our contracted hearts lose a beat.

Miss Him when a choked voice at
the crematorium recites the poem
about fearing no more the heat of the sun.

Miss Him when we stand in judgement
on a lank Crucifixion in an art museum,
its stripe-like ribs testifying to rank.

Miss Him when the gamma-rays
recorded on the satellite graph
seem arranged into a celestial score,
the music of the spheres,
the *Ave Verum Corpus* of the observatory lab.

Miss Him when we stumble on the breast lump
for the first time and an involuntary prayer
escapes our lips; when a shadow crosses
our bodies on an x-ray screen; when we receive
a transfusion of foaming blood
sacrificed anonymously to save life.

Miss Him when we call out His name
spontaneously in awe or anger
as a woman in a birth ward bawls
her long-dead mother's name.

Miss Him when the linen-covered
dining table holds warm bread rolls,
shiny glasses of red wine.

Miss Him when a dove swoops
from the orange grove in a tourist village
just as the monastery bell begins to take its toll.

Miss Him when our journey leads us
under leaves of Gothic tracery, an arch
of overlapping branches that meet
like hands in Michelangelo's creation.

Miss Him when, trudging past a church,
we catch a residual blast of incense,
a perfume on par with the fresh-baked loaf
which Milosz compared to happiness.

Miss Him when our newly-decorated kitchen
comes in Shaker-style and we order
a matching set of Mother Ann Lee chairs.

Miss Him when we listen to the prophecy
of astronomers that the visible galaxies
will recede as the universe expands.

Miss Him the way an uncoupled glider
Riding the evening thermals misses its tug.

Miss Him, as the lovers shrugging
shoulders outside the cheap hotel
ponder what their next move should be.

Even feel nostalgic, odd days,
for His Second Coming,
like standing in the brick
dome of a dovecote
after the birds have flown.

Dennis O'Driscoll was born in County Tipperary and at the age
of 16 became a civil servant in Dublin – and remained so for 40
years. Consequently he once referred to himself as 'Lord of the
Files'. Whereas personally sociable and warm, many of his poems
can be temperamentally compared to those of Philip Larkin in

their grumpy evocations of everyday life, of the misery and conso-
lations of work and their droll directness about provincial living:

> No, I don't want to drop over for a meal
> on my way home from work.
> No, I'd much prefer if you didn't feel obliged
> to honour me by crashing overnight.
> No, I haven't the slightest curiosity about seeing
> how your attic conversion finally turned out.[1]

A number of his poems reflect on mortality and he has a meta-
physical poet's ability to use wit as part of his mindfulness of
death. However, it deeply shocked the literary world when
O'Driscoll died in 2012 at the early age of 58.

He once said that 'one of the fundamental emotions in my
poetry is empathy. I have the deepest sense of compassion for
the bewilderment that people feel when forced to face, on a daily
basis, all of the daunting things that life throws at them'. His
poem 'Missing God' might be read with this well in mind, as it
attempts to give voice to what has been lost in a world where
the sense of the sacred has receded. Throughout the poem you
get no sense that the poet is judging this faith-diminished world
as being somehow dishonest, but we wonder whether the poem
is an ambiguous but prophetic warning against an impoverished
imagination and colourless universe. Is this a cry from a heart
that rejects faith but also needs it, a lament for a belief in God
that cannot be retrieved because the gaps and questions that God
once filled have been replaced, but now open up a melancholic
absence? After reading this poem I am left remembering a com-
ment made by the novelist Graham Greene: 'The trouble is I don't
quite believe my unbelief'.

This poem notes the dying embers of the faith that inspirited
poems of previous generations, such as Gerard Manley Hopkins'
'God's Grandeur', where the material world was perceived to
be charged with God's majesty and a deep-down freshness. It is
ironically written in the form of a religious Litany. A Litany is a
prayer form that often uses *anaphora* or word repetition, and 16

times, at the beginning of each stanza, O'Driscoll repeats the two words *Miss Him*. The two beats of these words are the poem's constant, like the beeps of a life-support machine or the short cries of intense despair from a lover forsaken, offering no false hopes for some sort of reanimated existence. The cumulative effect, however, does force a revaluation of the mentalities and emotions of a world that is no longer sacramental. There is no interconnectedness between outward signs and invisible grace here, just a marketplace universe that has suffered a traumatic loss and, perhaps, is in denial.

From the beginning of the poem we are given impressions of a productive and efficient world that has lost a sense of gratitude: *grace is no longer called for* as *farmed fish multiply*. The poet seems to understand that we have rebelled against a God who was some sort of *oppressive father*. He refers to God as a bearded hermit, an unworldly being who doesn't go through what the rest of us do. In another poem, 'Votive Candles', he spells this out with a daring metaphor:

what is left
of inflamed hopes

is a hard waxen mass,
a host;

the shard of soap
with which

God washes
His spotless hands.

The small burned-out votive candles, like small pieces of soap, are used by God to wash his hands clean of all responsibility, like Pontius Pilate before the passion of Christ.

'Missing God' then goes on to name the places, spaces and moments when the absence of God itself becomes a presence. These include a civil wedding where the focus of the altar is a bunch of flowers, *blossomy*, and where there is no intimation of something being *everlasting*. Likewise at the crematorium the *choked voices* try to console themselves with a reading from Shakespeare's 'Cymbeline' in which a repetition reminds us that we all come to dust. O'Driscoll seems to be plaintive about that situation, which the poet Anne Stevenson imagined, of a funeral without a minister, where all the words have nowhere to go, not addressed beyond themselves. 'Imagine them', she writes, 'circling and circling the confusing cemetery/ . . . roving the earth without anywhere to rest'.[2]

In another of his poems, O'Driscoll comments that:

God and humankind meet on uncommon ground
They just don't speak the same language[3]

This comes into view in 'Missing God' when he notes how we miss God when looking at a crucifix in an art museum and misunderstand *rank*. For the Christian, God empties himself in the incarnation and in a body-language we know as Jesus Christ, stretches open his arms in an embrace on wood in a cry of forsakenness. In that darkness, it is believed, God has never been nearer. Strangely, later in the poem the poet refers to blood *sacrificed anonymously to save life*. It is Christ who is anonymous now but frustratingly at a time when the freshness and radical nature of his teaching has the potential to transform a material competitive rank-infested slog of a life into a spiritual adventure of deepening relationships and trust. If it is true that we are just spending money we don't have on things we don't want in order to impress people we don't like, then the teachings of the one whose ribs now confuse us in a gallery are well overdue to be heard again. All this, though, to the weary casual observer in the museum, is lost or unknown.

Similarly those who *trudging past a church* and smelling incense, or hearing a monastery bell, have a stirring of something Other, a sense of strangeness that feels almost like home, but they move on. O'Driscoll says he feels *nostalgic*, an important word from the Greek *nostos* which, Odysseus-like, means a return to your homeland. He recognizes that this return appears impossible, as empty of hope as a dovecote from which the birds have fled. He also sees how the distraction of an overtly sexual culture (where lovers ponder their next moves outside a cheap hotel), an unthinking confidence in scientific rationalism, and a possessive obsession for objects such as smart kitchen chairs, all push us further into our own desires and *equations*. The magnetism of mystery we know as God no longer draws people out of this burrowing underground unless, feeling life is *a wheel skidding in snow*, or a breast lump is newly found, *an involuntary prayer/ escapes our lips*. It is likely, then, to be a prayer of need rather than of praise.

The person of faith reading this poem might feel overwhelmed by the picture O'Driscoll paints but may also feel sympathetic to what is being voiced. We know that those who are seeking the spiritual today, often without a vocabulary for the soul, feel that the Church is just too secular, too caught up in those things from which they want to be freed. There is no doubt that the community of Christian faith, having spent centuries on working out the *form* of Christianity, must now concentrate on what it is *for*. We are thrown back to basics – and if there is a crisis of faith then a good crisis must not go to waste. It is time for Christianity to do some stocktaking, self-scrutiny and distillation. In the Church we spend a great deal of energy on asking how we might be loyal to the past. Another question has emerged in the culture O'Driscoll interrogates: how might we be loyal to the future? What is it that might make belief in God a gift to the world again and not, as we seem to behave, just to religion? How might faith in God be generous in conversation and learning, instead of being defensive and dogmatic? So much talk of God has been punitive in focus over the centuries, a God out to take revenge on human depravity. It is surely time to start talking again, as the scriptures do, of a restorative God who takes it upon himself to uphold human dignity and asks us to join him. Although we have often begun with idolatry and ended in violence, for the Christian all must start in wonder and end in humility. The voices in the poem seem to have some consciousness that this might indeed be a way to understand the world and the human heart better.

So a poem like 'Missing Him' might be received gratefully as an invitation, asking how faith might express and translate itself now and in the years ahead. God goes missing so that we look for him. His silence is his defence against our idolatry.

Messengers

Louise Glück (b. 1943)

You have only to wait, they will find you.
The geese flying low over the marsh,
glittering in black water.
They find you.

And the deer –
how beautiful they are,
as though their bodies did not impede them.
Slowly they drift into the open
through bronze panels of sunlight.

Why would they stand so still
if they were not waiting?
Almost motionless, until their cages rust,
the shrubs shiver in the wind,
squat and leafless.

You have only to let it happen:
that cry – *release, release* – like the moon
wrenched out of earth and rising
full in its circle of arrows

until they come before you
like dead things, saddled with flesh,
and you above them, wounded and dominant.

In April 1980, the home of American teacher and poet Louise Glück was destroyed by fire. It was a distressing event in her life but:

> Gradually certain benefits became apparent. I felt grateful; the vivid sense of escape conferred on daily life an aura of blessedness. I felt lucky to wake up, lucky to make the beds, lucky to grind the coffee. There was also, after a period of devastating grief, a strange exhilaration. Having nothing, I was no longer hostage to possessions.[1]

Thirteen years later she addressed graduating students about the lives they were just about to begin. She reminded them that there was no question as to whether or not they will suffer in their life ahead. They will all suffer. At issue, she argued, is the meaning of suffering, or the yield:

> Despair in our culture tends to produce wild activity: change the job, change the partner, replace the faltering ambition instantly. We fear passivity and prize action . . . But the self cannot be willed back. And flight from despair forfeits whatever benefit may arise in the encounter with despair . . . The alternative? A life made entirely of will and ultimately dominated by fear. Such a life expresses itself in too prompt, too superficial adjustments of what can, in the external environment, be manipulated, or in a cautious clinging to those habits and forms which, because they are not crucial, cannot, in being lost, do much damage. The deft skirting of despair is a life lived on the surface, intimidated by depth, a life that refuses to be used by time, which it tries instead to dominate or evade. It is all abrupt movement or anxious cleaving . . .[2]

This may be helpful background if you have never encountered Louise Glück's poetry before. Classically restrained, terse but dramatically charged, it is a poetry that is calmly sure-handed with elaboration and the ornamental stripped away. She uses simple vocabulary with subtle impact. I find the experience of reading a poem by her similar to placing a shell right up next to your ear. You hear a far-off voice very close up, unearthly but human, distantly intimate. It is poetry that rarely consoles but which you sense, with its fatal truthfulness, is breaking up the ice on your surface.

She often uses biblical stories and metaphors in her work and over the years she has shown innovative development, from long poem sequences to giving flowers individual voices in dialogue with a poet-gardener and a gardener God ('The Wild Iris', 1992) and a more ironic tone in interrogating the failure of a marriage ('Meadowlands', 1996). Some find her poetry stylistically affected, the metaphors too abstract and the suggestiveness therefore disappointingly diminished. One critic, Peter Stitt, has argued that the poems are too difficult to comprehend because 'the maker has excluded too much'. I sense Glück might see this as an apt theological statement.

She was born in New York and her father was a first-generation American businessman of Hungarian descent. Her mother lost her first-born daughter and Glück acknowledges this as one major source of her work's focus on death and grieving. As a teenager Glück lived with anorexia, and a consequent seven-year programme of psychoanalysis taught her, she says, to analyse her own speech and to begin work as a poet. She has gone on to win a number of awards and was made the United States Poet Laureate in 2003. She has taught in a number of colleges and universities, helping her to survive the 'extended silences' she endures when it seems impossible to write poems.

'Messengers' comes from Glück's second volume of poetry called *The House on Marshland*, published in 1975 and comprising 35 short poems. It is the book widely thought to have established her distinct voice as a poet. The title makes me think of the parable of Jesus where he distinguishes between the man who built his house on sand and the one who built his on rock.[3] I think I am someone whose home is more on marshland, somewhere in between. As the writer and pastor Nadia Bolz-Webber once said to me, 'With me it's not a case of "I once was blind but now I see", more a case of "I once was blind and now I have really bad eyesight".' However we want to read the title of this book, though, it has tones of a spiritual amphibious terrain. The collection is divided into two sections named 'All Hallows' and 'The Apple Trees', so creating an Eden context to the poems, where all has been blessed and found good but which leads to a tree of bitten apples, to a move of human will and a loss of life. The mythology of Eden is of persistent interest in Glück's work.

The poem is set near a marsh. Its first two words *You have* are repeated later in the poem. They intone a sense of gift and ability – even, perhaps, triumph. The speaker is, typically for Glück, disembodied. So often in her work, even when she uses the word 'I' it is freed from autobiographical preoccupations. But here she uses *you* – six times. It lends a myth-like, experienced, even haunted authority to the voice – that echo in the shell I talked about earlier. We are being addressed – about what, though? The poem is called 'Messengers' and we wonder who these are. The deer, beautiful and unimpeded by their bodiliness, lit by sunlight? The geese, mobile in a world above, looking down on us, finding us? The shrubs, ageing and shivering in the wind? We wonder if the poet is *waiting*, drawn by the sight of the deer, and whether her own body, through anorexia, has been an impediment from which she needs release. The whole poem is made up of little rivers of images that lead out into an unknown sea of meaning. It feels intimate yet universal, symbolic but just out of reach.

The poem says that *you have only to let it happen:/ that cry – release, release – . . .* A cry can be a shout or it can be shedding tears. To release can be a liberation or might it mean 're-leasing' here, renewing our contract with the world, agreeing to different terms than the ones we have been inhabiting it with?

The Going

Thomas Hardy (1840–1928)

Why did you give no hint that night
That quickly after the morrow's dawn,
And calmly, as if indifferent quite,
You would close your term here, up and be gone
    Where I could not follow
    With wing of swallow
To gain one glimpse of you ever anon!

    Never to bid good-bye
    Or lip me the softest call,
Or utter a wish for a word, while I
Saw morning harden upon the wall,
    Unmoved, unknowing
    That your great going
Had place that moment, and altered all.

Why do you make me leave the house
And think for a breath it is you I see
At the end of the alley of bending boughs
Where so often at dusk you used to be;
    Till in darkening dankness
    The yawning blankness
Of the perspective sickens me!

    You were she who abode
    By those red-veined rocks far West,
You were the swan-necked one who rode

Along the beetling Beeny Crest,
    And, reining nigh me,
    Would muse and eye me,
While Life unrolled us its very best.

Why, then, latterly did we not speak,
Did we not think of those days long dead,
And ere your vanishing strive to seek
That time's renewal? We might have said,
    'In this bright spring weather
    We'll visit together
Those places that once we visited.'

    Well, well! All's past amend,
    Unchangeable. It must go.
I seem but a dead man held on end
To sink down soon. . . . O you could not know
    That such swift fleeing
    No soul foreseeing –
Not even I – would undo me so!

Claire Tomalin's insightful biography of Thomas Hardy[1] opens intriguingly with the death of his wife Emma. They had been married for 38 years but it had not been a happy relationship for a long time and Emma was now living upstairs in the attic. She was 72 and seemed very unwell. She didn't want the doctor but asked the young maid, Dolly, to fetch her husband. He climbed the stairs, went to the bed and spoke her name: 'Em, Em – don't you know me?' She was already unconscious and within minutes had stopped breathing. Tomalin then makes a memorable comment. 'This', she writes, 'is the moment when Thomas Hardy became a great poet.' She continues:

> . . . it was the death of Emma that proved to be his best inspiration. Filled with sorrow and remorse for their estrangement, he had her body brought down and placed in the coffin at the foot

of his bed, where it remained for three days and nights until the funeral. The gesture would have been remarkable in a lover who could not bear to be parted from the body of his mistress, but for an elderly husband who had for years been on bad terms with his wife it seems almost monstrously unconventional, until you realize that he was thinking of his situation differently. He had become a lover in mourning.[2]

'The Going' is the first poem about his bereavement and is dated just a month after her death in 1912, by which time he had discovered Emma's diaries in which she expressed her feelings that Hardy had been cruel to her which then led to his guilt and remorse. The poem appeared in a group of 21 collected elegies about Emma, their courtship, relationship and her death, simply called *Poems of 1912–13* but with a motto inscribed under the title: *Veteris vestigia flammae* – the relics of an ancient flame. Hardy had stopped writing the novels that had made him famous when his *Jude the Obscure* received such a negative response in 1895, not least from Emma. He recounts in the preface to the 1912 edition of the novel that it was even 'burnt by a bishop – probably in his despair at not being able to burn me'. He began writing and publishing poems, saying that he was always at heart a poet and had only ever written novels to make a living.

Between 1898 and his death in 1928 he published over 900 poems. They deal with common themes (birth, childhood, nature, locality, marriage, age, religious faith, doubt, death) in honest, unsentimental and occasionally ironic ways. They often appear serenely simple in style but have an emotional kick, and there can be a surprisingly modern feel to the sentiments being expressed. There's usually something very unexpected in a Hardy poem.

His main subject as a poet is his own experience, a poetic mythologizing of his life and the people and places that mean most to him. Growing up with a musical father, with whom he travelled about playing at entertainments, had taught him the power of the ballad; the poet Thom Gunn pointed out that Hardy absorbed and often used the devices of the ballad, particularly the unexplained voice that speaks or questions mysteriously.

Tomalin's definitive comment, though, is based on the belief that, after the death of Emma, Hardy's poetry shifted and developed into something quite startling, making the unconventional and metrically diverse elegies about her, according to the poet C. Day Lewis, 'some of the finest love poetry in our language'.[3] Hardy said he became 'in flower' as a poet during this time. He revisited his early love for Emma in his mind, writing to a friend that 'One forgets all the recent years and differences and the mind goes back to the early times when each was much to the other – in her case and mine intensely much'.[4]

'The Going' begins with a question that appears twice again in the poem: *why?* You can read this interrogation as bitterness or blame. He seems put out that Emma has died without letting him know in advance. He refers to her closing her term, as if she were a school or a shop finishing business for the day, and appears irascible that she was *indifferent* about him as she calmly passed away. The tone then changes in line five where he relates that he can't follow her and will never get a glimpse of her again. This 'doubleness', an inclusion of two tones with mixed feelings, inhabits the poem and makes it recognizably true to bereavement, which often experiences chaotic and changeable emotion, from anger and hurt to guilt and denial. Some wonder whether the rhyming bounce to the poem is inappropriate for its subject but Hardy interrupts the rhyme in a telling way. Lines one and three nicely end with a clear rhyme: *night* with *quite*. But then *dawn* has a jolted, uneasy rhyme with the word that haunts the whole poem – *gone*.

The second stanza relates the pains of loss – not being able to say goodbye or hear her voice again. Hardy was in his study as she lay dying upstairs, apparently unaware that she was so ill. But can that really have been the case? His words used to describe himself may be more accurate than we first think: *unmoved, unknowing.* He then adds a word to the title of the poem to make it *your great going* that *altered all.* Everything has changed in his world, including his heart.

He then questions the dead Emma again in the third stanza and implies that she is somehow to blame for making him believe he sees her outside where she used to spend time. Is she haunting him? She makes him *think for a breath* though she no longer breathes. Again the raw hurt changes in tone as he lets us in to the *darkening dankness* and *yawning blankness* of that empty garden that now sickens him. The rhythm and rhymes, assonance and alliteration, all intone a sinister aspect to Hardy's emptiness. Do we read it that he's hurting because he is missing her for herself – or because he is left living alone? Again, the mixture and lack of single feeling deepens the poem into his uncomfortable truths.

The fourth stanza gives another tonal shift. Hardy becomes nostalgic and recalls their early relationship, Emma's beauty and their easy, relaxed togetherness when *Life unrolled us its very best*. To reinstate this perfection the rhymes become crisp again but one can't help noticing the last three words of the last three lines: *me, me, best*. Is this what intruded and curdled the love they once shared? Was it his selfishness, his own final word, that ended their happiness?

Another *why?* opens the fifth stanza but this time there is a mutual blame as he refers to *we*. He's asking what went wrong but implies that things would have been put right if only they had gone visiting their old love-haunts. Again, there is a realism to the bereavement here as denial and avoidance of truths can take hold when we suffer a sudden loss of someone with whom we have had a complicated history, resentments and hate. His question sounds hollow. Doesn't Hardy see that there was much more that needed doing to repair their relationship than a trip out on a spring day? Nevertheless, yes, it might have helped.

In the last stanza it appears that he is beginning to learn things he didn't know about himself and his wife. The ironic use of the word *well* launches us into a resigned tone. Nothing can be repaired or amended now. Hardy called himself a 'meliorist', believing that individuals are powerless to affect their own lives and that only by accepting the fact can they have any hope of happiness. He lived in an extraordinary period of history. When he was born, the railway hadn't yet come to Dorset and yet by the year he died Walt Disney released the first Mickey Mouse film. In between, of course, was the First World War. He wrote in one poem:

Christmas: 1924

'Peace upon earth!' was said. We sing it,
And pay a million priests to bring it.
After two thousand years of mass
We've got as far as poison-gas.

In contrast to the Victorian ideal of progress, Hardy's novels and poetry portray human beings at the mercy of forces they have no ability to control, whether they are of nature, society or inner compulsion. Here, in the last stanza, the big dominating word *unchangeable* shadows the other words that then seem to break down. Sentences become short, the punctuation is unpredictable and the fluidity decomposes. The poem fragments. He is ready to sink and he admits that she would never have guessed that he would have reacted like this – and nor would he either. He is surprised to be affected by his wife's death: a truth that pushes us into the heart of the darkness that works through all the poem's lines. Emma once said of her husband that 'he only understands the woman he invents'. By the end of this poem we see that such a controlled comprehension has splintered and left him cut. It is a poem, to use a *Titanic* image, where the iceberg is lamenting the loss of the ship.[5]

One can read this poem as a fairly harsh, self-obsessed and questioning elegy or as a much softer, fragile, realistic poem of mourning's erratic sensations. Whichever one you tend towards, the shadow of the other reading will not be far way. This is typical of Hardy's desire in so many of his poems to hold contradictions and battling emotions together in an unresolved tension. It is a poem that grieves Emma's death, grieves the fact that their love ended and grieves the fact that he is alone and unable to change any of it. The poem holds its poise, with its almost hourglass-shaped verses, but its formal appearance is riddled with unpredictable syllables and its last stanza points to its own self-destruction. It is a portrait of Hardy himself.

Untitled

Emily Dickinson (1830–86)

This World is not conclusion.
A Species stands beyond –
Invisible, as Music –
But positive, as Sound –
It beckons, and it baffles –
Philosophy, don't know –
And through a Riddle, at the last –
Sagacity, must go –
To guess it, puzzles scholars –
To gain it, Men have borne
Contempt of Generations
And Crucifixion, shown –
Faith slips – and laughs, and rallies –
Blushes, if any see –
Plucks at a twig of Evidence –
And asks a Vane, the way –
Much Gesture, from the Pulpit –
Strong Hallelujahs roll –
Narcotics cannot still the Tooth
That nibbles at the soul –

If you try to copy out an Emily Dickinson poem on your computer, the auto-correct function will go into overdrive! It will not be able to deal with all the dashes, lack of punctuation and incomplete sentences. The same goes for many first-time readers of Dickinson's work. You can quickly get the sense of urgent rupture and volcanic alarm in many of her poems, of language being struck by lightning, but left rather pushed and puzzled as to what the poet is communicating. When she sent some poems to a friend to see whether he thought they had any value, Dickinson asked him if he thought the poems 'breathed'. You could be tempted to think on first encounter that they are more than breathing – they are hyperventilating. She is a poet of implication who provokes our intelligence by perplexing structures, elliptical imagery, aphorism and allusion. It's important to stick with these poems, though, to catch ourselves in the lightning flash and the electricity of her very original artistry. With deceptively simple stanzas, often in the metre used in hymns and nursery rhymes, our dull and moderate appropriation of the world is slapped awake by her work into something more emotionally charged and raw. Those who persevere with Dickinson often end up finding her to be one of the poets whose work most persistently re-navigates their mind and heart.

People found her work difficult to make sense of right from the start. Dickinson wrote 1,775 untitled short lyrics in her life and fewer than ten of these were published in her lifetime. She didn't write to be published. Seeking publication, she said, was as foreign to her mind 'as Firmament is to Fin' or, in one poem, 'Publication – is the Auction/ Of the Mind of Man'. She wrote with an investigative, self-critical and strenuous passion towards self-authenticity. She wrote to make invisible realities visible, but like hidden treasure her poems remained buried from view until her secret output was discovered after her death in 1886. Her sister found a mass of manuscripts arranged into groups and some of them were stitched together into little booklets or 'fascicles'. Preachers of the time often did the same with their sermons. The task of editing and collecting the poems was given to a family friend and to a man with whom Dickinson corresponded a great deal through her life. They brought out collections of her poetry but the poems were heavily edited to make them more 'sensible'. Rhymes had been smoothed, metre regularized and various words and metaphors changed. It was not until 1955, nearly 70 years after her death, that Dickinson's poetry appeared for the first time without any editorial adjustments.

It's not just the strangeness of her poetry that compels attention but also the strangeness of her life. Born in Amherst, Massachusetts, she was quickly seen to be a girl of quick wit and perception but she showed no real willingness to venture into the world. She described herself as 'small, like the Wren, and my hair is bold, like the Chestnut bur – and my eyes, like the Sherry in the Glass, that the Guest leaves'. Her father was a leading citizen in the town, a lawyer with a large library, and Dickinson eavesdropped on society through her father's connections and political life. She read his many books, and also wrote many letters, which are often very beautiful and poignant. When she wrote about her mother, for whom she and her siblings cared over some years before her death, but of whom we know much less than her father, she wrote: 'We were never intimate Mother and Children while she was our Mother – but Mines in the same Ground meet by tunnelling and when she became our Child, the Affection came – when we were children and she journeyed, she always brought us something. Now would she but bring us herself, what an only Gift . . .'[1]

She had occasional visitors. One described her as 'the very wantonness of overstatement', and said, 'I was never with anyone who drained my nerve power so much'. Dickinson was a lover of life, high-spirited, and a poet-surgeon who sliced into humanity's soul and its many unprocessed contradictions.

Dickinson can be abstract and intimate, elatedly ecstatic and emotionally numb, comic and uncomfortably pained. She can be savage, unsettling, epigrammatic, teasing, fresh, frustrating and energizing. She is playfully potent by way of indirection. She achieves compressed effects with her language and we often have to fill in the gaps to make sense of what she writes. We become like Bletchley Park decoders seeking undercover meaning in the unfamiliar phrasing, dots and dashes. Her poems often identify and define with cryptic metaphors. 'We see – Comparatively', she wrote. Sometimes we have what have been called 'unrecoverable deletions' where Dickinson doesn't give us a hint as to what the connection is between an image and an idea.

The endings of her poems, often done with a dash, can feel as if a window has been pushed open at night in a new place we've been taken to: we can feel the breeze but can't yet see where we are. We excitedly follow her, so in control of language and idiosyncratic as she is, but we get dizzy with her unpredictable threads, counter-intuitive logic and penetrating honesty. She is always the spider and never the fly. 'There is something about music that keeps its distance even at the moment that it engulfs us', composer Aaron Copland wrote in his book, *Music and Imagination*. 'It is at the same time outside and away from us and inside and part of us.'[2] The same could be said of Dickinson's poems that Copland set to music in 1950 in the song cycle, *12 Poems of Emily Dickinson*.

Dickinson's poems often have startling and effective first lines, and this poem is a good example. Others include: 'I heard a Fly buzz – when I died', 'I felt a Funeral, in my Brain', 'My Life had stood – a Loaded Gun –' and 'One need not be a Chamber – to be Haunted – '. *This World is not conclusion* is, for Dickinson's poems, very unusually followed by a full-stop, making the state-ment final with no doubt attached – as conclusive as the world is not. She confidently asserts that there is another world beyond our own, maybe an afterlife, or realities that are eternal rather than temporal. The assertion becomes qualified through the poem, though, as this invisible, positive species that is *beyond* confounds even the philosophers and the world's wisest. Originally Dickin-son referred to a 'Sequel' standing beyond, but she revised this, maybe in the light of Darwin's writings of around the same time, to *Species*. This takes the focus away from the other world being about time, after this life or in eternity, and instead stresses its functioning existence that can be scientifically explored.

The truth of what is beyond, we are told, both *beckons* and *baffles*. It invites us to be confused. The alliterative 'b' here creates a less esoteric conversational tone and followed by the colloquial *don't know* of philosophy we realize that it is both the educated and not so educated who are equally flawed in their understand-ing. All our cleverness and acquired *sagacity* must pass through a *Riddle, at the last –* (death?) before we are enlightened. Before this, however, scholars puzzle away and people have made themselves unpopular in their search and defence of the truth of this inconclusive life. By bringing *Crucifixion* into the poem we are immediately made to think of Christ who preached a kingdom 'not of this world'. We are then made to think through faith, rather than philosophy, and are told that it too *slips, laughs, rallies* and *blushes* – a better description of the life of faith in the twenty-first century can't be found! Dickinson notes that we can't resist plucking at twigs *of Evidence* to make us more certain. We go to church, where the *Vane* on its tower is looked to for a sense of direction but, of course, like all our thinking, the weather vane is blown around by the wind of passing currents. *Vane* can be heard as 'vain', something we become when we fail to recognize our limitations.

We stay in church towards the end of the poem as Dickinson talks of *much Gesture, from the Pulpit* and *Strong Hallelujahs* rolling. Her remarks about preachers were often wry: 'He preached upon "Breadth" till it argued him narrow', she observes in one poem. We become excited and even ecstatic in the beliefs and certainties we hold to about what lies beyond, or within, the reality we call 'the world' but, concludes Dickinson, all our religious and philosophical *narcotics* cannot still *the Tooth/ That nibbles at the soul* – all our dogma-clinging, ritual and clasped hands, it seems, dull the mind to a truth that cannot be ignored. Even the most assured of believers has, at the back of the busy meaning-making mind, relentless and inevitably unanswered questions as they look, say, at a coffin enclosed around an ended life or hear of a sudden death. The final dash of the poem, implying an open and continuous unknown into the future, is so different from the opening full-stop and hints that the questions that *nibble* don't end this side of the grave because we are just not in any position to get them answered with any certainty, no matter how much we fancy our own take on things. What we hold dearest is unable to be proved. The incomprehensible extinction of human beings by death inspired many poems from Dickinson. She was in a continual stand-off with the Riddle. Consequently, with an unsettling shift in the ear, you get the sense in so many of her poems that 'Truth' is 'Tooth'.

From early in her life, Dickinson refused to sign up to Christian conversion even when all her friends and family were caught up in local Christian revivals. 'I am standing alone in rebellion', she wrote to a friend. She resisted confinement of mind as much as she resisted the imprisonment of her womanhood to the conventions of her age. She wore white clothes throughout her life, as if she were her own bride, or that of poetry. There was an intellectual honesty in Dickinson that wouldn't allow her to be compressed. Throughout her poems, though, there is a conviction that certain abstractions like Virtue, Love and Hope were as real as anything visible. She was well versed in the King James translation of the Bible and with poets of faith such as George Herbert. She was drawn to the idea of personal immortality, but as one critic has commented, 'all of Dickinson's poems that resort to Christian imagery and language rework Christianity in some way – intellectually, blasphemously or comically'.[3]

I believe Dickinson's work has much to teach about Christian faith. I long for a theological language that is as fiery and sparked as her poetic language. Words that dare to speak of God should be bold in imagery, teasing of the mundane and conventional, but cautious of their own limited life-span and limping limits. There ought to be dashes everywhere interrupting our casual fluency and a lack of prosaic grammar charging through anything that speaks of the holiness of God. We need a language akin to the burning bush that blazes but doesn't allow us to come too close. This will be a language that points more than it defines, that deepens mystery rather than resolves it. To study Dickinson's poetry might just transform many sermons, theological teaching, liturgies and compromised church statements!

Equally, though, Dickinson reminds us in one of her poems that:

'Hope' is the thing with feathers –
That perches in the soul –
And sings the tune without the words –
And never stops – at all –

If certainty, not doubt, is the opposite of 'faith'; if 'hope', without final surety, 'sings the tune without the words'; and if 'love' is what moves us most but cannot be proved, then Dickinson's work reminds us that people who believe that these are the three things that last for ever,[4] who seek the freshness of God through them, are people always in the vocative. They will be men and women who are spiritually naked, in hiding, and who realize they and the world they inhabit are both incomplete and need to look beyond. They will realize, as Dickinson did, that we are injured and that hurt people often hurt people, becoming cruel. Left to ourselves we often destroy the things we love most and so, in this human reality of equal and damaging ignorance, we call out to a divine wisdom and life who ruptures this destructive pride and makes us, with all our endless opinions lying around our feet, once again know our need of God. This makes us poor in spirit, mourners of our lost confidences. We are converted back through life to a humane and purer heart on a path that makes us blessed.[5]

Tell all the truth but tell it slant –
Success in Circuit lies
Too bright for our infirm Delight
The Truth's superb surprise
As Lightning to the Children eased
With explanation kind
The Truth must dazzle gradually
Or every man be blind –

Dickinson energetically reminds us that Truth is a tricky business and that it might be best, as we set out to discover it, not to talk about what might or might not be 'true' but instead to begin to talk of what is or isn't honest. We need a new story, a new script, a new way of relating rather than binary fights of what is the case or isn't. Perhaps questioning our answers is more productive than answering our questions. Maybe Truth is something shared before it is understood, as anyone who has undergone psycho-therapy will recognize. Dickinson's thoughts about faith went from reverent to rebellious, from devout to demoralized – as many of us also experience – but there is a sense around in many of her poems that, as she writes: 'Faith – is the Pierless Bridge/ Supporting what We see/ Unto the Scene that We do not – '.

As her friends got carried away by noisy gesticulating preachers, Dickinson knew that re-birth starts elsewhere, somewhere more painful. Too much has to change in you, in me, in the heart, in the world, in the workplace, at home and in the communities of faith; too many contours pushed, pasts let go of, securities surrendered, habits broken, all our lives of endless stuff and competitions distilled and brought to their senses – all our insane mean defences let down – if God is to be truly glimpsed as Holy and the foundation of an authentic human life. It is a message I feel is very near to the one a cousin of Jesus preached by a river as he washed the confused with a baptism. Never let a crisis go to waste. Never let the puzzle and riddle of life's inconclusions lead us anywhere but hope. Yes, of course, our soul is nibbled by graceful irritants because unless we see that we are empty in and of ourselves there will be no open door in us for God and Truth to find.

Although Dickinson's immediate family accepted the poet's decision to keep the Sabbath staying at home rather than in church, her father once asked the Reverend Jonathan Jenkins, a local minister, to meet with his daughter and assess her spiritual health. His diagnosis was – 'Sound'.

The Sentry

Wilfred Owen (1893–1918)

We'd found an old Boche dug-out, and he knew,
And gave us hell, for shell on frantic shell
Hammered on top, but never quite burst through.
Rain, guttering down in waterfalls of slime
Kept slush waist high, that rising hour by hour,
Choked up the steps too thick with clay to climb.
What murk of air remained stank old, and sour
With fumes of whizz-bangs, and the smell of men
Who'd lived there years, and left their curse in the den,
If not their corpses . . .
There we herded from the blast
Of whizz-bangs, but one found our door at last.
Buffeting eyes and breath, snuffing the candles.
And thud! flump! thud! down the steep steps came thumping
And splashing in the flood, deluging muck –
The sentry's body; then his rifle, handles
Of old Boche bombs, and mud in ruck on ruck.
We dredged him up, for killed, until he whined
'O sir, my eyes – I'm blind – I'm blind, I'm blind!'
Coaxing, I held a flame against his lids
And said if he could see the least blurred light
He was not blind; in time he'd get all right.
'I can't,' he sobbed. Eyeballs, huge-bulged like squids
Watch my dreams still; but I forgot him there
In posting next for duty, and sending a scout
To beg a stretcher somewhere, and floundering about
To other posts under the shrieking air.

Those other wretches, how they bled and spewed,
And one who would have drowned himself for good, –
I try not to remember these things now.
Let dread hark back for one word only: how
Half-listening to that sentry's moans and jumps,
And the wild chattering of his broken teeth,
Renewed most horribly whenever crumps
Pummelled the roof and slogged the air beneath –
Through the dense din, I say, we heard him shout
'I see your lights!' But ours had long died out.

I am especially drawn to the work of Wilfred Owen because, although he died 50 years before I was born, we were both brought up in the same part of the world. His short life is well documented, and his poetry, as well as that of many other poets from the First World War period, has received more attention in Britain and across the world recently due to the centenary anniversaries of that horrendous world slaughter.

Owen was born in Shropshire. His mother was a devout Christian and she was a strong influence on Owen who, as a boy, became rather serious and straitlaced. He was only about ten years old when his 'poethood', as he called it, was born. While attending Shrewsbury Technical School he developed his interest in poetry and at the same time became preoccupied with religion. Sometimes on Sundays he would rearrange the furniture in his parents' home, and wearing a surplice and a cardboard bishop's mitre made by his mother would conduct Evensong for everyone – with a sermon. The Bible was to remain one of the main influences on Owen's poetry.

As time passed he also developed a passion for botany, geology and archaeology. In preparation to take his university entrance exam he worked as a lay assistant for the vicar of Dunsden but he found the conservative evangelicalism of the Reverend Herbert Wigan too constricting. Reading the atheistic Shelley and thinking through the evolutionary theory of Shrewsbury's own Charles Darwin, Owen's thoughts were liberalizing but, failing to get into university, he went to France instead to teach English in Bordeaux until, on August 1914, Germany invaded Belgium and war was declared.

Commissioned into the Manchester Regiment, Owen led his platoon into battle in January 1917. The experience of the horror of trench warfare, including being trapped for three days in a shelled cellar, began to take its toll. He wrote to his mother:

> I think the worst incident was one wet night when we lay up against a railway embankment. A big shell lit on the top of the bank, just two yards from my head. Before I woke, I was blown in the air right away from the bank! I passed most of the following days in a railway cutting, in a hole just big enough to lie in, and covered with corrugated iron. My brother officer of B Coy, 2/Lt Gaukroger lay opposite in a similar hole. But he was covered with earth and no relief will ever relieve him.[1]

Owen was observed now to be shaky, erratic and to have confused memory. He acquired a stammer which echoed what he would later describe as 'the stuttering rifles' rapid rattle'.[2] He was diagnosed as suffering from neurasthenia or 'shell-shock' and he was eventually sent to Craiglockhart War Hospital in the suburbs of Edinburgh. Suffering terrible nightmares, the influence of two people there helped Owen to piece himself back together. His doctor, Captain Arthur Brock, encouraged Owen to write in order to establish a connection with life again, and the soldier-poet Siegfried Sassoon, also at the hospital following his protesting open letter to his commanding officer as to the prolongation of the war, steered Owen's poetic voice and style to come into their own command.

In August 1918 Owen returned to France, leading the British Army's assault on the German's Beaurevoir-Fonsomme line. He was awarded the Military Cross for bravery and leadership but he would never get to wear the medal nor indeed see in print most of the poems he had been busily crafting through all these intense months. On 4 November, while helping his men to build a pontoon bridge under heavy fire at Ors, Owen was shot and killed. It was only a week later that the war ended. Indeed, the bells of Shrewsbury Abbey, ringing out for Armistice and victory that very day, could be heard by Owen's parents as they opened the door and received the telegram they had so feared, informing them of their son's death.

Virtually all the poems for which Owen is now remembered were written in a creative burst between August 1917 and September 1918. His self-appointed task was to speak for the men in his care, to show what he termed the 'pity of war' and to do this with a bleak realism and indignant energy.

Owen began writing 'The Sentry' while he was receiving treatment at Craiglockhart in 1917 and he developed it the following summer, finishing it eventually in France in September 1918. To understand its origins we can read a letter he wrote to his mother:

My dug-out held 25 men tight packed. Water filled it to a depth of 1 or 2 feet, leaving say 4 feet of air. One entrance had been blown in and blocked. So far, the other remained. The Germans knew we were staying there and decided we shouldn't. Those fifty hours were the agony of my happy life. Every ten minutes on Sunday afternoon seemed an hour. I nearly broke down and let myself drown in the water that was now slowly rising over my knees. Towards 6 o'clock, when, I suppose, you would be going to church, the shelling grew less intense and less accurate; so that I was mercifully helped to do my duty and crawl, wade, climb, and flounder over No Man's Land to visit my other post. It took me half an hour to move about 150 yards. In the Platoon on my left the sentries over the dug-out were blown to nothing. One of these poor fellows was my first servant whom I rejected . . . If I had kept him he would have lived, for servants don't do Sentry Duty. I kept my own sentries half way down the stairs during the more terrific bombardment. In spite of this one lad was blown down and, I am afraid, blinded.[3]

Like his famous poem 'Dulce Et Decorum Est', 'The Sentry' relates the fate of a young soldier in sickening circumstances and in the poet's presence. By focusing on one particular soldier he is

THE SENTRY ∾ OWEN

able to allow his particularity to represent all the other wounded and dead. With understated menace in line one we learn that the German enemy (*old Boche*) is only too aware of their position and vulnerability: *and he knew*. The weather conditions are awful, the rain causing *waterfalls of slime* and the *murk of air* calling to mind Lady Macbeth's comment that 'Hell is murky'. The understatement is not maintained, however, as Owen uncompromisingly tells the truths of the horrific event. His use of onomatopoeia and a barrage of words with an identical *u* sound (*buffeting, snuffing, thud, flump, thumping, pummelled, crumps, mud, ruck*) present us with the force of a relentless assault through the *shrieking air* and *deluging muck*. *Shrieking air* sounds as if the very air itself is terrified. His imagery is unforgettable and of nightmare quality with the alliterative *wild chattering of his broken teeth* and *Eyeballs, huge-bulged like squids*. The nightmare encroaches upon them without mercy as *shell on frantic shell* and whizz-bangs *found our door at last*. The poem provokes us to imagine the claustrophobic atmosphere of the dug-out, the fumes of cordite and the smell of fearful men. The erratic punctuation of full-stops, semi-colons and dashes breaking up the sentences, mirrors the movement of the chaotic atmosphere, the pain and confusions of lost meaning.

The poem's lines tend to be iambic with five stresses. All this is broken in line thirteen: *And thud! flump! thud! down the steep steps came thumping* as the collective experience of the men undergoes a violent change as their mate's body splashes down towards them followed by his rifle and other bits of metal and mud. The humanity of this man is reduced to being just another item that is savagely flung about in the turmoil of war.

In line three Owen uses the word *lit* to mean 'alighted' but it begins a 'light' theme to the poem, flickering through the noise and tremor of the onslaught's deep and haunting darkness. The candles, the cry of *I'm blind*, the flame held next to the sentry's eyes and the last line's *I see your lights!* inevitably bring to mind the words of Sir Edward Grey, the Foreign Secretary at the outbreak of the war: 'The lamps are going out all over Europe; we shall not see them lit again in our lifetime'.

The most moving line for me in the poem is line eighteen where, with all dignity and pretence of soldier-strength dissolved, the young man cries to his officer almost as a son to his father: *O sir, my eyes – I'm blind – I'm blind, I'm blind*. The politeness of the junior soldier stands in pitiful juxtaposition to the repeated realization that he can't see anything. Owen, however, has to forget the man in order to live up to his responsibilities and find a new sentry and to order a stretcher. He is somewhat alienated from the men by his rank and duties but it is clear that Owen, for all his authority, knows he is powerless and that the violence of war renders his commanding actions futile. The poem reveals a guilt: that of a man given charge of other men whose decisions cost them their lives. It was this vocation to lead men coupled with the inevitable inability to protect them that led to the shell-shock that so many officers suffered. We know from his letter to his mother that he had thought of drowning himself there to escape this insufferable situation. His sense of isolation is caught in the poem: *Those other wretches, how they bled and spewed,/ And one who would have drowned himself for good*, leading to the futility of the line *I try not to remember these things now*. This line has returned to a perfect iambic pentameter, amnesia bringing a peaceful calm. We know that the writing of this poem, begun in hospital, was part of Owen's process to try to subject his nightmares to his imagination in order that some shaping and extracting of value from the traumatic might, against all odds, be forged.

The poet tries to forget but the wounded soldier has the last word. His *moans and jumps* resurface and Owen finds himself haunted by the man shouting that he can now see the lights – to reassure his mates and himself – even though their lights are no longer lit. The man does not seem to know, or be able to admit, what his comrades see only too well. His shout is a last cry of empty hope and the final words, *But ours had long died out*, intimate the life within them all being extinguished by what they are enduring. Or, with another interpretation, was the man shouting near the point of death that he could see light in the distance, a religious overture, as the men are left in their purgatory?

By this time, Owen was infuriated by British clergy who were supportive of the war as if it were some holy crusade. The Bishop of London, Arthur Winnington-Ingram, in a notorious sermon, had urged the troops to 'kill Germans – do kill them; not for the sake of killing, but to save the world, to kill the good as well as bad, to kill the young as well as the old, to kill those who have shown kindness to our wounded, as well as those friends . . . I look upon it as war for purity. I look upon everyone who died in it as a martyr'.[4]

As each side of the conflict claimed their Christian identity, Owen could see that the message of Christ was being undermined by political and nationalistic jingoism. Truth is as much a casualty of war as anything else. He was angry that the institutional Church of his day, inseparable from the political rhetoric of the establishment, was betraying its true vocation by encouraging hatred and death. The Church was guilty of maintaining the hellish brutality of the evil it says it opposes:

> But cursed are dullards whom no cannon stuns,
> That they should be as stones.[5]

The nationalistic encouragement of the troops, so readily voiced by those at a safe distance back home sitting at desks or preaching in pulpits, was sickening to Owen. It was not sweet or fitting to die for your country as you looked at a man, at a friend, dying from poison-gas:

> If in some smothering dreams you too could pace
> Behind the wagon that we flung him in . . .
> If you could hear, at every jolt, the blood
> Come gargling from the froth-corrupted lungs . . .
> My friend, you would not tell with such high zest
> To children ardent for some desperate glory,
> The old Lie: Dulce et decorum est
> Pro patria mori.[6]

The poem by Owen that probably most draws on biblical allusion is his 'The Parable of the Old Man and the Young'. It follows the story in Genesis 22 of Abraham and his son Isaac. Although in the biblical account God has entered a covenant with Abram and given him the new identity of 'Abraham', in this poem Owen insists on calling him Abram as if the covenant of faithfulness has been forgotten or violated. The poem begins by seeming to retell the Genesis story and we expect it to relate the well-known end of the story with Abraham being told by an angel not to kill his son but to sacrifice a ram caught in the thicket nearby. Owen's ending has a shocking twist:

> When lo! an Angel called him out of heaven,
> Saying, Lay not thy hand upon the lad,
> Neither do anything to him, thy son.
> Behold! Caught in a thicket by its horns,
> A Ram. Offer the Ram of Pride instead.
>
> But the old man would not so, but slew his son,
> And half the seed of Europe, one by one.

Later letters and poems show Owen distinguishing between God the Father and Jesus: God, like his own father and the fathers of the nation, sending their sons off to die. Yet 'Christ is literally in no man's land'[7] and the damaged statues of Christ on his cross that the soldiers came across in France were, to Owen, representative of their own dismemberment and mortality. The fact that these crucifixes were shot and damaged revealed to him how the generals and clergy were peddling ideologies very distant from the message that Christ himself preached. His well-known poem 'At a Calvary Near the Ancre' reflects on a typical cross at a French road junction which he encountered in 1917:

> One ever hangs where shelled roads part.
> In this war He too lost a limb,
> But His disciples hide apart;
> And now the Soldiers bear with Him.

Near Golgotha strolls many a priest,
And in their faces there is pride
That they were flesh-marked by the Beast
By whom the gentle Christ's denied.

The scribes on all the people shove
And bawl allegiance to the state,
But they who love the greater love
Lay down their life; they do not hate.

Here Owen, like the soldier at the foot of Jesus' cross, is able to
see the righteous son of God when the chief priests of organized
religion are busy blessing armies. He sees truth in the teachings of
the man who is crucified, the man of sorrows who understands
what Owen and his colleagues are undergoing. Christ is here less
adored than respected but there is a mutuality, a recognition of
the greater power of love even when put to death, of the greater
integrity of the peace-loving even when being butchered. The poet
Robert Graves, after the war, commented that even when respect
for organized religion died among the men, reverence for Jesus as
our fellow-sufferer remained. In Owen's 'Soldier's Dream' Jesus
is the pacifist saboteur who does permanent damage to end the
hostility:

I dreamed kind Jesus fouled the big-gun gears;
And caused a permanent stoppage in all bolts;
And buckled with a smile Mausers and Colts;
And rusted every bayonet with His tears.

In 1918 Owen, encouraged by having met some literary giants
of his day, began to collect some poems into a book with the hope
of publication. In the preface he wrote: 'This book is not about
heroes . . . Nor is it about deeds, or lands, nor anything about
glory, honour, might, majesty, dominion, or power, except War.
Above all I am not concerned with Poetry. My subject is War, and
the pity of War. The Poetry is in the pity.'[8]

Lightenings viii

Seamus Heaney (1939–2013)

The annals say: when the monks of Clonmacnoise
Were all at prayers inside the oratory
A ship appeared above them in the air.

The anchor dragged along behind so deep
It hooked itself into the altar rails
And then, as the big hull rocked to a standstill,

A crewman shinned and grappled down the rope
And struggled to release it. But in vain.
'This man can't bear our life here and will drown,'

The abbot said, 'unless we help him.' So
They did, the free ship sailed, and the man climbed back
Out of the marvellous as he had known it.

When Seamus Heaney was awarded the Nobel Prize for Literature
in 1995, the citation famously paid tribute to his combination of
'lyrical beauty and ethical depth which exalt everyday miracles
and the living past'. This beautifully captures the poetic artistry of
the man who became one of the most significant poets of the last
century and whose recent death is such a great loss.

Heaney was a native of County Derry in Northern Ireland but
lived for many years in Dublin. He wrote over twenty volumes of
poetry and insightful criticism and was a popular anthologizer.
His work is hugely varied; each volume he produced seemed to

146

have a new form of writing in it with a different task and a fresh style. Just when you thought you knew how Heaney wrote poems he would bring out a new collection and you had to think again, finding yourself persuaded by yet another truthful voice. He once spoke of his falling in love with language:

> I had already begun a journey into the wideness of the world. This in turn became a journey into the wideness of language, a journey where each point of arrival – whether in one's poetry or one's life – turned out to be a stepping stone rather than a destination.[1]

This mobility and creativity, so infused with the influence of literary predecessors, as well as the political, historical and geographical complexities of Ireland, made him a rare poet acclaimed as much by the Academy and critics as by the general reader. He often quoted Gerard Manley Hopkins' belief that 'description is revelation'. His alert perspectives were indeed luminous. Whether his poems were being heard by the Nobel Prize audience, quoted by President Clinton at historic agreements or read by grim-faced commuters on the inside of Tube trains in the London Underground, it was his rich simplicity, earthed humanity and his ability to sound out the private heart caught in changing times, 'feelings into words' (the title of an early essay by him), that made him a poet of such remarkable range and poignancy.

Heaney ended his Nobel Lecture laying out his belief in:

> poetry's power to do the thing which always is and always will be to poetry's credit: the power to persuade that vulnerable part of our consciousness of its rightness in spite of the evidence of wrongness around it, the power to remind us that we are hunters and gatherers of values, that our very solitudes and distresses are creditable, in so far as they, too, are an earnest of our veritable human being.[2]

He liked to quote Yeats, that the effort of poetry's metaphors is 'to hold in a single thought reality and justice', or, to use his own line from 'The Cure of Troy', to make 'hope and history rhyme'.[3]

The poem I've chosen here is taken from Heaney's collection *Seeing Things* (1991). It is a book affected by the death of his father, a re-inspecting of the world in the aftermath of such a loss. It has two bookends holding the rest together. It opens with a poem inspired by the passage in Book VI of Virgil's *Aeneid* about the golden bough that acts as Aeneas' ticket into the underworld as he seeks the shadow of his father. The collection ends with a poem based on the story in Dante's *Inferno* where Charon (whose name, appropriately for a collection named *Seeing Things* means 'of keen gaze') initially refuses to take Dante into his boat that takes the souls from the realm of the living to the dead. Jefferson Hunter, reviewing the book for the *Virginia Quarterly Review*, maintained that this book takes a more spiritual approach. 'Words like "spirit" and "pure" . . . had never figured largely in Heaney's poetry,' Hunter explained. However, in *Seeing Things* Heaney uses such words to 'create a new distanced perspective and indeed a new mood' in which '"things beyond measure" or "things in the offing" or "the longed-for" can sometimes be sensed, if never directly seen'.[4]

Within *Seeing Things* there is a 48-poem sequence called 'Squarings'. The poems are somewhat square in shape with 12 lines each and five beats per line, placed in 12 poem units. Each poem is title-less, allowing them to play off each other with an uncontained, numinous energy. In one of the poems we get insight into the title of the sequence: a player takes 'squarings' when positioning himself to shoot a marble in the playground, full of 'anglings, aimings, feints and squints'.[5] The poem ends: 'You squinted out from a skylight of the world'.

The unit our poem is taken from is named 'Lightenings'. Again, the title needs attention – as they always do with poems. So much can be lost when reading poetry by casually passing over the title. A 'lightening' can be an unburdening or an illumination, even a flash in the sky, but it can also refer to a flaring of the spirit at the moment before death. All these senses blend together in the poem and in the whole collection itself.

Poem viii in 'Lightenings' is based on several medieval stories about miracles that were believed to take place in Ireland. There are various versions of a legend in which a ship appears in the sky and lets down an anchor which then gets caught on something – often a church or a tombstone – and a man is seen coming down from the ship to try to release it. Later versions set the miracle in the important monastery of Clonmacnoise, by the Shannon, that had a reputation for such wonders. The legend eventually developed a dialogue in which the curious monks took hold of the sailor from the sky, but he shouts, 'Let hold of me for God's sake! You are drowning me!' – not a unique response to being in some churches perhaps. They let him go and he swims back to board.

Heaney's poem says the ship appeared when the monks were *all at prayers* in the oratory. The ship appears and the anchor gets caught on the altar rail, the place that Heaney in another later poem says he 'knelt and learnt almost/ Not to admit the let-down to myself'.[6] It is ironically both the place of communion with God, as you kneel and receive bread and wine, and a railed excluding barrier to the holy sanctuary. 'Unroofed' is a word used in the first poem of the sequence and here we get an unroofed world. The image of the ship floating on the air suggests that the divide between heaven and earth is like the surface of the sea and we are in its depths. This ship with its other-worldly crew (are they angels?) sends a man down into our life but the wise abbot can see he *can't bear our life here and will drown* and shrewdly gets his monks to help the man free the anchor so that he can quickly return to his ark. Just as we are concluding that the man probably wasn't able to bear our life because it is too polluted or distant from his heavenly country with no transcendent oxygen, we are told that he climbs back *out of the marvellous as he had known it*. That is, this world that he had found himself in is a place of wonder and, in a place of prayer, he was able to see this better than those of us who live here.

The idea that we are living in an unfathomable and fascinating sea of life was caught in a line of a poem by Richard Wilbur that I had printed on my ordination card: 'All that we do/ Is touched with ocean, yet we remain/ On the shore of what we know'.[7] We tend to seek the 'miraculous' in the un-ordinary, the unusual and incongruous, but here we are shown that our life itself, our world and atmosphere, is the real miracle. The fact that we miss this or can be indifferent to it is equally miraculous. Strangely, a religious belief can often encourage us to be wary of life by insisting that our real 'home' is in heaven. When a believer in Jeanette Winterson's novel *Oranges Are Not the Only Fruit*[8] goes on a beach mission she goes into the sea and her fellow churchgoers think she is drowning when they see her waving her arms. She is rescued but is not happy about it because she was not waving for help but waving goodbye; she wanted to be in heaven with God. She was drowning herself out of the world. In some respects this is what each Christian does at baptism – but only to come up again out of the water with new breath and new purpose, to live as one who is saved for the world, not from it.

There is another Christian resonance to this poem. The man who climbs down into our world can be seen as a Christ figure, entering our thick air in incarnation, and who, having seen and announced the wonders of the kingdom, escapes all that the world might do to him and takes his place over a sea that has been changed by his presence for ever. Those committed to prayer are those who allow him to sail free as they enjoy the mysteries of the deepened life. The fact that in some stories the anchor was trapped on a tomb adds even more Christ-like reflection to it.

When Heaney spoke of the poem, however, he felt it was about 'two orders of knowledge which we might call the practical and the poetic . . . the frontier between them is there for the crossing'.[9] When his friend and fellow poet Dennis O'Driscoll interviewed him about his work, Heaney said: 'You could think of every poem in "Squarings" as the peg at the end of a tent-rope reaching up into the airy shadows, but still with some purchase on something earthier and more obscure'.[10] Unroofed. It's not a bad way of describing faith.

In another of Heaney's poems, 'Postscript',[11] he writes of a journey that was able to 'catch the heart off guard and blow it open'. The poems of *Seeing Things* are aware of open secrets that a faith in God also blows your heart open to – the overspilling density and gift of what is, of that liberated energy to be gained by a more generative seeing and of the interconnection of the experiencing self and all created being. What the poet Jane Hirshfield says about writing poetry could also be said of the one who has been called to that visionary strangeness known as discipleship and sets about trying to see the world through the eyes of Jesus Christ the story-teller who is Word of God:

> . . . the eyes of ordinary seeing close down and the poem rushes forward into the world on some mysterious inner impulsion that underlies seeing, underlies hearing, underlies words as they exist in ordinary usage. The condition is almost sexual, procreative in its hunger for what can be known in no other way. All writers recognize this surge of striking; in its energies the objects of the world are made new, alchemised by their passage through the imaginal, musical, world-foraging and word-forging mind.[12]

The English poet and critic Lachlan MacKinnon wrote a typically astute tribute to Heaney on his death:

> Many – perhaps most – poets betray in their work or their lives some original wound their art tries to heal. The great puzzle with Heaney was that one could never tell what that hurt was, or whether there was one. His purpose, though, was less to describe than to convey an ethical vision. As Oxford's Professor of Poetry from 1989 to 1994, he said that 'In order that human beings bring about the most radiant conditions for themselves to inhabit, it is essential that the vision of reality which poetry offers should be transformative, more than just a printout of the given circumstances of its time and place' . . . Engaging, funny, conscientious, wise; Seamus leaves us much to miss personally. However, his unfailing integrity and his unshowy dedication to an art he knew was greater than himself were exemplary. A little bit of him will survive in any decent poet's conscience, while his work will feed the imaginations of generations to come.[13]

Heaney is buried in his birthplace, Bellaghy, County Derry. Words from his poem 'The Gravel Walks' are inscribed on his gravestone:

> Walk on air against your better judgment.[14]

Holy Sonnet XIV

John Donne (1572–1631)

Batter my heart, three-person'd God; for you
As yet but knock, breathe, shine and seek to mend;
That I may rise, and stand, o'erthrow me, and bend
Your force to break, blow, burn and make me new.
I, like an usurp'd towne, to another due,
Labour to admit you, but Oh, to no end,
Reason, your viceroy in me, me should defend,
But is captiv'd, and proves weak or untrue.
Yet dearly I love you, and would be loved faine,
But am betroth'd unto your enemie:
Divorce me, untie, or break that knot againe,
Take me to you, imprison mee, for I
Except you enthrall me, never shall be free,
Nor ever chaste, except you ravish me.

It was one line in John Donne's poetry that got me hooked on him
for life. I came across it in his Holy Sonnet XIX when I was at
school and trying to work out something of who I was and what
I wanted to be and, incidentally, not making a very good job of
it. Over thirty years later I still seem to be engaged in the same
project and the line still captures: 'Oh, to vex me, contraryes meet
in one'. It seemed then, as it seems now, that the 'contraryes' of
being human are quite overwhelmingly complex.

One thing I did know as a schoolboy was that I wanted to be
a priest and that much has come true. The 'contraryes' of being a
Christian and of being an ordained minister only add, however, to

those of being a human being. Existentialists have often identified those two basic anxieties we have: first, of not becoming our true self and, second, of indeed becoming our true self. Add to this the paradoxes of a life of faith and it can all get a bit much! Watching myself a little more carefully over the past years, I can see in retrospect that the times when I have had very strong religious beliefs have often been the times when I have had no faith. I can see also that the God I wish would unveil himself with greater clarity often reveals himself uncompromisingly either in darkness or alarmingly unexpected ways. Infuriatingly, God is not dictated to by my agenda nor by my impatience. In the Gospels, Jesus found faith where least expected (in foreigners, sinners and the unclean, for instance) and found it absent where it should have been flourishing (religious professionals and his disciples). I have sympathies with both groups because living in my head too much means God can quickly become an object that I chatter about and have opinions on rather than the Subject to whom I am to relate most deeply in order to shape a life around trust and love.

All in all, I have now come to terms with the fact that my Christian faith will not so much answer all my questions as question all my answers. This might be a lonely and somewhat forlorn conclusion to make if it were not for others, explorers of the soul such as John Donne, who have given voice to so many of these human and spiritual experiences way before I had them, and through the richness of their recognition and interpretation they cut a path towards a happier acceptance of them. One scholar, Joan Webber, has argued that 'Donne, as a writer, was only good at one thing, though that one thing was very intense and valuable. He was good at communicating his own experience . . .' I don't agree that this is all he was good at – but I'm pleased he was.

Nothing is as difficult as not deceiving yourself. To read the poems and prose of John Donne is to encounter many of the man's various contradictions. It is therefore also to come face to face with ambiguity of meaning, with puns and secrecies. Donne referred to his own 'riddling, perplexed, labyrinthical soule'. There is what he called a 'maze of corridors' in his breast. There is an honesty about things we can find difficult to talk about. He knew, for example, that he was always being distracted in prayer and that he could 'neglect God and his angels for the noise of a flie, for the rustling of a coach, for the whining of a dore . . . a memory of yesterday's pleasures, a fear of tomorrow's dangers, a straw under my knee, a noise in mine ear, an any thing, a nothing, a fancy'. As he himself said, 'It is not the depth nor the wit nor the eloquence of the Preacher that pierces us but his nearnesse'. It is the same for the poet. Donne feels very near as I read him.

Donne's colliding confusions, so often the focus of his intense introspection, are at the very heart of his creativity. His experiences as truth-seeker and self-seeker, as passionate lover of women and pious lover of God, as a man of consistent ambition who nevertheless had an overpowering sense of death's inevitability, as a betraying apostate and also an admired priest and preacher, all these disconnected splinters of his being alive were brought into some sort of unity in his poems. This is how it works. As T. S. Eliot put it:

> When a poet's mind is perfectly equipped for its work, it is constantly amalgamating disparate experience; the ordinary man's experience is chaotic, irregular, fragmentary. The latter falls in love, or reads Spinoza, and these two experiences have nothing to do with each other, or with the noise of a typewriter or the smell of cooking; in the mind of the poet these experiences are always forming new wholes.[1]

Donne's talent as a writer, though, has over the centuries been a topic of heated debate. A neat summary of this discussion has been made by C. A. Patrides: 'Donne was much praised in his life time, underpraised thereafter, and over praised (in the twentieth century)'.[2] Although not all of Donne's contemporaries thought Donne a good poet (King James is said to have quipped that Donne's verses 'were like ye peace of God they passed all understanding'), it is true that many of them perceived Donne's avant-garde modernity and thought him original. 'To the awe of thy imperious wit', wrote one, 'our stubborne language bends.'[3]

Donne was a 'Copernicus in poetrie', after whom the universe of verse would never be the same.

Later commentators such as Samuel Johnson disliked metaphysical poets such as Donne who, he thought, wrote poetic 'conceits' aimed at showing off the poet's cleverness rather than laying truth before the reader who, consequently, 'though he sometimes admires, is seldom pleased'.[4] Making a similar point, Simmel Goldberg said that Donne's 'brain went to his head'.[5]

More recently C. H. Sisson revitalized some interest in Donne's themes in his own poem 'A Letter to John Donne' and he perhaps captures something of Donne's talent and energies that shaped his work:

> I understand you well enough, John Donne
> First, that you were a man of ability
> Eaten by lust and by the love of God (. . .)[6]

And if that doesn't make you want to read him, then I don't know what will.

Donne was born in London and remained a city man throughout his life. He was not a 'pastoral' poet and never could be as he always complained when he wasn't at the heart of metropolitan goings-on. His father was an ironmonger who lived to see his son for only four years. His mother was a daughter of a poet and playwright and a descendant of Sir Thomas More, and her family was heroically committed to the Roman Catholic faith. Donne had two uncles who were Jesuit priests, and his great-uncle, Thomas Heywood, was a Catholic martyr. His brother Henry gave refuge to a priest and died of the plague in Newgate prison awaiting trial. The Catholic faith shaped his childhood and stayed with him as he studied at Hart Hall in Oxford. He then proceeded to Lincoln's Inn where he made a name for himself as a widely read wit who, though never called to the bar, ensured that he called on the Court and played the romantic and servile games necessary for social acceptance. Eventually he secured a post as one of Sir Thomas Egerton's secretaries. Egerton was Lord Keeper of the Great Seal, Master of the Roll and a Privy Counsellor. The contacts Donne made through his work for Egerton were important to him, but things went wrong when, in 1601, he married Ann, the 15-year-old niece of his employer in a secret ceremony. Ann's father, Sir George More, was furious and refused to acknowledge the marriage and to make financial provision. Egerton dismissed Donne from his service.

The marriage was legally valid and it proved to be a strong loving backbone to what now became a vulnerable life both socially and financially. He looked for patrons wherever he could, even when it meant long journeys abroad, in 1605 and 1611, away from his wife and young children. He eventually acquired a house in Mitcham and started to seek favour at Court again. He was not successful at landing the appointments he desired, particularly those at the King's disposal. He continued to write, however, and often for payment. He wrote letters, verses, theological essays and continued to study law, philosophy and literature, but he was also plagued by a great deal of ill health and consequent despair.

Donne had always been interested in theological matters and had moved, for whatever reasons, towards the Church of England and away from his Roman Catholicism as the years had passed. In the end Donne 'resolved to make my Profession Divinite' and was ordained in Old St Paul's Cathedral on 23 January 1615. He was appointed Chaplain in Ordinary to the King, made a Doctor of Divinity by Cambridge University, and then Reader of Divinity at Lincoln's Inn. Here he learned the art of preaching, crafting with the poet's eye and orator's tongue the sermons that captured, and still do, the Christian's ear.

Ann died in 1617 and this shattering event made Donne reflect at a deep level on his faith, his humanity, and his God. He seems to have wanted to be considered for the appointment of Dean of St Paul's, and for once his wish came true. He was installed in November 1621 and took upon himself the many responsibilities that the position entailed, while enjoying at the same time the security and status that it brought. It was a fruitful period of his life but ill health cropped up again and he grew generally and painfully weaker. He eventually died in 1631 at the age of 59, survived by six of his 12 children. According to his friend Izak

Walton his last words were: 'I were miserable if I might not dye' and 'Thy Kingdom come. Thy will be done'.

Although I have enjoyed Donne's poetry now for a long time and have found myself returning to his poems very frequently, it is only recently that I have started to re-read his sermons. They are startlingly fresh and, although long and often full of classical reference and Latin phrases, are direct, earthy and unafraid to tread confidently through the shadows that our humanity casts. I find myself using lines from his poems and sermons in my own preaching: 'He can bring thy Summer out of Winter, though thou have no Spring'; 'That music of thy promises, not threats in thunder, may awaken us to our just offices'; 'I shall be made thy Music'; 'Only our love hath no decay'; 'Look Lord, and find both Adams met in me'; 'As West and East in all flat maps (and I am one) are one, so death doth touch the Resurrection'.

In an essay on Lancelot Andrewes, T. S. Eliot lamented that Donne was one of those people 'who seek refuge in religion from the tumults of a strong emotional temperament which can find no complete satisfaction elsewhere',[7] and about whom 'there hangs the shadow of the impure motive'. This may or may not be true. Regardless, the fact is that much of Donne's theological imagery resonates and continues to give voice to many parts of the contemporary soul. He does probably grasp ideas through intuition rather than logic, but so do many of us. We often know more than we can say. Donne is not a systematic theologian. And there again, many of us are grateful for this, suspicious as we are of the business of forcing the Mystery of God into the confines of a culturally conditioned philosophical framework. Instead of a system, Donne presents a theological vision and it is noticeable that sight is the pre-eminent sense in his work. He constantly searches for images and representations that feed faith and allow it to grow towards God. If there is no easy system to dissect, however, it does not mean that we cannot discern what were obviously important theological themes for Donne. Indeed, Jeffrey Johnson argues in a fascinating book that there are very clear distinguishing features in Donne's theological vision.[8]

First, there is his belief in the Trinity as the fundamental doctrine for regulating Christian faith and practice. Within the nature of God lies community that enlarges itself into creativity and an embrace of humanity. In a sermon of 1624 he refers to the 'sociablenesse, the communicablenesse of God'. Belief in the Trinity should also be the unifying belief for all Christians of differing traditions. Donne says that the Trinity is undermined by seeing 'Christians scratch and wound and teare one another, with ignominous invectives, and uncharitable names of Heretique, and Schismatique' – a lesson that might need to be re-learned . . .

Second, Donne stresses the vitality of prayer and especially of liturgical common prayer. Such prayer affirms belief in the grace of God and is a manifestation of the unity of the Church. Prayer is the way we 'batter Heaven', wrestle with God and dare some 'religious impudency' as we forge our relationship with the Creator. Donne very much gives the impression that for him, as for Thomas Aquinas, prayer is 'an appetitive act' where desire and prayer become synonymous and where only love can effect our union with God. 'Churches are best for Prayer', he writes, 'that have least light:/ To see God only, I goe out of sight:/ And to scape stormy dayes, I chuse an Everlasting night.' Prayer is where we uncomfortably learn the dialogue between human weakness and divine faithfulness.

Third, as already mentioned, Donne emphasizes the need for pictures and images in our fashioning of a theological vision. The love of the world 'is but a smoke' that 'putts out our eyes'; whereas the eye of Christ is like the eye of the ostrich that, according to legend, with one look 'is said to hatch her young ones, without sitting'. He also describes baptism as an 'eye-salve to all, by which they may mend their eye-sight'. In the sacrament of baptism the visible and invisible fuse to give birth to a new reality.

Fourth, Johnson argues that Donne was convinced of the theological imperative of repentance. Tears, like the baptismal water, bring new life. They are a gift for which we should pray, 'Pour new seas in mine eyes'. In preaching on Christ's declaration that he calls not the righteous but sinners, Donne comments: 'Are ye to learn now what that is? He that cannot define Repentance, he that cannot spell it, may have it; and he that hath written whole books, great Volumes of it, may be without it. In one word, (one word will not do it, but in two words) it is Aversio, and Conversio; it is a turning from our sins, and a returning to God.' Donne's beautiful image for the voice of repentance is 'a groaninge not a roaringe, the voice of the Turtle not of a Lyon'.

Finally, like most Christians of his generation, Donne gave much thought to the doctrine of grace, what he terms the 'soule of the soule'. God gives initial grace and we must pursue present grace in order for the work of salvation to have effect. The Word and the Sacrament enable this process, and the presence of Christ becomes truly present in those who abide by the Word and eat and drink the Sacrament worthily. Word and Sacrament are the signs of the love relationship that God has with his people. This relationship is caught in a moving passage in one of his sermons: 'Truly to me, this consideration, That as his mercy is new every morning, so his grace is renewed to me every minute, That it is not by yesterdaies grace that I live now, but that I have . . . My daily bread, my hourely bread, in a continuall succession of his grace, That the eye of God is open upon me, though I winke at his light, and watches over me, though I sleep.'[9]

In his 'Devotions upon Emergent Occasions' Donne reflects: 'I have not the righteousness of Job, but I have the desire of Job: I would speak to the Almighty, and I would reason with God'. The critic D. J. Enright tried to summarize this: 'God is to be feared and revered, but a man's a man for all that.'[10] I suppose that is why I am attracted to Donne's work at the end of the day. You are left in no doubt that God is holy and gracious and that his love transforms; but you are also convinced of the fragility and pomposity of being human. To face both is to know many con-solations and difficulties, and it is these, for me learned most in his poetry and sermons, that make me return to him time and time again. To use an overused and somewhat inaccurate caricature, I find myself liking the young, sassy, audacious Jack Donne as well as the reflective, tearful, ambitious Dr Donne. I feel I know both of them quite well. And when it does all get too much as a priest, and when doubts set in about the self and the vocation, I am reminded of Donne's reminder to a newly ordained cleric that he is there to 'open life' – rather like the work of a good poet.

The 19 'Holy Sonnets' were written by Donne most probably in 1609–10, around the time of his move towards the Church of England. 'Holy Sonnet XIV' is a variation of the Petrarchan sonnet form where its 14 lines are divided into an eight-line octave and a six-line sestet. It ends with a rhyming couplet. It reveals a truth about Donne (and indeed many of the so-called metaphysical poets) – he thought in metaphors. There are three central images to the poem as it calls on God to come and brashly take charge over his life because, well, this is John Donne, and God's got his work cut out in trying to save him of all people.

Strong action is needed to save this poet from his sin and so the poem opens in an urgent imperative mood: *Batter my heart.* Say these words aloud and they even sound like a frantic knocking. Up to now God has, like a craftsman with a metal vessel, sought to *mend* Donne. He's tapped it to see where it's worn thin, breathed on it before polishing it and sought to make it *shine*. But this is not enough. Paradoxically, if Donne is to rise he needs to be overthrown. Again, read the poem aloud and see how disruptive the word *o'erthrow* is to the rhythm, creating an interruption akin to that which Donne wants to his life. If he is to be saved by God it will mean more than a quick repair job. His soul-vessel needs to be re-created and so he prays that God will *bend/ Your force to break, blow, burn and make me new*. All the *b*'s here sound like the barrage of destruction necessary for rebirth. In fact the poem has many 'plosives', consonant sounds that are formed by completely stopping airflow. In phonetics, a plosive consonant is made by blocking a part of the mouth so that no air can pass through (e.g. *b*, *d*, *g*). By using them it's as if life as it has come to be and breathe has to die in order to live again. In one of his sermons he says: 'I consider . . . myself a piece of rusty copper, in which those lines of the Image of God which were imprinted in me in my Creation are defaced and worn, and washed and burnt, and ground away, by many, and many, and many sins'.[11]

Donne then admits that his heart is like a besieged town with a foreign ruler. He labours to admit the true king but it doesn't work. That king, God, has left in him a viceroy or ambassador. This is reason or logic and it should be enough to persuade Donne to avoid sin but, just like every other part of him, it proves *weak or untrue*. He confesses that he loves God and wants to be loved in return but it feels as if he is betrothed to an invader or enemy (the word 'Satan' is derived from the Hebrew for 'enemy'). He prays again, this time that God will *Divorce me, untie, or break that knot againe*. It's an abusive marriage and he needs to be released from it if he is to be truly free.

The alarming eroticism at the end of the poem has Donne appealing to God to come and imprison him so he can't be at large to get up to more mischief. The truest freedom will come from serving God's commands to love. He then petitions God to *enthrall* and *ravish* him. Donne will never be pure unless God abducts him and has his way with him. Behind the poem might well be a vision such as that found in Isaiah 1.21–27 where metal becomes purified through God's creative resilience and the city that has sold itself to buyers regains its original faithfulness: 'How is the faithful city become an harlot . . . thy silver is become dross . . . I will turn my hand upon thee, and purely purge away thy dross, and take away all thy tin . . . afterward thou shalt be called the faithful city.'

Working in St Paul's Cathedral, I now look at John Donne every day. He was Dean of St Paul's for ten years and towards the end of his life he posed for a monument to be made of him by the sculptor Nicholas Stone. Having remarkably survived the Great Fire of 1666 that destroyed the old St Paul's, the memorial was eventually placed in the Dean's Aisle. Never one to take death lying down, Donne is shown standing and perched on a funerary urn, shrouded in a sheet that has been gathered into two decorative ruffs at the head and feet. Cocoon-like, he appears to rise out of the urn with his eyelids shut and his mouth in a benign, half-smiling expression. The Dean's Aisle is where the clergy robe before a service. Donne hovers over us as we plump up our surplices and get in line, reminding us that the imagination is not a vestigial organ in the Christian but is there to be used for God and for good. It is a haunting reminder of the Dean whose mind constantly sought to rise out of the deathly soil towards the brightness of his God. The fact that Donne's effigy survived the Great Fire was not lost on the writer Virginia Woolf:

> We still seek out Donne even if we cannot see how so many different qualities meet together in one man. But we have only to read him, to submit to the sound of that passionate and penetrating voice, and his figure rises again across the waste of the years more erect, more imperious, more inscrutable than any of his time. Even the elements seem to have respected that identity. When the fire of London destroyed almost every other monument in St Paul's, it left Donne's figure untouched, as if the flames themselves found that knot too hard to undo, that riddle too difficult to read, and that figure too entirely itself to turn to common clay.[12]

God-Box

Mark Doty (b. 1953)

They give us a white cube, a paper box,
the kind that might hold a small gift,
and ask us to write or draw on its surface
our image of the divinity, whatever
that might be.
                        We're here, we have,
in principle, already agreed.
Daniel's octopus is a Buddha,
Glenn's highest self a blazing star,
though no marker's adequately golden.
In my future blue one hand blooms
from the next in a rush of wind
from another life.
                        Step two: Write
on an index card what you most want
to be released from, fold it,
place it inside, close the lid. That's it,
that's the end of the exercise.

Walking home on Sixth, thinking
Its intention not artifact that matters,
I'm inclined to toss the thing away,
but I wind up walking blocks
holding this coffer only a little bigger
than my hand. Steam blurs
a bank's bright windows;
glassy slab of winter twilight

over the stairs to the subway,
then I'm down in the station, restless,
walking the long platform,
                              and here's
the unknowable of music too far
to name. Keep walking, a violin,
sonorous, emotive. Closer: resolute travelers
facing the tracks but the rest of us
turn toward the man whose powers
concentrate on his instrument,
from which pours
                      – how is it possible? –
an aching distillate so exact
I don't need to go anywhere.
CD for sale in the velvet cavity
beside his shoes, two dollar bills,
gleaming change.
                      Odd bit of movement
across the tracks, so I can't help but look
toward the platform: a tall black man
– why does his darkness
seem to matter? – cradling a violin
that isn't there, invisible chin-rest
beneath his jaw, immaterial body resting
on the shoulder of his coat, and the bow
that isn't there lifted and lowered
precisely.
                      Not mimicry; he knows the music.
On my side of the double tracks
the tunnel fills with an embodied grief,
too poised to be an outcry, contained,
larger than any single suffering,
and the man on the other side
makes nothing, no sound at all,
but answers adequately.
What did I write on that card?
One blue hand folding out of another,

one golden octopus,
one embattled star,
this box in these hands,
that have done so much
to harm myself,
                    this box.

My sister once said, in response to a memoir I'd written, 'What you got wrong made it that much more you.' That's become an aphorism for me, a motto in favour of going forward in the dark, allowing our stumbling and groping to be themselves an act of self-portraiture. As a Zen-practitioner friend of mine likes to say, 'The obstacle in the path is the path'.[1]

Mark Doty's first collection of poetry was published in 1987, the year I left school. I remember that time as one of increased fear in Britain due to the rise of HIV/AIDS. We watched scary advertisements on our televisions with large gravestones that told us not to die of ignorance. There was a homophobic backlash in society. Gay people with the virus were thought by many to have got what they deserved, the Chief Constable of Greater Manchester Police referring to people 'swirling about in a human cesspit of their own making'. Section 28 of the Local Government Act 1988 prohibited local authorities in England and Wales from 'promoting' homosexuality. It also labelled gay family relationships as 'pretend'. At a time when some newspapers were discussing whether HIV could be transmitted through sitting on toilet seats, it was a vitally important thing that Diana, Princess of Wales, did when she visited a hospital and shook hands with Shane Snape, a patient living with AIDS. The fact that she shook hands without wearing any gloves, he said, 'meant more to me than anything'. I think of George Herbert's 'Love took my hand . . .'

It was not an easy time, then, to come home, switch off the television and tell my grandmother, who brought me up as a child, that I was gay. She smiled and said she thought she had known for a little while and she had only been worried about one thing.

I was convinced she was going to say 'AIDS'. But no. 'I have just been worried that you would never feel able to tell me,' she said.

This loving response is the opposite of the one given to me by the official Church of England over my years of ministry. Generally over those 25 years it has been the unspoken agreement that I can have a ministry as a gay person but I mustn't talk about my sexuality in case it creates a fuss – and if that happens I can't expect the backing of the Church leadership. As society has become more accepting of LGBT people, and able to see the discrimination they have suffered for something they did not choose but simply discovered about themselves, the Church rightly finds itself shamed about this state of affairs. At the moment the Church is paralysed as to how to be honest and embracing of the many LBGT people who minister, serve and worship in churches, and the even more who love them and want the best for them in life. Many of us remain committed to helping the Church challenge homophobia within its own structures as well as in other parts of the world. This is all based on a hatred that the Church has contributed to over many centuries and that therefore it must now take responsibility to correct. It is not enough to write PR statements saying, 'But we are not homophobic' when the evidence is stacked high against you. Unless the Church sees what most in society can see, as was the case with the issue of women in the episcopate, there will continue to be moral outrage about the Church's discrimination. When someone hits you and says 'sorry' at the same time, we call it domestic abuse. Institutions can be guilty of this abuse and the Church especially so at the moment.

In this present twilight world of mixed messaging in the Church of England, private support but public negativity from most bishops, for instance, and where a power lies in the fear of exposure it all generates, especially in those employed and housed by the Church, it is understandable that many of us have needed to find writers who have voiced something of our experience. We have needed, to use Kafka's image, writers whose work acts like a pickaxe in the ice, tracing out a more authentic, honest path towards a place where we might live in a better and more wholesome light – even if there is a cost. Over the last twenty or so years, Mark Doty has been one of those writers for me.

The son of an army engineer, Doty spent his childhood moving from suburb to suburb. As he grew up he became frightened of his sexuality and quickly married at the age of 18 to hide. The marriage did not last long. He moved to New York where he met and fell in love with Wally, with whom he lived for 12 years before Wally died of AIDS-related causes in 1994. His experience of growing up gay, of many friends dying young in those early days of the virus, as well as living with and caring for Wally in his illness before he died, has shaped much of Doty's work. Michael Schmidt has written that Doty's poems 'come back from an abyss' and, right from when his first collection was reviewed, it was seen that Doty is a gay poet who turns his experience into 'an example of how we live, how we suffer and transcend suffering'.[2] Pain is an individual and private hurt but Doty breaks it open into universal recognitions of truth. His collections *My Alexandria* (1993) and *Atlantis* (1995) both delve into desire and the pain of life's losses, especially through Doty's descriptions and responses to Wally's sickness and death, but there is a courage in his writing that is able to extract beauty out of the living moments. It is a part-translation of the truth that the poet Wallace Stevens voiced when he said that 'death is the mother of beauty'. The evocative title of the memoir Doty wrote about his bereavement is called *Heaven's Coast* (1997).

Patricia Hampl wrote of Doty that 'when he sees the ocean – the salt spray hits you'. It is this ability to describe, of making the familiar strange and the strange familiar, both internally and externally, that makes him so accomplished. He is the first American to receive the T. S. Eliot prize for poetry and has recently written a short book about this art of poetic description.[3] His language is intelligent but accessible, elegantly simple, luminously crafted and assured. There is a strong visual quality to his work, often daring in its complex syntax, and although he writes in free verse there is never a sense that his poetry is unmoored. Indeed, some more critical readers find him too much of a detached observer of himself, but his contained and unhidden self-questioning has, to my mind, a music that is conscious of the notes but that, nevertheless, plays a heart-melody that enters us with striking lyrical power. Philip Levine has summed this up well: 'If it were mine to invent the poet to complete the century . . . I would create Mark Doty just as he is, a maker of big, risky, fearless poems in which ordinary human experience becomes music'.[4]

Doty's latest collection is the searching *Deep Lane* (2015) and it is one of my favourites. Two long-vowelled monosyllables, such as 'Deep Lane', in English usually convey some sadness or ominous intrigue. This is true of this book but there is also a more settled and contented, even grateful sense to many of the poems. There are nine of them called 'Deep Lane' in the volume, and like the nine circles that the poet Dante descends in his 'Divine Comedy' halfway through life's path, here Doty also descends. In fact the book begins with a poem that sees him on his knees in the garden pulling up wild mustard by the roots. He has written about *Deep Lane*:

This is my book of descents: into the soil, in anticipation of both growth and mortality; into desire and its driving hungers; into the past with its ravenous ghosts; grief and its seemingly permanent woundings. Because I gave myself permission not to strive for affirmation, it may be the darkest of my books. I pushed myself to keep digging, to come face to face with the difficult. Still, it's by no means a joyless book. I find hope and pleasure in the persistence of – spirit, soul, an energetic response to reality? – in the face of struggle. Resilience, for me, often lies in language, in the work of giving form and voice to how it feels to be in one's own skin.[5]

His poem 'God-Box', found in the middle of the book, exemplifies so much of what Doty says here. It appears to take place in some sort of therapeutic workshop, the participants being asked to take a small white box on which they are asked to write or draw *on its surface* their image of the divinity. At the end of the day, that's all any of us can do when it comes to imagining God, merely scratching the surface on one side of a multi-sided mystery: *no marker's adequately golden* and yet this exercise might be inviting them to treasure something that holds *a small gift*. The poet draws a hand that *blooms* from other hands in *a rush of wind/ from another life*.

The group is then asked to write on a card what they most want to be released from. Everything we want lies on the other side of fear. To name those fears is the first step to salvation. The cards are placed in the little divine box, so becoming invisible. The lid closes shut. Walking home, the writer is tempted to throw the box away because the exercise made its point but he holds on to it. He sees *winter twilight*, goes down into the New York subway, restless, and down there on the platform he finds a man playing a violin, selling CDs and presumably trying to earn some cash. The beauty of the music Doty calls *an aching distillate so exact/ I don't need to go anywhere*.

In the New York subway the tracks separate the two platforms so you can see passengers opposite you waiting to travel in the other direction. Doty looks across and sees a black man holding an imaginary violin and pretending to play the music that is still being played by the man he has been observing: *the bow/ that isn't there lifted and lowered/ precisely*. That last word shows the intensity of what the man is enacting on that opposite platform. This is *not mimicry*, we are told. The man knows the music. He knows the ache, the distillation, the place from which the tune comes. This recalls to my mind the lines of the poet Mary Oliver: 'that greatest of love affairs, a violin/ and a human body'.[6] As one plays and the other responds in a shared recognition the tunnel *fills with an embodied grief,/ too poised to be an outcry*. This could be a description of Doty's poetry. The man with no violin makes no sound but *answers adequately*.

Doty asks himself what he wrote on that card. His private fear remains private. We are not told what was on it. But as he sees the beauty of human empathy, of the momentary harmony of shared hearts and hurts down underground, he remembers the depictions of the divine: shared hands, the extended reach of an octopus, the light of a star seen together on a dark night. In *hands,/ that have done so much/ to harm myself* Doty sees *this box*.

Demeter

Fiona Benson (b. 1978)

Up in shorn Drake's Meadow the hay bales shine.
They're shreathed in plastic tubing, and the plastic
is slack at each end then tight round the bale
like a film. My daughter is compelled –
she must fit her arms round each bale, or pull
at their silver tails and I cannot draw her home.
I head down the path hoping she'll come
but when I look back she's gone and my own voice
snags at her name like barbed wire on skin.
When I see her again she's halfway down the field
emerging from behind another bale
as if they were portals or wormholes to pass her
through this sun-bleached meadow – impossible –
her mouth is bruised with blackberry juice
and she keeps disappearing, as if into hell through the shadow
of a hay bale – Demeter will be screaming soon,
cutting her wrists with broken glass,
rubbing in dirt, turning the world to darkness and ice
she misses her daughter so much (pathological) –
black ice on the school run, shuddering cars,
bodies through glass – she can't bear it and I
can't stand it – not that small smashed body on the road
nor the germs – septicaemia, meningitis –
her small blotched body in my arms –
nor the men preparing underground rooms –
bare mattress and a bucket, concealed stairs –
what mother could find you there,

digging up the pavement with her nails –
I can't bear it and I cannot pray enough
to spare it, I'll pray to any listening god
to keep her safe from harm, I go and pick
my daughter up and carry her protesting home.

In Greek mythology Demeter is the goddess of the harvest, fertility and agriculture. Her virgin daughter Persephone was abducted and taken to the underworld by Hades. Demeter was distraught with grief and worry, searching for her everywhere. As she was obsessional in her search and lost all interest in everything but her daughter, so the weather failed and the harvest died. It looked as if life itself would become extinct and so Zeus sent his messenger to find Persephone and bargain for her return. She was allowed to return on the understanding that she spent certain months of the year with Hades, and it was during these months that her mother Demeter would once again be overcome with loss and grief, forgetting to look after the harvest. This, conclude the myths, is how the seasons came to be.

Fiona Benson's poem, named after the goddess of agriculture, is set in a hay meadow. It forms part of her debut collection called *Bright Travellers* and is a poem, she has said, 'about how becoming a mother turns you into a crazy person'. *Bright Travellers* comprises 45 poems and they range in theme from dark-age Devon to Temperance Lloyd, one of the last women to be executed for alleged witchcraft in England. There is also a poignant sequence of poems that explores the relationship between Vincent Van Gogh and his lover, using the titles of his paintings as each poem's diving board. Benson is a versatile poet, often using trimmed lines and keeping balance through her visceral topics by sparingly shaped and contained forms.

Many of Benson's poems lead us into the heartlands of violence and loss. She writes from the gut about her miscarriages and other losses that make a world of 'hardened survivors'.[1] The first poem in the collection is called 'Caveat':

But consider the cactus:
its thick hide
and parched aspect

still harbour a moist heart;
nick its rind, and sap
wells up like sugared milk

from the store of water
held beneath its spines,
its armoury of barbs.

And, once a lifetime,
when the slant rains fall
there is this halo of flowers.

Like the cactus, we develop tough exteriors and protective barbs
to get us through a life that, frankly, is not for beginners. Benson's
work, though, shows that there are still refreshments and clarified
moments that remind us of the heart's capacity to be thankful –
and share itself – even when fractured.

One can imagine the mother in 'Demeter', having suffered mis-
carriages in the past and now enjoying her daughter's presence on
a walk in a field. Looking round and finding that she can't see her
creates mad panic and the worst possible imaginings of what can
happen to a child – from car accidents and illness to abduction
and abuse:

I can't bear it and I cannot pray enough
to spare it, I'll pray to any listening god
to keep her safe from harm . . .

She goes and picks up her protesting daughter and takes her home,
safe out of all trouble.

Benson has called this a 'heifer in a china shop' poem. It
screams with disproportionate fear and alarm. You can imagine
her daughter looking at her mother wondering what all the fuss
is about – somewhat like the boy Jesus in St Luke's Gospel when

his parents eventually find him after three days of panic (I often wonder if the memory of passionate protection gave rise to Jesus' story in later life about a man whose son goes off and leaves him bereft and who then does all he can to celebrate his return when 'what was lost is found'). In her poem 'Cave Bear' the grief of losing its cub makes the 'massive slab' of its mother's heart give way, her skull discovered calcified and embedded so many years later. Benson's father was in the army and she has noted that because the family moved around such a lot when she was young, 'home has been people for me, not a place'. The thought that the people who matter most to her might be taken away is nothing less than a ruptured sense of who and where she is, a homelessness, such as made Demeter so wretched and lost.

One of the striking features of Benson's writing is the honesty of emotion: 'Sometimes, I feel embarrassed but you just have to get over that. You cannot let ego interfere, you have to be truthful'.[2] She has spoken about working against the resistances that suggest what is right and proper and of how it is important not to 'enforce an epiphanic uplift' but to leave it earthbound, unwinged and untempered, if that is the authentic place in which to be. 'She never forgets how vivid our loves can be or how tangible we are', her former teacher John Burnside has written. Equally, she never forgets that when we lie about how we feel, when we know more than we tell, we live in fear of losing control and seek to make everything simpler than it is. Often liars have many friends but they remain lonely. Benson knows that in lying to others we end up lying to ourselves. There is a bravery to her work and a rawness that does justice to our complexity.

The American poet Adrienne Rich gave a talk in 1975 on 'Women and Honor: Some Notes on Lying'[3] which ended with this insight:

> When someone tells me a piece of the truth that has been withheld from me, and that I needed in order to see my life more clearly, it may bring acute pain, but it can also flood me with a cold, sea-sharp wash of relief. Often such truths come by accident, or from strangers.

It isn't that to have an honorable relationship with you, I have to understand everything, or tell you everything at once, or that I can know, beforehand, everything I need to tell you. It means that most of the time I am eager, longing for the possibility of telling you. That these possibilities may seem frightening, but not destructive, to me. That I feel strong enough to hear your tentative and groping words. That we both know we are trying, all the time, to extend the possibilities of truth between us.

The possibility of life between us.

There is no doubt that Benson works hard, as all good poets do, to extend the possibilities of truth between us. It is a lesson that those of us who are part of faith communities should try to imitate more. The Church often talks about truth but is less good at honesty. We can build and support an institutionalized form of truth that is ultimately delusional and destructive. This convenient but untruthful 'truth' can be about the deeper and more chaotic parts of what makes us human, but it can also be part of signing up to a PR culture of soundbite and salesmanship that sees the world as a competition to be won. The reason that God is frightening, on one level, is not because God is angry and out to get us but that God is real and we, so much of the time, are not. God's reality exposes our cover. Though painful, divine judgement is ultimately liberating to us, an act of love not revenge, because at last who we really are is exposed and taken seriously, honestly. There can be no salvation before recognition, as John the Baptist preached so many years ago.

Many mornings of the week, as Morning Prayer is being said in hushed and reverent tones in a chapel at St Paul's Cathedral, a woman comes in carrying all she owns in a few large bags. She stands nearby and lights a candle before the icon of Jesus and then she lets him have it! She stands there shouting, berating him for whatever appears justified that day. As the clergy continue their politeness to God, this woman unearths the pain of us all and adds it to our prayers with an exhilarating, honest energy. She is, in so many ways, one of the priests of the cathedral – offering a truth to the unseen God of what it is to be an alive human being with a hurt heart.

I long for the day when more theology will be written with an experiential transparency, a placing on the table of private moments and uncertain doubts, and a fierce resistance to polite thinking, as if God can be taken in like the others we try it on with, as if, that is, at the end of the day we are not all hardened survivors.

most of us are not this brave
our whole damn lives;
teach me to admit
a touch more light.[4]

Prayer

Jorie Graham (b. 1950)

What of the   quicksand.
My desperate eye   looking too hard.

Or of the eye   of the world
looking too   hard

for me. Or, if you prefer, *cause*,

looking to take in
what could be sufficient –

Then the sun goes down   and the sentence

goes out. Recklessly towards the end. Beyond
the ridge. Wearing us as if lost in

thought with no way
out, no eye at all to slip through,

none of the hurry or the between-
hurry thinkings to liquefy,

until it can be laid on the tongue

– oh quickness – like a drop. Swallow.
Rouse says the dark.

It has been said that for Jorie Graham the world 'is like a vast text deserted by its author late in the process of composition'.[1] We might also wonder if she similarly abandoned many of her poems in mid-construction and that the publisher decided to print them anyway to see what we made of them. Her poems can be notoriously difficult to make sense of, not only complex but wilfully obscure. If you try to type out this poem, 'Prayer', on your computer, it will go into spasms trying to correct your grammar and spacing, as it does with Emily Dickinson's poems. This is language – but not as we know it. It is language that throws us completely off balance. Her poems are known for the many gaps in her lines, large spaces of unspokenness that force themselves between the words (as in life) but which can appear so wide that, without some sort of bridge to cross, we can't follow her in her meaning. It is at these moments that your teeth begin to clench in frustration and you wonder if it is worth the effort to read her work.

Jorie Graham was born in New York City the daughter of a journalist and a sculptor. She was raised in Rome, and educated in French schools. She studied philosophy at the Sorbonne, Paris, and then film-making back in New York. She is currently the Bolyston Professor of Rhetoric and Oratory at Harvard University and the successor of Seamus Heaney in the post. Graham has won many literary awards including the Pulitzer Prize in 1996 and, more recently, the 2012 Forward Poetry Prize for best collection, being the first American woman to win one of Britain's most prestigious poetry prizes.

One of Graham's strongest advocates is the literary critic Helen Vendler. In an exploration of a Graham poem entitled 'From the New World' (a haunting overlaying of the stories of her own grandparents in a care home, a young girl who came out of the gas chamber having somehow survived and asking for her mother, and the trial of a man who ordered her subsequent rape),[2] Vendler describes the tissue of Graham's poetic language coming to us 'in a zigzag of half-articulated suspicions, invocations, silences, hints, glimpses, stumblings, and contradictions – the very picture of the mind making meaning'.[3] This is a helpful way of approaching a poem by Graham, imagining yourself surrounded by the pieces of an important jigsaw of being, aware that there may be missing pieces (those gaps again), and alert to the fact that Graham is inviting us to resist easy assimilations of the world in order to force out of us new responses to it. Hers is an uncompromising exercise of reality-repair, or what the poet Elizabeth Bishop termed 'constant re-adjustment'.

Graham's poems explore the big themes of philosophy, history, science, mythology and language. The fractured, incomplete and disjointed sense of the poems reveals the dualities and polarities of life and perception, the creative and destructive tensions, the stillness and motion, the interior and exterior. So many of the gaps in the lines seem to admit that things are as yet inconceivable or misunderstood and look to us for help, perhaps, as to how we might fill in the spaces to enable a deeper and more unified understanding. In her introduction to *The Best American Poetry 1990* she writes of how she wants 'to clean the language of its current lies, make it capable of connecting us to the world'. One critic, Calvin Bedient, commented that Graham is 'never less than in dialogue with everything'.[4]

Can the same be said about prayer? Words written about prayer are often consoling and peaceful, bringing a sense of internal order to the reader. Graham, in this poem, articulates a form of prayer that has left any stable moorings behind and has pushed out to sea with her usual collage of half-truths, asides, parenthetical remarks, sense perceptions and momentary meanings. We may prefer writing with more predictable structures when it comes to prayer, but might this disjointed collision of experience be a closer resemblance to our capability in prayer than some pious formulaic precision? After all, it has been said that with our inevitable limitations and ignorance when it comes to comprehending this divine-infused world, we shall probably spend eternity thanking God for the prayers he didn't answer.

As we have seen, a poem cannot be paraphrased. Where would one begin with this one anyway? Graham's work always pushes the consequences of the words, not the closures. It's as if she wonders why we would surrender a good question for the sake of a mere answer. So perhaps it is best to think first of the gaps that occur in the first half of the poem, forcing us to slow down, breathe and encounter the words in small units. After all, prayer is a bridge that reaches out over space and time, as well as between the wounds within us and that 'great Heart of my own heart'. The title of the poem, 'Prayer', makes us question who it is we feel subject to in this day and age, and whether we relate to objects, among them maybe even a thing-God. If so, a prayer would be a ritual in which the words have nowhere to go, whereas for the person of faith, prayer is the relationship to the Subject, the one to whom I am to relate most deeply, the source of being and loving cause who makes reality ultimately trustworthy. It is interesting that Graham has written a number of poems with the same title. This one is taken from her collection entitled *Swarm*. The question of prayer persists through her work: to whom or to what are human beings accountable?

Having slowed down through the spacing in the first line, the word *quicksand* appears key. In fact as you move through the poem words appear that define the work of quicksand – *take in, goes down, lost in, no way out, slip through, liquefy, swallow*. Quicksand can symbolize so much of our times: shifting and mobile, something we sink into without trace, our identity eaten up by dangerous illusions. The word *eye* is also vital to the poem. Prayer here seems connected to a looking, a discernment for what is real in a world where both the natural order (the sun going down) and our attempt to order it more (the sentence) have their habitual cycles and ends. All our understanding involves a stepping into a commitment but it must also entail an exiting from it. We must see the *cause* of things. We must understand that we have a will. The poem scrutinizes the way I look at the world subjectively (hear how *eye* and *I* sound the same), how that world stares back at me objectively and whether in the midst of this there might be some causation perceived or demanded. How can we begin to understand anything without a prior unlearning, a recognition of the shallow quicksand we are sucked into and where our years and days go native to a life we cannot recognize? Is there *no way/ out*? Nothing *beyond/ the ridge*?

The image of something being *laid on the tongue* in a poem called 'Prayer' inevitably makes us think of communion, the bread that feeds the soul by making it more hungry for God. We *swallow* to show our commitment to the faith the broken bread celebrates but we do it, as it were, in the dark. We are made up of, and surrounded by, doubts and incomprehension. We long for drops that bring *quickness*, life, freshness. The last line of the poem hints that such darkness on the spiritual adventure is a place of birth. It is the place where we are roused, are woken up, distilled and amended. Anyone who has found themselves lying on a hospital bed, in a darkness of the as-yet-unknown, similarly knows that new understandings are created there that seem so obvious and true we wonder why we never saw or embraced them before. Prayer may be a word for this process of distillation, in whatever dark places it occurs. It is the necessary work that must take place in the heart and through the mind's eye, an opening up of the clenched-fist life, if we are not just to hurry *recklessly towards the end*.

Here, as in all Graham's poems, we are made to perceive that it is more authentic to be hurt by the truth than be comforted by a lie. A Christian can readily agree. God cannot work with unreality, and our prayer must be the lifelong way we painfully and liberatingly learn to face what is and the grace that makes it so full of potential.

The Starlight Night

Gerard Manley Hopkins (1844–89)

Look at the stars! look, look up at the skies!
  O look at all the fire-folk sitting in the air!
  The bright boroughs, the circle-citadels there!
Down in dim woods the diamond delves! the elves'-eyes!
The grey lawns cold where gold, where quickgold lies!
  Wind-beat whitebeam! airy abeles set on a flare!
  Flake-doves sent floating forth at a farmyard scare! –
Ah well! it is all a purchase, all is a prize.

Buy then! bid then! – What? – Prayer, patience, alms, vows.
Look, look: a May-mess, like on orchard boughs!
  Look! March-bloom, like on mealed-with-yellow sallows!
These are indeed the barn; withindoors house
The shocks. This piece-bright paling shuts the spouse
  Christ home, Christ and his mother and all his hallows.

In 1875 a ship ran aground near the mouth of the Thames. It was called the *Deutschland*, and because there was a severe storm its distress signals were not seen and the ship was stuck, badly destroyed by the waves, until the next day – by which time a quarter of the passengers had drowned. These included five Franciscan nuns. Gerard Manley Hopkins, an intelligent, gentle and artistic Jesuit, and a convert from the Church of England, was greatly affected on reading about the tragedy. He had not written much poetry for seven years, believing at the time that it was incompatible with his vocation, but when his superior suggested that an elegy should be written for the nuns, Hopkins began work with a renewed energy and with a new 'sprung' rhythm. The result was 'The Wreck of the Deutschland' of 1876. Hopkins continued writing and, though only a few friends knew about it and the public would not see any of his poems published until 20 years after his death, so started the journey that made him into one of the most innovative, experimental and influential British poets.

I remember well the first time I heard a Hopkins poem being read out loud. I didn't understand a word of it as I sat there but I was mesmerized by a running cavalcade of compound words that flashed images so quickly and tantalizingly that I was left, at the end, emotionally winded and unsure as to what had just happened. I later learned that the often busy verbal fireworks of a Hopkins poem ask of us a slower reading, a heightened attention, which pays off, albeit with friction and frustration, with the thrilled reward of a world re-seen. Hopkins, in his tight clerical clothes and disciplined life, changed traditional poetics with an extraordinary revolutionary force. His oddities are deliberate and uncompromising. As he disrupts our expectations of language we are given perceptions we had not dreamed of. He plays with sounds but, like most play, it isn't trivial. It's an invitation into a fresh world lying deep in an old world. He begins poems with stressed syllables and then asks us to read accented stresses – rather than a regular alternation of stressed and unstressed syllables. He dazzles with elliptical phrasing, compressed imagery, assonance, alliteration, half-rhymes, dialects, convoluted syntax, elaborate metrical notations and coined phrases. Like light through a prism, a whole spectrum of possible meanings streams through his words. From his reading of the philosopher Duns Scotus and his teachings about the 'this-ness' of things, Hopkins developed the now famous concepts of 'inscape', a term he styled to describe the inward, distinctive, essential quality of a thing, and 'instress', which refers to the force that gives a natural object its inscape and allows that inscape to be seen and expressed by the observer. His well-known sonnet 'The Windhover', for example, seeks to capture the inscape of creation as a means of knowing and praising God.

If we find it difficult to appreciate a Hopkins poem, we are not alone. When he sent 'The Wreck of the Deutschland' to his friend Robert Bridges the reply was not positive. Bridges found the poem virtually incomprehensible and said he would not for any money read the poem ever again. Even 30 years later, when Hopkins was dead and Bridges was now the Poet Laureate, Bridges edited his friend's poems in a first collection and wrote to Hopkins' sister that although the 'Deutschland' read better in type, he wished 'those nuns had stayed at home'. In his introduction he commented: 'The poem stands logically as well as chronologically in the front of his book, like a great dragon folded in the gate to forbid all entrance'.[1]

Hopkins once began a poem to celebrate his younger brother's wedding. It is known as his 'Epithalamion'. It isn't dated but is likely to have been written in 1888. In it he imagines some 'brancy bunchy bushybowered wood' where a 'candycoloured, where a gluegold-brown/ Marbled river, boisterously beautiful' is the summer bathing scene of some lads from the town. Into the scene walks 'a listless stranger' who sees how the boys 'With dare and with downdolphinry' are 'earthbound, airworld, water-world thorough hurled, all by turn and turn about'. Watching them gives him a 'sudden zest/ Of summertime joys' and he finds a neighbouring pool for himself whose water 'with heavenfallen freshness down from moorland still brims'. He gets into the pool and lets the 'Flinty kindcold element' break across his body where he becomes 'froliclavish, while he looks about him, laughs, swims'.

He then briefly makes this a metaphor for wedlock but the poem is incomplete and it ends. It strikes me, though, that this poem contains a perfect image of Hopkins the priest and his poetry. Often feeling himself to be a stranger in life, and protected somewhat by his ministry and piety, as a poet he was released and unconfined. Like the man in the water endlessly looking about him and letting the elements break on him, doused in heaven's freshness, his words are riotously, gratefully 'froliclavish'. They laugh and swim. To read him is to jump in too.

This is especially true of his most widely known shorter poems on nature, many of which were written during the early years of his priesthood. These include poems such as 'Pied Beauty', 'God's Grandeur', 'Inversnaid', 'Spring' and the poem I have chosen here, 'The Starlight Night', written in 1877.

There are 14 exclamation marks in this poem. It is a poem on alert, almost giddy! It opens with an injunction, repeating the same verb four times – *look, look, look up, look* – as if no one has ever seen what he's looking at. He breathlessly goes on to describe the stars set above him. They are *fire-folk, circle-citadels* (like medieval fortresses), *elves' eyes* and *wind-beat whitebeam* (trees with white blossom) and *airy abeles* (trees also known as white poplars whose leaves have white undersides and so glisten when the breeze brushes them). He then uses the surprising image of the stars being like startled birds that quickly fly up from *a farmyard scare*. The birds are *flake-doves*, like snowflakes playing in the light or small sparks of ash blown up from a fire into the darkness. The poet then stops himself and says *Ah well!*, both a description of how good it is but also that he cannot continue describing what he sees because words ultimately fail. All he can say is that it is *all a purchase, all is a prize*. It is desirable, longed for, a sight to be won and possessed for ever by buying or bidding for it. The currency here, though, is not monetary exchange but *prayer, patience, alms, vows*. These all ask of us, demand of us, in order for the world to be gained. If creation's grandeur is not to be missed then a life needs to develop serious habits that humble the self before its divine Source. You need to sell everything you have to gain the pearl of greatest price (Matthew 13.45).

The poem then has three more requests to *look* and he refers to the *May-mess, like on orchard boughs* that alliteratively invites us to see the spring-like abundant mess of the stars. The yellow willows of March with their catkins that release a golden dust like flour are brought in to add to the physical sensory delight of the sky that is the reason for the poet's ecstasy. He then says that all this natural beauty is a barn to house *the shocks* or bundles of cut grain. This is an old Christian symbol for the souls who have been harvested by love. The sky is full of God's redeemed. But the barn also houses the Good Shepherd in a home with outer *piece-bright paling*. Paling is a picket-fence; 'beyond the pale' originally meant 'going beyond the fence'. This sky paling is *piece-bright*, glimmering, and on the ear sounds like 'peace-bright'. Paling can also mean fading or declining – as the stars do as the Son (sounding as 'sun') appears in the final line, their brightness giving way to the glory of God, Christ, his mother and all the saints. By referring to Christ as *spouse* we see that this is a marriage of heaven and earth in a divine creativity that leaves us longing for better words and fuller understanding. Has the stable of Bethlehem become the barn of creation? Has the one star that led the magi to Christ become the starlight night that leads us to him again?

We could leave Hopkins here, looking up at the dark night and praising the God of creation. This would not be the complete picture, though. Because as well as looking up at the stars, he also looked into a disabling darkness that brooded in his mind and heart and deeply fell over many of his days. The 'Sonnets of Desolation' or 'Terrible Sonnets' are a group of untitled poems probably written during 1885–86 and were found after his death. There are six poems, usually referred to by their opening words: 'To seem the stranger', 'I wake and feel', 'Carrion comfort', 'Patience, hard thing', 'My own heart' and this one, 'No worst':

No worst, there is none. Pitched past pitch of grief,
More pangs will, schooled at forepangs, wilder wring.
Comforter, where, where is your comforting?
Mary, mother of us, where is your relief?
My cries heave, herds-long; huddle in a main, a chief
Woe, wórld-sorrow; on an áge-old anvil wince and sing –
Then lull, then leave off. Fury had shrieked 'No lingering! Let me be fell: force I must be brief.

O the mind, mind has mountains; cliffs of fall
Frightful, sheer, no-man-fathomed. Hold them cheap
May who ne'er hung there. Nor does long our small
Durance deal with that steep or deep. Here! creep,
Wretch, under a comfort serves in a whirlwind: all
Life death does end and each day dies with sleep.

Again, Hopkins' language and poetic shaping give such an extravagance of feeling that you feel he is about to break. His poems are as varied in their response to life as the psalms of scripture. 'The Starlight Night' and 'No worst' are similar expressions of wonder and despair as are 'the heavens are telling the glory of God and the firmament proclaims his handiwork' (Psalm 19) and 'My God, my God, why have you forsaken me?' (Psalm 22). As with the Psalms, Hopkins keeps a relationship with God through his questioning despair rather than a sense of being answered. His spiritual life can feel as if letters to his God are constantly left unopened and get no reply ('Like dead letters/ Sent to dearest him that lives alas! away'[2]), yet he still addresses the envelopes. It is debated as to whether Hopkins was suffering depression when he wrote these late sonnets. The statement 'Hold them cheap/ May who ne'er hung here' is as true today as it ever was, depression not being understood or taken as seriously as it ought to be by families, friends, workplaces and society. To live with faith and with depression can be especially paralysing because therapy can sometimes suggest that your depression is caught up with your faith's worldview, and the Church can often hint that if only you had real faith your depression would go.

Hopkins is, then, a poet for all seasons and even of extreme weathers. He is the poet who celebrates God as 'beauty's self and beauty's giver'[3] but who can wake and feel 'the fell of dark, not day'. He prays to a God who so often appears silent and indifferent: 'O thou lord of life, send my roots rain'.[4] It can't have been easy for the zealous convert, the Jesuit priest and poet of God's grandeur to have voiced the spiritual disappointment and aloneness he often endured. He told Bridges that he wrote some of the desolate sonnets in blood, but to have pity on his own heart meant being as kind to himself as Christ calls us to be with our neighbours. His faith demanded honesty of him. It was this honesty with his God that enabled him to survive the worst and understand the true interplay of light and darkness that Christian faith witnesses to. It is an honesty that has helped carry many of us through the devotions and derelictions of faith, and for this reason when I was ordained I decided to have a line from 'The

Wreck of the Deutschland' printed at the bottom of my ordination card:

For I greet him the days I meet him, and bless when I understand.

Sunday School, Circa 1950

Alice Walker (b. 1944)

'Who made you?' was always
The question
The answer was always
'God.'
Well, there we stood
Three feet high
Heads bowed
Leaning into
Bosoms.

Now
I no longer recall
The Catechism
Or brood on the Genesis
Of life
No.

I ponder the exchange
Itself
And salvage mostly
The leaning.

Alice Walker is best known for her landmark novel *The Color Purple* (1982). As well as being a Pulitzer prize-winning author, activist and feminist she is someone for whom 'poetry is medicine'.

She was born in the US State of Georgia, the youngest of eight children to poor black parents during the days of segregation. When she was eight years old she was wounded in her right eye by a BB gun fired by one of her brothers. Although the shot was deliberate, Walker protected her brother from their parents' anger by saying it was an accident. Her family didn't have a car and so it took a week for her to be seen by a doctor, by which time she had lost the sight in that eye. Scar tissue formed and she became very shy and self-conscious. She retreated into herself and took solace in nature and books. Later in life she was able to see how her injury had allowed her to 'really see people and things, really to notice relationships and to learn to be patient enough to care about how they turned out'.[1] She also learned the personal cost of bearing a lie as a child, and how traumatized wounded and laughed-at children can be. This has fuelled her lifelong hatred of war, violence and abuses of human dignity. She has said that becoming an artist was the way she sought to help people see that human beings can change: 'Life gives you a gift from every disaster that you survive'.[2]

When she left home her mother gave her three things: a suitcase, a typewriter and a sewing machine. Walker says that these were just right for her because she was able to travel, write and make her own clothes – not having to fit into other people's outfits. She married a white civil rights lawyer and this inter-racial marriage led to a lot of threatening harassment, not least from the Ku Klux Klan. Walker began to write and became a civil rights activist. That activism, her defence of human rights and the rights of all living beings, has continued throughout her life. She is committed to breaking 'all the rules that are bad':[3]

Even when we feel we can't change things, it's important to have awareness of what has happened. If you are unaware of what has happened, it means you're not alive in many respects. And to be unalive in many places within yourself means you are missing a lot of the experience of being on this planet. And this planet is not to be missed.[4]

While I was writing this book I visited my friend Bishop Gene Robinson in Washington. He told me he had recently been to see the makeshift memorial set up in a street in Ferguson, Missouri, for Michael Brown, a young, unarmed black man killed by a policeman. As he stood reflecting on events he saw a cardboard box standing like a pillar. It had been painted black, and written in gold letters were the words: 'They tried to bury us. They didn't know we were seeds.' Gene was moved by the resiliency of these words because, as he says, as a gay person most of what he knows and understands about his own community's fight for equality comes from what he has learned from the black civil rights movement even though he is fully aware that his 'white privilege' works to protect him from the full knowledge of the extent to which he is rewarded for the colour of his skin.[5]

He researched the origin of the words on the cardboard box and discovered they had been borrowed from the 1990s Zapatistas' fight for indigenous people in Mexico. And the Zapatistas had got them from the writings of Dinos Christianopolous, a living Greek poet, who had been marginalized by the Greek literary community throughout his life because of his sexuality. He had written in the 1970s: 'You did anything to bury me. But you forgot I was a seed.'

The spirit of these words is very much the spirit of Alice Walker. She has said that she understands her work as a 'prayer to and about the world',[6] and she seeks in her poetry and in her life to 'honour the difficult'. She is resilient in the fight for the recognition of dignity, that of the human and that of the natural world. She is adamant that no person is your friend who demands your silence. The poem I have chosen is taken from a collection called *Revolutionary Petunias and Other Poems*,[7] which she prefaces by saying:

> These poems are about Revolutionaries and Lovers; and about the loss of compassion, trust, and the ability to expand in love that marks the end of hopeful strategy. Whether in love or revolution. They are also about (and for) those few embattled souls who remain painfully committed to beauty and to love even while facing the firing squad.[8]

'Sunday School, Circa 1950'[9] was written when in her thirties and like many of the poems in the collection revisits her Southern past. Her parents brought her up as a Methodist but Walker was soon to have questions:

> For a long time I was confused. After all, when someone you trust shows you a picture of a blond, blue-eyed Jesus Christ and tells you he's the Son of God, you get an instant image of his father: an older version of him. When you're taught God loves you, but only if you're good, obedient, trusting, and so forth and you know you're that way only some of the time, there's a tendency to deny your shadow side. Hence the hypocrisy I noted early in our church.[10]

She concluded that 'it is fatal to love a God who does not love you'.[11] That is, any God created to enlarge the tribal borders of someone else and oppress you and those like you is to be unapologetically rejected. When asked once about what she thought of Jesus Christ she answered:

> I think we should just kidnap Christ and go off with him; he's the best of the whole bunch. I say that having struggled for many years trying to deny him, get rid of him, or ignore him, because he is a captive of the church and they use him for absolutely everything . . . And I feel a great love for Jesus as a teacher and as a very feminine soul . . . His tenderness, his caring quality always makes me think of someone who was raised by his mother. I mean, he's the son of a feminist.[12]

In this poem we see Walker picturing herself as a child *three feet high* being asked who made her and knowing that only one answer was allowed: *God*. She and the other boys and girls had been taught to bow their heads and lean reverently as they went under this interrogation where God was always the answer. Later in life, she reflects, she has no recall of the Catechism of belief she was made to remember. It presumably has long failed to resonate. She no long broods on the *Genesis/ Of life*. By giving the word

'Genesis' a capital letter she evokes the book of the Bible that contains the ancient mythology of the world's making. By following this with *No*, sitting alone on one line, she gives her definitive response to the creationist belief, still popular in the American South, that reads those myths in a literalist way.

The poem leads us to where Walker is now in her response to her churchgoing past. She writes that she ponders *the exchange*, the questioning of who she is and how she is made with the invocation of the divine name. I was reminded when reading the end of this poem recently of the important book *Between the World and Me* by Ta-Nehisi Coates.[13] Coates explores the racial history of America in form of letters to his 14-year-old son, where, for instance, some of his hopes for his child are expressed: 'My wish for you is that you feel no need to constrict yourself to make other people comfortable'.[14] He lays out at the beginning of the book that he doesn't think he has ever found any satisfactory answers of his own to the important questions, but he knows that to keep asking them is vital because every time a question is asked it is 'refined'. Coates encourages his son to pursue 'a constant questioning, questioning as ritual, questioning as exploration rather than the search for certainty'.[15]

For Walker to *ponder the exchange* of whether life is a divine gift and the being of the creator salvages in her the reverential *leaning* rather than any dogma or certitude, a movement that acknowledges the sacred nature of the question and of those intimations of ours, what T. S. Eliot called the 'hints and guesses',[16] which lead us to ask it and not ignore it. Walker is by no means an orthodox Christian believer, but the fact that she believes in the world so much leads her to both a political activism and a spiritual seriousness willing to scrutinize the language games and power bids of the religious.

Like many, I was moved by the opening words of Rowan Williams' small book *Writing in the Dust: Reflections on 11 September and its Aftermath*. He writes:

Last words. We have had the chance to read the messages sent by passengers on the planes to their spouses and families in the desperate last minutes; and we have seen the spiritual advice apparently given to the terrorists by one of their number, the thoughts that should have been in their minds as they approached their death they had chosen (for themselves and for others). Something of the chill of 11 September lies in the contrast. The religious words are, in the cold light of day, the words that murderers are saying to themselves to make a martyr's drama out of a crime. The non-religious words are testimony to what religious language is supposed to be about – the triumph of pointless, gratuitous love, the affirming of faithfulness even when there is nothing to be done or salvaged.[17]

He goes on:

We'd better acknowledge the sheer danger of religiousness. Yes, it can be a tool to reinforce diseased perceptions of reality . . . our religious talking, seeing, knowing, needs a kind of cleansing . . . God always has to be rediscovered. Which means God always has to be heard or seen where there aren't yet words for him.[18]

Alice Walker takes it upon herself to explore how 'clean' our religion is but without surrendering the truth that the world and the miraculous life it nurtures is a consistent and joyful cause in the human soul for wonder and humility.

Landay, Afghanistan

I call. You're stone.
One day you'll look and find I'm gone.

This small poem was recited by a teenage Afghan girl called
Rahila Muska. She lived in Helmand, a Taliban stronghold, and
like many young and rural women in Afghanistan, she wasn't
allowed to leave her home. Her father fearfully took her out of
school, the education of women being viewed as dishonourable
by the Taliban and therefore making her liable to kidnap or rape.
Formalized poetry of a high style is revered in Afghan culture but
the type of poem that Rahila enjoyed is called a 'landay'. They
are short folk poems, couplets recited or sung by women native
to the Pashtun areas of eastern Afghanistan and western Pakistan.
The landay is ancient but alive. It is a secretive and anonymous
tradition where a woman who is supposed to be invisible, com-
pliant and silent makes her heart, life and angry protests known.
Some trace landays as far back as to Bronze Age immigrants from
Indo-Aryan people, from around 1700 BCE. The great immortal
themes of landays tend to be love, war, loss, a woman's pride in
her lover's courage, grief and often a teasing of a man's cowardice
in battle and in bed:

A landay has only a few formal properties. Each has 22 syllables:
nine in the first line; 13 in the second. The poem ends with the
sound *ma* or *na*. Sometimes landays rhyme, but more often not.
In Pashto, they lilt internally from word to word in a kind of
two-line lullaby that belies the sharpness of their content, which

is distinctive not only for its beauty, bawdiness, and wit, but also for its piercing ability to articulate a common truth about love, grief, separation, homeland, and war. Within these five main tropes, the couplets express a collective fury, a lament, an earthy joke, a love of home, a longing for the end of separation, a call to arms, all of which frustrate any facile image of a Pashtun woman as nothing but a mute ghost beneath a blue burqua.[1]

Rahila liked to listen to poetry programmes on the radio and would often phone in to a live chatline run by a women's literary group called Mirman Baheer. Here girls from the provinces could read out their work or talk to other poets. Rahila was a popular and frequent caller. One day in spring 2010, Rahila phoned in from a hospital bed in Kandahar to say that she'd set herself on fire in anger. Her brothers had beaten her after discovering that she wrote poetry. To many Afghan women, poetry is forbidden because it implies a freedom of will and her brothers were brutal in punishing her. Rahila, with all the resilience and strength she had shown in her poems, set herself alight and, soon after her phone call on the radio, she died.

Although she didn't write this landay, Rahila often recited it on the programme. Landays have no one author. Women remember just some of these short poems, out of the thousands that exist, that are especially relevant to their own particular life and struggle. Rahila didn't author this landay, she didn't own it nor did she write it down. It therefore cannot be destroyed and it continues to embody her as much as it survives her.

The American poet and journalist Eliza Griswold read about Rahila's death and decided to go to Afghanistan to research the story. She travelled with photographer Seamus Murphy and some translators. Rahila's real name turned out to be Zarmina, and as her story unravelled, Griswold became more and more interested in the significance of landays to the Afghan women and decided to tour around the region to collect them from the memories of the often illiterate women she met in refugee camps, private homes and secret places. She was in a good tradition. Both the missionary Jens Enevoldsen and the intellectual Sayd Bahodine Majrouh collected landays before her. Griswold wanted to see the enormous diversity of these short poems and translate them for an English-speaking readership. The result is her fascinating book *I am the Beggar of the World*.[2] She discovered that old and contemporary landays opened a closed window on aspects of Afghan life, including the impact of the last decade of war and subsequent pull-out of Western troops on the lives of Afghan women.

One of the enjoyable elements of landays that Griswold encountered was their flexibility and their adaptability to be brought up to date. For example:

> How much simpler can love be?
> Let's get engaged. Text me.

and

> Leave your sword and fetch your gun.
> Away to the mountains, Americans have come.

Others have the feel of being as old as humankind itself:

> Your eyes aren't eyes. They're bees.
> I can find no cure for their sting.

> When sisters sit together, they always praise their brothers.
> When brothers sit together, they sell their sisters to others.

or

> May God make you into a riverbank flower
> so I may smell you when I go to gather water.

> I'll kiss you in the pomegranate garden. Hush!
> People will think there's a goat in the underbrush.

Some of them have all the feel of the erotic poetry of the biblical Song of Songs. These poems, with their prescribed form and subtle subjects, are historically and culturally central to Afghanis and address those timeless topics of passion and love – whether composed centuries ago or in the present as a woman grieves the death of dear ones killed in a drone strike. These are poems that were not composed and recited for Western readers' benefit. They are part of the cultural reality and centuries-old vitality of Afghani culture that we get to glimpse in these tough little couplets of resilience and survival.

> Separation, you set fire
> in the heart and home of every lover.

I find the story of Zarmina very moving. I wanted her story to end this book. A teenage girl on the other side of the world to me decides that she is willing to die to witness to the importance of poetry and its celebration of the whole uncensored human person in a whole and uncensored world. It was the language, the creativity and associative freedoms of poems that made her 'feel' that self and world when others tried to forbid her. I see in her story too the poet of Galilee nailed to the cross, the man whose words were taken to court and put on trial. And in Zarmina, and in all who bear the cost of liberating, perplexing, defiant, truthful words, in good and dark days, I see the holy God of truth's beauty reflected.

I have to come to a place in my own life where, inspired by poets such as Rahila and the others in this book, I can celebrate the perception that God is in this world as poetry is in the poem and that a life can be worse spent than pursuing the footfalls of this puzzling and transforming intuition.

Further Reading

W. H. Auden, *Collected Poems*, Faber, 2004.

Fiona Benson, *Bright Travellers*, Jonathan Cape, 2014.

Liz Berry, *Black Country*, Chatto and Windus, 2014.

Elizabeth Bishop, *Poems*, Chatto and Windus, 2011.

Humphrey Carpenter, *W. H. Auden: A Biography*, Faber, 2014.

Emily Dickinson, *The Complete Poems*, ed. Thomas H. Johnson, Faber, 1976.

The Complete Poems of John Donne, ed. Robin Robbins, Longman, 2010.

Mark Doty, *Deep Lane*, Jonathan Cape, 2015.

Mark Doty, *Fire to Fire: New and Selected Poems*, HarperPerennial, 2009.

Mark Doty, *Heaven's Coast: A Memoir*, Vintage, 1997.

John Drury, *Music at Midnight: The Life and Poetry of George Herbert*, Allen Lane, 2013.

Carol Ann Duffy, *Collected Poems*, Picador, 2015.

Choosing Tough Words: The Poetry of Carol Ann Duffy, ed. Angelica Michelis and Antony Rowland, Manchester University Press, 2004.

U. A. Fanthorpe, *Selected Poems*, Enitharmon Press, 2013.

U. A. Fanthorpe and R. V. Bailey, *From Me to You: Love Poems*, Enitharmon Press, 2007.

Louise Glück, *Faithful and Virtuous Night*, Carcanet Press, 2014.

Louise Glück, *Poems 1962–2012*, Farrar, Straus and Giroux, 2013.

Brad Gooch, *City Poet: The Life and Times of Frank O'Hara*, Alfred A. Knopf, 1993.

Jorie Graham, *From the New World: Poems 1976–2014*, HarperCollins, 2016.

Jen Hadfield, *Almanacs*, Bloodaxe Books, 2005.

Jen Hadfield, *Nigh-No-Place*, Bloodaxe Books, 2008.

Jen Hadfield, *Byssus*, Picador, 2014.

The Gift: Poems by Hafiz, the Great Sufi Master, trans. Daniel Ladinsky, Penguin, 1999.

The Green Sea of Heaven: Fifty Ghazals from the Diwan of Hafiz, trans. Elizabeth T. Gray, White Cloud Press, 1995.

Thomas Hardy, *Selected Poems*, Penguin Classics, 1993.

Olav H. Hauge, *Don't Give Me The Whole Truth, Selected Poems*, trans. Robin Fulton and James Greene with Siv Hennum, Anvil Press Poetry, 1985.

Olav H. Hauge, *The Dream We Carry: Selected and Last Poems of Olav H. Hauge*, trans. Robert Bly and Robert Hedin, Copper Canyon Press, 2008.

Seamus Heaney, *New Selected Poems 1966–1987*, Faber, 2002.

Seamus Heaney, *New Selected Poems 1988–2013*, Faber, 2015.

The English Poems of George Herbert, ed. Helen Wilcox, Cambridge University Press, 2007.

Dominic Hibberd, *Wilfred Owen: A New Biography*, Weidenfeld and Nicolson, 2002.

Gerard Manley Hopkins, *Poems and Prose*, Penguin Classics, 2008.

I am the Beggar of the World: Landays from Contemporary Afghanistan, trans. Eliza Griswold, photographs by Seamus Murphy, Farrar, Straus and Giroux, 2015.

Hilly Janes, *The Three Lives of Dylan Thomas*, Robson Press, 2014.

Louis MacNeice, *Collected Poems*, Faber, 2007.

Robert Bernard Martin, *Gerard Manley Hopkins: A Very Private Life*, Flamingo, 1992.

Dennis O'Driscoll, *Dear Life*, Anvil Press, 2014.

Dennis O'Driscoll, *Stepping Stones: Interviews with Seamus Heaney*, Faber, 2008.

Dennis O'Driscoll, *New and Selected Poems*, Anvil Press, 2004.

Frank O'Hara, *Selected Poems*, Carcanet Press, 2005.

Mary Oliver, *New and Selected Poems, Volumes 1 and 2*, Beacon Press, 2004.

Mary Oliver, *A Poetry Handbook*, Harcourt, 1994.

Alice Oswald, *Falling Awake*, Faber, 2016.

Alice Oswald, *Memorial*, Faber, 2012.

Alice Oswald, *Dart*, Faber, 2010.

The Poems of Wilfred Owen, ed. Jon Stallworthy, Chatto and Windus, 1990

Jo Shapcott, *On Mutability*, Faber and Faber, 2010.

Jo Shapcott, *Her Book: Poems 1988–1998*, Faber and Faber, 2006.

Jon Stallworthy, *Louis MacNeice*, Faber, 1995.

John Stubbs, *Donne: The Reformed Soul*, Penguin, 2007.

The Collected Poems of Dylan Thomas, ed. John Goodby, Weidenfeld and Nicolson, 2014.

R. S. Thomas, *Collected Poems: 1945–1990*, Weidenfeld and Nicolson, 2000.

R. S. Thomas, *Collected Later Poems, 1988–2000*, Bloodaxe Books, 2004.

M. Wynn Thomas, *R. S. Thomas: Serial Obsessive*, University of Wales Press, 2013.

Colm Toibin, *On Elizabeth Bishop*, Princeton University Press, 2015.

Claire Tomalin, *Thomas Hardy: The Time-Torn Man*, Penguin, 2006.

Helen Vendler, *Dickinson: Selected Poems and Commentaries*, Belknap Press, 2010.

Alice Walker, *Hard Times Require Furious Dancing: New Poems*, New World Library, 2010.

The World has Changed: Conversations with Alice Walker, ed. Rudolph P. Byrd, The New Press, 2010.

Notes

Believing in Poetry

1 'Names', Wendy Cope, *Serious Concerns*, Faber, 1992, p. 85.
2 *Poems that Make Grown Men Cry*, compiled by Anthony and Ben Holden, Simon and Schuster, 2014; *Poems that Make Grown Women Cry*, compiled by Anthony and Ben Holden, Simon and Schuster, 2016.
3 'Entirely', Louis MacNeice, *Collected Poems*, Faber, 2007, p. 171.
4 This helpful image comes from David Orr, *Beautiful and Pointless*, HarperPerennial, 2012, p. xv.
5 Emily Dickinson, poem 1212, 'A Word is Dead' by Emily Dickinson from *Poems by Emily Dickinson* (Third Series), ed. Thomas Wentworth Higginson and Mabel Loomis Todd, Little Brown, 1896.
6 Marilynne Robinson, *Gilead*, Picador, 2006, p. 177.
7 For a study of Jesus' figurative preaching see *The Preaching of Jesus: Gospel Proclamation, Then and Now*, William Brosend, Westminster John Knox, 2010.
8 For more exploration on this theme see the very helpful essay 'Poetic Ways of Being Religious' by Peggy Rosenthal in *The Oxford Handbook of Religion and the Arts*, Oxford University Press, 2014, p. 146.
9 'Poetry and Religion', Les Murray, *Collected Poems*, Carcanet, 1998, p. 267.
10 Padraig O'Tuama, *In the Shelter: Finding a Home in the World*, Hodder and Stoughton, 2015, p. 176.
11 D. H. Lawrence used this image about the novel in D. H. Lawrence, 'Morality and the Novel', *Selected Literary Criticism*, ed. Anthony Beal, Heinemann, 1967, p. 110.
12 Thomas Howard, *Dove Descending: A Journey into T. S. Eliot's Four Quartets*, Ignatius Press, 2006, p. 21.
13 From 'The Incarnate One', Edwin Muir, in *The Penguin Book of Religious Verse*, ed. R. S. Thomas, Penguin, 1963, p. 55.

14 From Asphodel, 'That Greeny Flower in Asphodel', *That Greeny Flower and Other Love Poems*, New Directions Publishing Company, 1994.

15 Poem 466, Emily Dickinson. For a study of this poem see Dickinson, *Selected Poems and Commentaries*, Helen Vendler, Belknap Press, 2010, p. 222.

16 Thomas Merton, *Message to Poets in Selected Essays*, ed. Patrick F. O'Connell, Orbis, 2013, ch. 12.

17 For an insightful exploration of first impressions, see Adam Phillips' *Two Lectures on Expectations in Side Effects*, Penguin, 2006, pp. 218–62.

18 Benedict Nightingale, *The Future of Theatre*, Phoenix, 1998, p. 39.

19 Rowan Williams, *What is Christianity?*, SPCK, 2015, p. 21.

20 Commentary on 1 Epistle of St John, quoted in John Burnaby, *Amor Dei: A Study of the Religion of St Augustine*, Wipf and Stock, 2007, pp. 96–7.

21 From Seamus Heaney, 'The Government of the Tongue', *Finders Keepers: Selected Prose 1971–2001*, Faber, p. 190.

22 Jane Hirshfield, *Nine Gates: Entering the Mind of Poetry*, Harper-Perennial, 1998, pp. 3–22.

23 Ibid., p. 7.

24 Glyn Maxwell, *On Poetry*, Oberon Books, 2012.

25 Ibid., p. 16.

Paternoster

1 'Jaunty Voice from the Isles', interview with Luke Leitch, *The Times*, 14 January 2009.

2 Ibid.

3 K. Koch, *Making Your Own Days: The Pleasures of Reading and Writing Poetry*, Simon and Schuster, 1998, p. 28.

4 Jen Hadfield, *Nigh-No-Place*, Bloodaxe Books, 2008.

5 'Hedgehog, Hamnavoe', ibid.

6 Jane Hirshfield, *Nine Gates: Entering the Mind of Poetry*, Harper-Perennial, 1998, for further exploration of this idea.

7 'Blashey-wadder', *Nigh-No-Place*, op. cit.

8 'Still Life with Longjohns', ibid.

9 Susan Mitchell, 'Havana Birth', *Rapture*, HarperCollins, 1992.

10 www.poetryarchive.org.

Procedure

1 'Jo Shapcott: the book of life', *The Guardian*, 27 January 2011.
2 Virginia Woolf, *On Being Ill: With Notes from Sick Rooms by Julia Stephen*, introductions by Hermione Lee and Mark Hussey, afterword by Rita Charon, Paris Press, 2012.

North Haven

1 Quoted in Colm Toibin, *On Elizabeth Bishop*, Princeton University Press, 2015, p. 109.
2 Robert Lowell, 'Watchmaker God', *The Anthology of Contemporary American Poetry*, ed. Helen Vendler, I. B. Tauris and Co., 2008, p. 108.
3 Helen Vendler, *Last Looks, Last Books*, Princeton University Press, 2010, p. 105.
4 Ibid., p. 105.
5 *On Elizabeth Bishop*, op. cit.
6 Ibid., p. 1.
7 Ibid., p. 101.
8 Ibid., p. 113.
9 Ibid., p. 14.

Tripping Over Joy

1 From 'Laughter', in Daniel Ladinsky, *I Heard God Laughing: Poems of Hope and Joy*, Penguin, 2006, p. 65.

Prayer Before Birth

1 Jon Stallworthy, *Louis MacNeice*, Faber and Faber, 1995, p. 329.
2 Dennis O'Driscoll, *The Outnumbered Poet*, Gallery Books, 2013, p. 152.
3 Taken from a sermon preached at St Alban's Cathedral on 26 December 2005 and broadcast on BBC Radio 4.

Song VIII

1 W. H. Auden, *Selected Poems*, selected and ed. Edward Mendelson, Vintage International, 2007, p. xv.
2 Helen Vendler, *Part of Nature, Part of Us: Modern American Poets*, Harvard University Press, 1980, p. 95.
3 Wendy Moffat, *E. M. Forster: A New Life*, Bloomsbury, 2010, p. 132.

4 From 'The Truest Poetry Is the Most Feigning' in W. H. Auden, *Collected Poems*, ed. Edward Mendelson, Faber and Faber, 1976.

Getting It Across

1 From U. A. Fanthorpe and R. V. Bailey, *Me to You: Love Poems*, Enitharmon Press, 2007.
2 Eddie Wainwright, *Taking Stock*, Peterloo, 1994.

Do not go gentle into that good night

1 Seamus Heaney, 'Dylan the Durable? On Dylan Thomas', in *The Redress of Poetry*, Faber, 1995, p. 134.

Bird

1 From the poem 'Black Country', in Liz Berry, *Black Country*, Chatto and Windus, 2014, p. 6.

Raptor

1 Quoted at www.poetryfoundation.org/bio/r-s-thomas.
2 Dennis O'Driscoll, *Stepping Stones: Interviews with Seamus Heaney*, Faber, 2008, p. 113.
3 R. S. Thomas, 'The Empty Church', *Collected Poems: 1945–1990*, Dent, 1993, p. 349.
4 Matthew Arnold, 'Dover Beach'.
5 R. S. Thomas, 'Tidal', *Selected Poems*, Penguin Modern Classics, 2003, p. 248.
6 'The Other', *Collected Poems: 1945–1990*, p. 457.
7 'The Moon in Lleyn', ibid., p. 282.
8 'Kneeling', ibid., p. 199.
9 John Updike, *Self-Consciousness*, Knopf, 1989, p. 229.
10 'Pilgrimages', *Collected Poems: 1945–1990*, p. 364.
11 Ernesto Cardenal, quoted in Michael Paul Gallagher, *Dive Deeper: The Human Poetry of Faith*, DLT, 2001, p. 77.
12 John Powell Ward, *The Poetry of R. S. Thomas*, Seren Books, 2000, p. 113.
13 'Adjustments', *Collected Poems: 1945–1990*, p. 345.
14 *Selected Poems*, op. cit., p. 229.

15 Colin Meir, 'The Poetry of R. S. Thomas', in *British Poetry Since 1970: A Critical Survey*, ed. Peter Jones and Michael Schmidt, Carcanet Press, 1980, p. 6.

The Journey

1 Stanley Kunitz, quoted on www.maryoliver.beacon.org.
2 Les Murray, 'The Dream of Wearing Shorts Forever', *Collected Poems*, Carcanet, 1998, p. 234.
3 Anthony Mansousos, 'Mary Oliver', in *Dictionary of Literary Biography: American Poets Since World War II*, ed. Donald J. Greiner, Gale Research, 1980, p. 114.
4 Mary Oliver, *Winter Hours: Prose, Prose Poems and Poems*, Houghton Mifflin Company, 1999, p. 102.
5 See 'The Ponds', in *New and Selected Poems*, Beacon Press, 2004, p. 93.
6 Sermon 68,6 of St Augustine.
7 'I Happened to be Standing', *A Thousand Mornings: Poems*, Penguin, 2013, p. 3.
8 Mary Oliver, *Long Life: Essays and Other Writings*, Da Capo Press, 2004, p. 9.

Prayer

1 Peter Forbes, 'Winning Lines', *The Guardian*, 31 August 2002.
2 Carol Ann Duffy, 'Mrs Darwin', *Selected Poems*, Penguin, 1994, p. 147.
3 Eavan Boland, *The Independent*, 25 July 1993.
4 *Desert Island Discs*, BBC Radio 4, 12 July 2015.

To the Harbormaster

1 Brad Gooch, *City Poet: The Life and Times of Frank O'Hara*, Alfred A. Knopf, 1993, p. 288.
2 Introduction by Mark Ford to Frank O'Hara, *Selected Poems*, Alfred A. Knopf, 2008, p. xi.
3 Introduction by Bill Berkson to Frank O'Hara, *Poems Retrieved*, City Lights, 2013, p. xvii.
4 *City Poet*, op. cit., p. 8.

Wedding

1 See www.jeanettewinterson.com: 'Oswald 3'.
2 Sir Andrew Motion, 'Resetting the Human Compass: The Use and Value of the Arts', Gresham College Lecture, 4 July 2012.
3 *Poetry Book Society Bulletin*, Spring 1996.

Missing God

1 From his poem 'No, Thanks', in Dennis O'Driscoll, *Exemplary Images*, Anvil Press, 2002, p. 70.
2 From 'The Minister', in Anne Stevenson, *The Collected Poems 1955–1995*, Oxford University Press, 1996, p. 62.
3 'Intercession', in Dennis O'Driscoll, *Reality Check*, Anvil Press, 2007, p. 18.

Messengers

1 Louise Glück, *Proofs and Theories: Essays on Poetry*, Ecco Press, 1994, p. 99.
2 Ibid., p. 134.
3 Matthew 7.24–27.

The Going

1 Claire Tomalin, *Thomas Hardy: The Time-Torn Man*, Penguin, 2006.
2 Ibid., pp. xvii–xviii.
3 C. Day Lewis, 'The Lyrical Poetry', in *Thomas Hardy: Poems Quoted in Poetry Criticism*, Volume 8, ed. Drew Kalasky, Gale Research Inc., 1994, p. 132.
4 Tomalin, op. cit., p. xviii.
5 Joseph Brodsky, *The Essential Hardy*, Ecco Press, 1995, p. 44.

Untitled

1 Milton Meltzer, *Emily Dickinson: A Biography*, Twenty-First Century Books, 2006, p. 97.
2 Aaron Copland, *Music and Imagination*, Harvard University Press, 1980, p. 10.
3 Helen Vendler, *Dickinson: Selected Poems and Commentaries*, Harvard University Press, 2010, p. 16.
4 1 Corinthians 13.13.

5 See Matthew 5.3–12.

The Sentry

1 *Collected Letters, Wilfred Owen*, ed. Harold Owen and John Bell, Oxford University Press, 1967, p. 452.
2 'Anthem for Doomed Youth'.
3 *Collected Letters*, op. cit., p. 427.
4 Quoted in Michael Burleigh, 'How God was enrolled in Europe's holy war', *The Times*, 6 August 2014.
5 From 'Insensibility'.
6 From 'Dulce et Decorum Est'.
7 *Collected Letters*, op. cit., p. 461.
8 James Anderson Winn, *The Poetry of War*, Cambridge University Press, 2008, p. 18.

Lightenings viii

1 www.nobelprize.org. 'Seamus Heaney – Nobel Lecture: Crediting Poetry', Nobel Media AB 2014, 24 June 2015.
2 Ibid.
3 Seamus Heaney, *The Cure at Troy: A Version of Sophocles' Philoctetes*, Faber, 2002.
4 Quoted but with no other reference at: www.poetryfoundation.org/poems-and-poets/poets/detail/seamus-heaney.
5 Seamus Heaney, 'Lightenings, iii', *Opened Ground: Poems 1966–1996*, p. 360.
6 Seamus Heaney, 'The Loose Box', *Electric Light*, Faber, 2001, p. 15.
7 Richard Wilbur, 'For Dudley', in *The Hudson Review*, Volume XXI, No. 4.
8 Jeanette Winterson, *Oranges Are Not the Only Fruit*, Vintage, 1991. Compare the reversal she makes here of the existential poem 'Not Waving but Drowning', in Stevie Smith, *A Selection*, Faber, 1983, p. 128.
9 Dennis O'Driscoll, *Stepping Stones: Interviews with Seamus Heaney*, Faber, 2008, p. 322.
10 Ibid., p. 320.
11 'Postscript', *Opened Ground*, op. cit., p. 444.
12 Jane Hirshfield, *Ten Windows: How Great Poems Transform the World*, Alfred A. Knopf, 2015, p. 8.
13 Lachlan MacKinnon, 'Seamus Heaney: A Poet of Unfailing Integrity', *Daily Telegraph*, 1 September 2013.

14 'The Gravel Walks', *Opened Ground*, op. cit., p. 423.

Holy Sonnet XIV

1 T. S. Eliot, *Selected Essays*, Faber and Faber, 1951, p. 287.
2 C. A. Patrides, *Figures in a Renaissance Context*, ed. Claude J. Summers and Ted-Larry Pebworth, University of Michigan Press, 1989, p. 112.
3 'An Elegy upon the Dean of St Paul's, Dr John Donne', Thomas Carey, *The Works of the English Poets*, Volume V, Samuel Johnson, London, 1810, p. 214.
4 *The Works of Samuel Johnson*, Volume II, ed. Arthur Murphy, New York: Harper Brothers, 1857, p. 8.
5 Stevie Davies, *John Donne*, Northcote House, 1994, p. 13.
6 C. H. Sisson, 'A Letter to John Donne', *Selected Poems*, Carcanet, 1981, p. 24.
7 T. S. Eliot, *Essays Ancient and Modern*, Harcourt, Brace and Co., 1936, p. 21.
8 Jeffrey Johnson, *The Theology of John Donne*, D. S. Brewer, 2001.
9 *The Sermons of John Donne*, eds Evelyn M. Simpson and George R. Potter, 10 Volumes, University of California Press, 1953–62, VIII. 16.480–5.
10 See introduction to *John Donne*, selected and edited by D. J. Enright, Everyman's Poetry, Phoenix, 2012.
11 *The Complete Poems of John Donne*, ed. Robin Robbins, Longman, 2010, p. 554, notes 2–4.
12 From the essay 'Donne after Three Centuries' by Virginia Woolf, in *The Complete Poetry and Selected Prose of John Donne*, ed. Charles M. Coffin, New York: The Modern Library, 2001, p. viii.

God-Box

1 *Poetry Book Society Bulletin*, Summer 2015, 05: Mark Doty.
2 Michael Schmidt, *Lives of the Poets*, Weidenfeld and Nicolson, 1998, p. 618.
3 *The Art of Description: World into Word*, Graywolf Press, 2010.
4 Schmidt, op. cit., p. 617.
5 *Poetry Book Society Bulletin*, op. cit.
6 Mary Oliver, *And Bob Dylan Too, A Thousand Mornings: Poems*, Penguin, 2013, p. 17.

Demeter

1 Interview with *Granta* magazine: http://granta.com/interview-fiona-benson/.
2 'The Confessional', interview in *The Economist*, 12 January 2015.
3 Adrienne Rich, *Arts of the Possible*, Norton and Co., 2001, p. 30.
4 Fiona Benson, 'Sunflowers' *Bright Travellers*, Jonathan Cape, 2014, p. 22.

Prayer

1 William Matthews, *Contemporary Poets* (5th edition), St James Press, 1991, p. 357.
2 Jorie Graham, *From the New World, Region of Unlikeness: Poems*, Echo Press, 1991, p. 12.
3 Helen Vendler, *Soul Says: On Recent Poetry*, Belknap Press, 1995, p. 231.
4 www.poetryfoundation.org/poems-and-poets/poets/detail/jorie-graham.

The Starlight Night

1 Robert Bridges, *Poems of Gerard Manley Hopkins*, Humphrey Milford, 1918.
2 Gerard Manley Hopkins, 'I wake and feel the fell of dark, not day', *Poems and Prose*, Penguin, 1985, p. 62.
3 'The Leaden Echo and the Golden Echo', ibid., p. 52.
4 'Thou art indeed just, Lord, if I contend', ibid., p. 67.

Sunday School, Circa 1950

1 World Authors 1995–2000, 2003. Biography Reference Bank database.
2 *Desert Island Discs*, 19 May 2013, BBC Radio 4.
3 Ibid.
4 *The World has Changed: Conversations with Alice Walker*, ed. Rudolph P. Byrd, The New Press, 2010, p. 1.
5 See Gene Robinson, 'I am Gay and I am Black Lives Matter', *Huffpost Religion*, The Blog, 13 July 2015.
6 Alice Walker, *The Same River Twice: Honoring the Difficult*, New York: Scribner, 1996, p. 38.

7 *Revolutionary Petunias and Other Poems*, Harcourt Brace Jovanovich, 1971, p. 11.

8 Ibid., Introduction.

9 I am very grateful to my friend Allan Sandlin for introducing me to this poem.

10 Alice Walker, 'The Only Reason You Want to Go to Heaven is That You Have Been Driven Out of Your Mind', *On the Issues* magazine, Spring 1997.

11 Ibid.

12 *The World has Changed*, op. cit., p. 127.

13 Ta-Nehisi Coates, *Between the World and Me*, Text Publishing Co., 2015.

14 Ibid., p. 107.

15 Ibid., p. 34.

16 T. S. Eliot, 'The Dry Salvages', *Four Quartets*, Faber, 1944, p. 37.

17 Rowan Williams, *Writing in the Dust: Reflections on 11 September and its Aftermath*, Hodder and Stoughton, 2002, pp. 1–2.

18 Ibid., pp. 4–5.

Landay, Afghanistan

1 *I am the Beggar of the World: Landays from Contemporary Afghanistan*, trans. Eliza Griswold, photographs by Seamus Murphy, Farrar, Straus and Giroux, 2015, p. 3.

2 Ibid.

Acknowledgements

'Names' by Wendy Cope, copyright © Wendy Cope. Reprinted by permission of Faber and Faber Ltd.

'Names' by Wendy Cope, reprinted by kind permission of United Agents LLP on behalf of Wendy Cope.

'Entirely' by Louis MacNeice, from *Collected Poems*, Faber and Faber (2007). Reprinted by permission of David Higham Associates Ltd

'A word is dead' by Emily Dickinson, from *Poems* by Emily Dickinson (Third Series), ed. Thomas Wentworth Higginson and Mabel Loomis Todd (1896).

'Religion and Poetry' by Les Murray, from *Learning Human: New Selected Poems*, Carcanet Press (2001). Reprinted by permission of Carcanet Press.

'Religion and Poetry' by Les Murray, from *Learning Human: New Selected Poems*, Carcanet Press (2001). Reprinted by permission of Farrar, Straus and Giroux, LLC.

'The Incarnate One' by Edwin Muir, from *One Foot in Eden*, Faber and Faber (1956). Reprinted by permission of Faber and Faber Ltd.

'I dwell in possibility' from *The Poems of Emily Dickinson*, ed. Thomas H. Johnson, Cambridge, Mass.: The Belknap Press of Harvard University Press, copyright © 1951, 1955 by the President and Fellows of Harvard College. Copyright © renewed 1979, 1983 by the President and Fellows of Harvard College. Copyright © 1914, 1918, 1919, 1924, 1929, 1930, 1932, 1935, 1937, 1942, by Martha Dickinson Bianchi. Copyright © 1952, 1957, 1958, 1963, 1965, by Mary L. Hampson.

'Paternoster' by Jen Hadfield, from *Nigh-No-Place*, Bloodaxe Books (2008). Reprinted with permission of Bloodaxe Books, on behalf of the author. www.bloodaxebooks.com

'Procedure' by Jo Shapcott, copyright © Jo Shapcott. Reprinted by permission of Faber and Faber Ltd.

'Vision and Prayer' by Dylan Thomas, from *The Poems of Dylan Thomas: The New Centenary Edition*, Orion (2014). Reprinted by permission of David Higham Associates Ltd.

'Vision and Prayer' by Dylan Thomas, from *The Poems of Dylan Thomas*, copyright ©1952 by Dylan Thomas. Reprinted by permission of New Directions Publishing Corp.

'Let Evening Come' by Jane Kenyon, from *Collected Poems*, copyright © 2005 by The Estate of Jane Kenyon. Reprinted with the permission of The Permissions Company, Inc. on behalf of Graywolf Press, Minneapolis, Minnesota, www.graywolfpress.org

'Bird' from *Black Country* by Liz Berry. Published by Chatto & Windus. Reprinted by permission of The Random House Group Limited.

'The First Path' from *Black Country* by Liz Berry. Published by Chatto & Windus. Reprinted by permission of The Random House Group Limited.

'Homing' from *Black Country* by Liz Berry. Published by Chatto & Windus. Reprinted by permission of The Random House Group Limited.

'Birmingham Roller' from *Black Country* by Liz Berry. Published by Chatto & Windus. Reprinted by permission of The Random House Group Limited.

'Raptor' by R. S. Thomas, from *No Truce with the Furies*, Bloodaxe Books (1995). Reprinted by permission of Bloodaxe Books, on behalf of the author. www.bloodaxebooks.com

'The Empty Church' by R. S. Thomas, from *Collected Poems 1945–1990*, The Orion Publishing Group (2000). Reprinted by permission of Orion Books.

'Tidal' by R. S. Thomas, from *Collected Later Poems*, Bloodaxe Books (2004). Reprinted by permission of Bloodaxe Books, on behalf of the author. www.bloodaxebooks.com

'Kneeling' by R. S. Thomas, from *Collected Poems 1945–1960*, The Orion Publishing Group (2000). Reprinted by permission of Bloodaxe Books, on behalf of the author. www.bloodaxebooks.com

'More than Enough' by R. S. Thomas, from *Collected Later Poems*, Bloodaxe Books, 2004. Reprinted by permission of Bloodaxe Books, on behalf of the author. www.bloodaxebooks.com

'The Moon in Lleyn' by R. S. Thomas, from *Collected Poems 1945–1960*, The Orion Publishing Group (2000). Reprinted by permission of Orion Books.

'This world is not Conclusion' by Emily Dickinson, from *Poems by Emily Dickinson* (Third Series), ed. Thomas Wentworth Higginson and Mabel Loomis Todd (1896).

'Hope' by Emily Dickinson, from *Poems by Emily Dickinson* (Second Series), ed. Thomas Wentworth Higginson and Mabel Loomis Todd (1891).

'Tell all the truth but tell it slant', from *The Poems of Emily Dickinson*, ed. Thomas H. Johnson, Cambridge, Mass.: The Belknap Press of Harvard University Press, copyright © 1951, 1955 by the President and Fellows of Harvard College. Copyright © renewed 1979, 1983 by the President and Fellows of Harvard College. Copyright © 1914, 1918, 1919, 1924, 1929, 1930, 1932, 1935, 1937, 1942, by Martha Dickinson Bianchi. Copyright © 1952, 1957, 1958, 1963, 1965, by Mary L. Hampson.

'Lightenings VIII' by Seamus Heaney, copyright © Seamus Heaney Estate. Reprinted by permission of Faber and Faber Ltd.

'VIII' from 'Lightenings' from 'Squarings' from *Opened Ground: Selected Poems 1966–1996* by Seamus Heaney, copyright © 1998 by Seamus Heaney. Reprinted by permission of Farrar, Straus and Giroux, LLC.

'God Box' from *Deep Lane* by Mark Doty, published by Jonathan Cape. Reprinted by permission of The Random House Group Limited.

'God Box' from *Deep Lane: Poems* by Mark Doty, copyright © 2015 by Mark Doty. Used by permission of W. W. Norton & Company Ltd.

'Demeter' from *Bright Travellers* by Fiona Benson, copyright © Fiona Benson. Reproduced by permission of the author c/o Rogers, Coleridge and White Ltd, 20 Powis Mews, London W11 1JN.

'Caveat' from *Bright Travellers* by Fiona Benson, copyright © Fiona Benson. Reproduced by permission of the author c/o Rogers, Coleridge and White Ltd, 20 Powis Mews, London W11 1JN.

'Sunflowers' from *Bright Travellers* by Fiona Benson, copyright © Fiona Benson. Reproduced by permission of the author c/o Rogers, Coleridge and White Ltd, 20 Powis Mews, London W11 1JN.

'Prayer' by Jorie Graham, from *Poems*, Carcanet Press (2000). Published by permission of Carcanet Press Limited.

'Prayer' from *Swarm* by Jorie Graham, copyright © 1999 by Jorie Graham. Reprinted by permission of HarperCollins Publishers.

'Sunday School, Circa 1950' by Alice Walker, from *Collected Poems*, Orion. Reprinted by permission of David Higham Associates Limited.

As always, I am indebted to Ann Ruby for her patience and help.